Sharing Federal Funds for State and Local Needs

PRAEGER SPECIAL STUDIES IN
U.S. ECONOMIC AND SOCIAL DEVELOPMENT

Sharing Federal Funds for State and Local Needs

GRANTS-IN-AID AND PPB SYSTEMS

**Selma J. Mushkin
John F. Cotton**

**with the assistance of
Gabrielle C. Lupo**

PRAEGER PUBLISHERS
New York · Washington · London

The purpose of the Praeger Special Studies is to make specialized research monographs in U.S. and international economics and politics available to the academic, business, and government communities. For further information, write to the Special Projects Division, Praeger Publishers, Inc., 111 Fourth Avenue, New York, N.Y. 10003.

PRAEGER PUBLISHERS
111 Fourth Avenue, New York, N.Y. 10003, U.S.A.
5, Cromwell Place, London S.W. 7, England

Published in the United States of America in 1969
by Praeger Publishers, Inc.

Library of Congress Catalog Card Number: 70-98936

Printed in the United States of America

CONTENTS

PREFACE

THIS STUDY of the fiscal interdependence of the national government, the states, and local communities through the instrumentality of grants-in-aid is a complement to the "5-5-5 Project" conducted in 1967-68 by the State-Local Finances Project of The George Washington University.[1] In the 5-5-5 Project we sought to demonstrate the usefulness and feasibility of planning, programming, budgeting systems (PPBS) for state, city, and county. In undertaking the complementary study we had two purposes in mind: (1) to explore methods of equating city needs and revenue sources; (2) to examine the potential consequences of introducing PPBS into the partnership of governments that is basic to a federal system.

In regard to the first purpose, present-day city officials face difficult program planning problems even under fairly favorable conditions. And when revenue resources are extremely meager—as they are in many cities of our nation—relative to general urban blight and to poverty in core neighborhoods, planning may be overwhelmed by frustration. A large injection of new resources from the state and nation is a precondition to rational choice of local programs; otherwise, the cities can be expected to continue to place resources where they will have little long-run payoff. The problems are enormous and compelling, yet the local property tax levies available for their solution are usually insufficient for reasonable allocation in a workable time frame.

The difficulties can be illustrated by an analogy between control of urban blight and control of disease. A public health physician knows very well that spreading the cost of hookworm control over a five-year period, treating, say, only 20 percent of the population each year, will do very little toward eliminating the disease. Reinfection will in fact occur continually from some part of the 80 percent not being treated in any one period. Thus the five years of resource expenditure will have been wasted and futile.

[1] The 5-5-5 demonstration was financed by a Ford Foundation Grant to the State-Local Finances Project. The present complementary study was done in response to a contract for the U.S. Bureau of the Budget; some of its content is drawn from study material originally undertaken on behalf of the National Governors' Conference. The views expressed by the authors do not necessarily reflect the views of the Bureau of the Budget or of the National Governors' Conference.

In regard to our second purpose, we define a PPB system as fundamentally a tool for dividing up scarce fiscal resources among competing claims and claimants on a rational basis. The in-depth analysis by which such systems question program purposes and assess relative costs and effectiveness of alternative ways of satisfying basic objectives may be expected to shift program initiative from the national government to states and localities. Many state and local program proposals have formerly been responses to action of the U.S. Congress on new offerings of federal assistance. As state, city, and county staffs turn to an analytical search for alternative ways (better or less costly) to carry out the public's business, state and local governments should be able to initiate program designs that are appropriate to the specific characteristics—political, economic, and social—of those governments. An essential purpose of our federal system of government will be fulfilled if the notion of the fifty states as fifty research laboratories is given practical effect.

In the past, state and local officials have often asked: How can we get our maximum share of the federal grant dollars that are offered or available? At present, as the new analytical tools assist states, cities, and counties to formulate objectives and examine relative costs of optional programs, some federal offerings will undoubtedly be rejected. Grants may not meet specific state or local purposes, or not meet them as well, as effectively, or as cheaply as other options. Some governments, on examining the grant "carrot," may not find it to their taste because it is too small, or because the strings attached to it exact too high a program price. Nevertheless, some city governments that are hard pressed for funds may continue to be undiscriminating in reaching out for federal assistance. In any case, the query of state and local officials is likely to change from *how* to get the most federal dollars, to *which* of the federal offers will help provide the *most wanted* public services at the *least cost*.

Such a change in the response of states, cities, and counties would have implications for federal grant policy. State and local performance under cooperative programs would become a test of the federal grant design by providing a yardstick for judging the appropriateness of that design for the national purpose. Moreover, through in-depth program analysis within a PPB system, more assurance is given that federal revenue resources will be efficiently used by many states and cities, without the conditions and requirements that accompany grant programs.

SCOPE OF THE STUDY

The general lines of the analyses in the chapters that follow were determined by the study's intention to complement the demonstration on planning, programming, budgeting systems in the five states, five cities, and five counties of the 5-5-5 Project. Some of the topics for analysis, however, were chosen at the special request of the U.S. Bureau of the Budget. For example, the study presents detailed information to illuminate the specific problems of unused federal grant offerings, and it summarizes the experience of various jurisdictions with grants-in-aid. This experience was assembled from (1) our discussions of intergovernmental problems with selected state, city, and county officials and (2) questionnaire responses. Also at the request of the Budget Bureau, we have summarized the research done so far on the substitution of federal for state funds and on the stimulatory effects on state expenditures of federal grant offerings.

Other topics were included in view of the concerns of the National Governors' Conference. The study titled "New Directions in Federal Aid Policy," which was prepared in 1967 by the State-Local Finances staff for the National

Governors' Conference, served as a take-off point for our 1968 role as volunteer staff for the Conference's Committee on Revenue and Taxation. In that role we were able to carry out a survey on the status of present packaging of federal aids in the states and on possible other packaging that might serve state purposes if further authority for joint funding and packaging were provided under the proposed Joint Funding Simplification Act (S. 2981 and H.R. 12631) introduced in August 1967. The possible applications of this new authorization were of direct interest to both the Budget Bureau and the Governors' Conference, because President Johnson and the Conference had earlier urged the Congress to enact such legislation.

A summary of the survey findings is contained in this volume, but for reasons of space we have not included the state-by-state responses. However, details of the responses were included in the testimony of Governor Philip Hoff of Vermont, as Chairman of the National Governors' Conference Committee on Revenue and Taxation, before the House Subcommittee on Executive and Legislative Reorganization, June 10 and 11, 1968.

CONTENTS SUMMARY

In Chapter 1 of the study, after a brief review of the intergovernmental fiscal pattern that has emerged from the past, we ask: Is there a set of concepts on which the present pattern rests? What are the possible directions of fiscal interdependence in the years ahead and what principles or concepts underlie these new directions? The chapter then summarizes recent adaptations of grants-in-aid that give federal support and guidance to state and local program development and outlines some optional ways in which federal assistance may be extended. Chapter 2 views the functions of grants-in-aid from the perspective of the national government; Chapter 3 examines and evaluates some principles of grants-in-aid design. The next three chapters analyze selected aspects of grants-in-aid structure: Chapter 4 examines the diversity of matching provisions and their meaning for state and local decision; Chapter 5 discusses problems of measuring "need" and resources in relation to the yardsticks required to convert *ad hoc* fiscal remedies to objective formulas for grant allocation; Chapter 6 presents problems related to state and local budget distortion and a review of findings of studies dealing with the fungibility of federal funds. The next three chapters outline and review various prescriptions for federal aids: Chapter 7, "packaging," Chapter 8, grant consolidation, and Chapter 9, the overhead or general support grant, as an additional and new instrument for distributing federal revenues to achieve public services that will be more responsive to demands and needs in states and cities. Chapter 10 reviews intergovernmental tax cooperation and the use of tax credits as a way of encouraging more adequate funding of state and local services. Chapter 11 is a brief summary.

ACKNOWLEDGMENTS

The approach toward a theory of federal grants-in-aid in Chapter 3 is solely the work of John Cotton.[2] After reviewing the recent theoretical work that calls for a sharp division in function between categorical (conditional) grants and unconditional grants, he has formulated a stronger conceptual framework for categorical grants that could be the basis for assuring national minimum program standards. The contribution that Chapter 6 makes toward an understand-

---

[2] Unless otherwise identified, each of the persons named in this section is a staff member of the State-Local Finances Project.

ing of (1) the budgetary distortion produced by federal grants and (2) the unconditional grant's role in overcoming this budgetary impact is also John Cotton's. The summary of studies on substitution and stimulatory effects of grants-in-aid in the latter part of Chapter 6 was prepared by Clifford Reid. I share with Gabrielle Lupo the responsibility for the research and summary findings presented in Chapter 5, which in effect had long been in the making, since its subject is one we have studied in its various aspects for a number of years. This is a research area that has been substantially illuminated, but much remains to be done if more precise tools are to become available for measuring comparative requirements for federal financial assistance. Chapter 10 is the work of Mrs. Lupo, but draws heavily on draft materials on tax credits prepared by George Roeniger of the Committee on Economic Development; we are grateful to Mr. Roeniger and the CED for this assistance. The study's Appendix, which reviews expenditure determinants research, is the work of Roy Bahl, formerly of West Virginia University and now with Fiscal Affairs Department, International Monetary Fund. Karen Nelson helped us compile grants-in-aid data, and Beatrice Crowther spent many hours on figure verification. Free-lance consultant Kathleen Sproul edited the study's final draft and saw it through to publication.

L'ENVOI

To dispose of any misunderstandings before they arise (and are voiced), let me say that we are quite aware that the study takes only an initial step toward analysis of the potential effects of PPB systems—when in full operation in states, cities, and· counties—on federal grant-in-aid design. We do, however, believe it is an important step. We anticipate little disagreement from competent analysts on the theory we develop here, but will welcome review and suggestions for its improvement. On the recommended prescriptions for federal grant policy, we anticipate nothing *but* disagreement, and we reserve the right to alter them as we learn more about them from operational PPB systems.

September 1968
SELMA J. MUSHKIN, *Director*
State-Local Finances Project

CHAPTER 1

Intergovernmental fiscal trends and prospects

PLANNING, PROGRAMMING, BUDGETING SYSTEMS

PROGRAM PLANNING AND FINANCING are twin parts of governmental machinery. The gearing of these parts depends upon the shape and size of each. If one is not in shape to fit the other, substitute parts are required to make the machinery of government operate effectively. Substitutes for planning, when the planning is too small or too jagged, have been federal controls and requirements as a condition for federal financial assistance; the substitutes for self-financing through state or local taxes have been public prices on the one hand and intergovernmental grants-in-aid on the other. The substitutes for deficiencies in financing have been program purposes, unrealized.

A federal system of government has, not one set of gears, but several, and there must be capacity for meshing the machinery of one government with the other. The political scientist long ago discarded the concept of a rigid division of responsibility among governments. The economist's formulation of a "mix" of governments to further public services was developed much later.[1] In brief, this formulation runs in familiar terms. The voter in making his decision with respect to public services, their quantity and quality, decides as well about the "mix" of governments. He turns, not exclusively to the state, but to the national government, the state, and his community, as needed to get what he wants. He does this within our political structure through group action, joining the vested interests that seek, for example, better water quality, hot school lunches, improved maternal and child health, crime control, juvenile delinquency protection, or job opportunities and job training.

This multijurisdictional pressure of voters as an aspect of the federal system is often overlooked. It means that when individuals are not satisfied with the type or levels of services they are receiving, they shift gears and change the mix of governments to get the preferred results. The people who would foreclose such a shifting and urge that local programs be financed exclusively by local taxes are those inclined to favor lower taxes rather than enlarged public services. One concept of the public market place is that individuals move to those com-

---

[1] See Selma J. Mushkin and Robert F. Adams, "Emerging Patterns of Federalism," *National Tax Journal*, Vol. 19 (September 1966), pp. 225-47.

munities which offer them the public services they seek at the tax price they are willing to pay; by the selection of the place of residence, their preferences are recorded.[2] However, expressing preferences by choosing the "mix" of government is often a more suitable and convenient answer than moving to another community.

The factors that determine these preferred choices among the mix of governments are partly efficiency criteria (that is, efficient use of scarce personnel skills and of economies of scale or economies of operation); partly criteria of flexibility of governments in the face of citizen desires to influence governmental action (that is, speed in gaining action, the proper differentiation of services that will tailor them to the demands of specific groups, and the extent of group access to power centers); and partly criteria of equity (that is, the fairness of distribution of public services as well as of taxes).

It may be useful here to describe the function of each of the twin parts—program planning and financing—and the intergovernmental role of each. The functions of program planning are: (1) to steer toward the purposes and directions sought, (2) to anticipate and predict, (3) to quantify the dimensions, (4) to describe the factors at work, (5) to make clear the interactions of those factors, and (6) to explain why, what, how, for whom—and what else. Thus, program planning helps to define, for the voters and those who make the decisions on the voters' behalf, what needs doing, with what purpose in mind, for whom, and with what effect. The functions of financing are: (1) to constrain public use of limited economic resources, (2) to achieve a fair distribution of tax burdens, (3) to equate public payments with public benefits. Thus, financing sets the constraints within which planning is translated into the choices to be made; once the choices are made, financing becomes the means for implementing them.

In August 1965, in recognition of the interrelated functions of financing and program planning, President Johnson directed national agencies to apply a modern management system of planning, programming, and budgeting. In March 1967 he carried the directive further:

This system—which proved its worth many times over in the Defense Department—now brings to each department and agency the most advanced techniques of modern business management . . . [and] is forcing us to ask the fundamental questions that illuminate our choices. . . .

Under PPBS, each department must now:

- Develop its objectives and goals, precisely and carefully;
- Evaluate each of its programs to meet these objectives, weighing the benefits against the costs;
- Examine, in every case, alternative means of achieving these objectives;
- Shape its budget request on the basis of this analysis and justify that request in the context of a long-range program and financial plan.[3]

State and local governments have responded to the steps taken by the national government. In May 1966 the Governor of California issued a directive to California agencies similar to that issued in 1965 by the President to the national government. Over the course of the months following, a number of states and cities also began implementing PPB systems. In 1967-68, in addition to the five cities participating in the intergovernmental cooperative demonstration known as the "5-5-5 Project," New York City and Philadelphia initiated

[2] Charles M. Tiebout, "An Economic Theory of Fiscal Decentralization," in National Bureau of Economic Research, *Public Finances: Needs, Sources, and Utilization* (Princeton University Press, 1961).

[3] *The Quality of American Government*, President's Message to the Congress, March 17, 1967.

the system. By the middle of 1968 some ten states and fifty-five local governments (cities and counties) had begun working to improve the process of decision making through program analysis and longer-range program and financial planning.[4]

Implementation of planning, programming, budgeting systems has important implications for federal grant-in-aid policies. Some changes in policy are already indicated by the greater emphasis on evaluation of programs and methods as a condition of specific federal aids. Evaluation of program effects is becoming a part of congressional and agency reviews. Some newer grant programs are especially designed to yield better information on program outputs. The improvement of the process of decision making will, as time advances, take deeper root in intergovernmental relations. It will add one more dimension to the changes in governmental contours that are now taking place.

THE CLIMATE OF CHANGE

The rapidly accelerated pace of urbanization and congestion; new technology in industry, agriculture, and transportation; the awakened concern about civil rights; structural changes in the labor market which are closing avenues for the unskilled and demanding more professional and technical training—all have contributed to adaptations in the fiscal tools of intergovernmental relations.

Burgeoning demands for public service have pressured increases in federal support of state and local programs and changes in the way in which states and localities conduct the public business. The number of governmental units is being pruned; in the period 1962-67, the units with separate taxing and expenditure powers were reduced from 90,000 to 80,000 (approximate). Local governments are dealing with problems of fragmentation by organizing regional authorities and by contracting for and purchasing each others' services. In some instances, state direction has been proffered to localities to assure, for example, adequate water to supply the requirements of industry and households. Increasingly, states are assuming all, or a great measure of, responsibility for welfare payments and for education. The complex interdependency of contiguous states and their responsibility for such services as transportation, water, recreation, higher education, and economic development has triggered numerous interstate compacts. Reapportionment of state legislatures has been compelled by Supreme Court decisions on the one-man, one-vote rule. States and cities have been reorganizing to reduce the numbers of separate departments, bureaus, and agencies and thereby to strengthen the administrative capacity of governors and mayors. In short, many forces within this present climate of change are working to equate the capacity to govern with the dimensions and magnitude of the public problems facing all levels of government.

CHANGES IN GRANT AMOUNT AND DESIGN

For many decades the national government has given support and encouragement to public services and facilities administered by states and localities. The fiscal tool labeled the "grant-in-aid" is not a single instrument but a variety of instruments that have been forged in many shapes and sizes to stimulate provision of new public products and to improve methods of delivering them as public services. National government encouragement to states predates the Constitution; under the Articles of Confederation, for example, land grants were used to encourage the building of schools. The monetary grant has had almost ninety years of trial and use, beginning with the 1879 grant to provide books

---

[4] Based on a preliminary and incomplete tabulation of a July 1968 survey made under the auspices of the National League of Cities and the U.S. Conference of Mayors.

Table 1–1. **RATIOS OF STATE-LOCAL OWN FUNDS TO FEDERAL PAYMENTS, SELECTED YEARS 1942, 1957, 1962, 1966**

States	1942	1957	1962	1966
Alabama	7.7	4.0	3.2	2.6
Alaska	a	3.1	2.0	1.3
Arizona	5.6	6.8	5.0	3.9
Arkansas	7.8	4.3	3.1	2.6
California	11.2	8.3	6.1	5.1
Colorado	5.9	5.8	5.2	4.2
Connecticut	15.1	17.5	8.3	6.9
Delaware	8.4	10.0	9.2	5.7
District of Columbia	5.5	4.6	2.7	2.7
Florida	11.2	9.0	8.1	6.1
Georgia	8.9	6.0	4.1	3.9
Hawaii	a	5.8	4.2	3.9
Idaho	5.8	5.3	3.7	4.0
Illinois	13.5	13.5	7.9	7.1
Indiana	10.0	13.7	8.3	7.5
Iowa	12.0	9.2	7.1	6.0
Kansas	8.3	7.5	6.7	5.7
Kentucky	8.1	5.9	3.9	3.1
Louisiana	9.8	5.8	4.1	3.6
Maine	9.4	7.3	5.4	4.1
Maryland	13.9	10.9	7.2	7.0
Massachusetts	13.3	12.9	8.1	6.3
Michigan	13.1	11.7	7.9	6.9
Minnesota	10.0	9.2	7.2	5.2
Mississippi	6.8	4.9	3.8	3.2
Missouri	7.3	5.1	4.6	4.0
Montana	7.0	4.6	3.8	3.1
Nebraska	7.5	7.3	5.7	5.2
Nevada	2.9	4.7	4.5	3.5
New Hampshire	9.8	9.8	4.6	5.0
New Jersey	22.8	20.7	10.5	8.6
New Mexico	6.5	3.4	3.5	2.4
New York	25.3	17.2	13.1	10.6
North Carolina	11.3	5.1	5.6	4.7
North Dakota	10.2	7.1	5.1	4.5
Ohio	11.2	11.5	6.9	5.8
Oklahoma	5.9	4.7	3.7	3.3
Oregon	7.5	6.2	4.3	3.5
Pennsylvania	11.0	14.6	8.1	6.2
Rhode Island	14.4	7.2	6.4	4.5
South Carolina	5.6	6.5	4.7	4.3
South Dakota	7.8	5.0	3.2	3.6
Tennessee	8.5	6.0	3.9	3.4
Texas	9.3	6.8	6.2	5.0
Utah	4.8	5.8	4.0	3.1
Vermont	8.3	6.6	2.5	2.7
Virginia	10.5	9.8	5.2	4.2
Washington	5.9	7.9	6.0	5.0
West Virginia	7.8	6.9	4.2	2.7
Wisconsin	13.5	13.1	7.9	8.6
Wyoming	5.0	3.0	2.3	2.0

a Not available.

SOURCE: U.S. Bureau of the Census, Governments Division, as cited in Selma J. Mushkin and Robert F. Adams, "Emerging Patterns of Federalism," *National Tax Journal*, Vol. 19 (September 1966), p. 240.

been taken to augment the supply of personnel in the health professions. Manpower training programs have received new authorizations. The concentrated programs of the Office of Economic Opportunity's "war on poverty" have provided aids for such innovations as the "Head Start" projects through which disadvantaged 3- to 5-year-olds are prepared for elementary schooling. Community action has been fostered to deal with neighborhood problems, and more recently has been buttressed by the "Model Cities" approach in which the gamut of national, state, and local activities are directed toward elevating whole target areas depressed by poverty and dilapidated dwellings. National legislation has called for community mental health programs to help the states cope with problems of mental illness and to give new direction to those isolated mental hospitals that have so long been known as the "Shame of the States."

FROM 50-50 TO 90-10

As the scope of federal aids has broadened, the pattern of cost-sharing between governments has altered. Federal shares of public service or facility cost have been increased, and matching ratios have become more diverse. Moreover, matching ratios have been applied as if they were a precise tool for encouraging (1) organizational changes in government or (2) provision of services considered of high national priority. This use of matching, as if it were finely tuned to public decision, is a new departure. For example, federal shares for college construction are a third of the total cost; however, if a public community college facility is being constructed, they are raised to 40 percent. Administrative costs for welfare are shared on a 50-50 basis, but, for administrative services that offer possibilities of preventing poverty, a 75 percent matching is provided by the federal government. The federal share for certain community services is increased if the facilities are provided on a metropolitan-wide basis.

Variations in matching for closely related activities are illustrated by the shares of federal, state, or community in highway facilities. Building of primary and secondary roads may be undertaken with 50 percent sharing of costs by the federal government. Urban highways also may be financed on a 50-50 basis. Grants for acquisition construction and improvement of capital facilities and equipment needed for urban mass transportation systems are made up to 66⅔ percent of "net project cost." The cost of removing nonconforming signs on highways as part of the control of outdoor advertising programs can be met by a 75 percent federal grant. No matching is required within the allocation for landscaping and scenic enhancement of roads. Road construction in redevelopment areas may be assisted with the addition of another 10 percent of federal funds to the prevailing matching ratios within an overall 80 percent federal participation ceiling. It was the interstate system with its 90 percent federal grant for highway construction that jarred the traditional 50-50 matching provision. That program, enacted in 1956, paved the way for .the oft-repeated question: Is a highway more important than "x" public service?

Increasingly since 1956, federal aids have been provided without matching or with 66⅔ percent to 90 percent federal sharing of costs. The national government, for example, is authorized to finance up to 90 percent of the cost of Neighborhood Youth Corps projects, Adult Basic Education, and Community Action Programs. The federal share ranges up to 80 percent of the cost of neighborhood legal services (except in very poor communities where grantees may be relieved of all or nearly all of their matching requirements). The training program to give work experience to those in poverty-stricken communities calls for up to 90 percent federal sharing of the cost. Operation Mainstream, directed toward establishing work-training and employment projects for chronically unemployed poor adults, also permits sharing up to 90 percent.

The wide variation in matching ratios even for the largest federal grant programs is illustrated in Chapter 4, Table 4-3.

THE 400 PLUS

The number of separate federal aids has been vastly increased, adding to the complexity of intergovernmental fiscal patterns. This problem has been the subject of debate over a long period, but by now most people agree that remedial action is necessary to curb the proliferation. In 1966, for example, Budget Director Charles Schultze emphasized in testimony before the Senate Subcommittee on Intergovernmental Relations that federal aid "is being provided through too many narrow categorical grant and loan programs." [6]

Trying to count the total aids to states and localities is a complex numbers problem, because the count depends heavily on what is being defined as a separate and distinct program or grant authorization. Various counts have been made, however; the most recent of these places the number in excess of 400.[7]

The excessive number of separate grants has become a costly information problem both to the national government and to the states and localities. The problem is discussed in Chapter 7; here we merely call attention to the several catalogs of federal assistance programs. One of these was assembled by the Legislative Reference Service of the Library of Congress; another, developed initially by the Office of Economic Opportunity, is now an interagency effort spearheaded by OEO. The Advisory Commission on Intergovernmental Relations has recently initiated a bibliography of catalogs on grants-in-aid.[8]

Representative William V. Roth of Delaware, speaking before the House on June 25, 1968, recounted his research on federally operated programs providing assistance to the public:

We found that only the largest cities and states and universities have the necessary money and staff required just to keep abreast of the programs from which they might benefit. . . .
. . . My State has a full-time Federal liaison man because of the complexity of dealing with the Federal Government. The universities likewise have individuals who spend a large share, if not all, of their time seeking Federal funds. Even within school districts I have found that on the staff of a high school a major portion of one person's time may be spent soliciting Federal funds.
It would indeed be valuable to have a study of the costs incurred, both in time and money, by our state and local governments just soliciting Federal funds. In fact, in this nation of specialists, an entire new breed of consultants has suddenly materialized as a result of the vast proliferation of Federal assistance programs. This new breed of specialists demands and receives fees or salaries into five figures because of its high degree of knowledge in specialized areas of Federal programs. There is, in other words, in our Federal Government a sort of information crisis.[9]

---

[6] *Creative Federalism,* Hearings Before the Senate Subcommittee on Intergovernmental Relations, Nov. 16-21, 1966 (Government Printing Office, 1967), p. 390.

[7] I. M. Labovitz, *Number of Authorizations for Federal Assistance to State and Local Governments Under Laws in Force at Selected Dates During 1964-1966* (Library of Congress, Legislative Reference Service, July 5, 1966).

[8] Library of Congress, Legislative Reference Service, *Catalog of Federal Aids to State and Local Governments,* (GPO, April 15, 1964), Supplement, (Jan. 4, 1965), Second Supplement (Jan. 10, 1966); *Catalog of Federal Assistance Programs,* (Office of Economic Opportunity, June 1, 1967): *Catalogs and Other Information Sources on Federal and State Aid Programs: A Selected Bibliography,* (Advisory Commission on Intergovernmental Relations, May 1968).

[9] *Congressional Record,* Vol. 114, No. 109, pp. H5434-35.

ENLARGED ROLE OF TECHNICAL ASSISTANCE

Intergovernmental cooperation in the provision of public services has also taken the form of professional consultation and technical help to states and communities. In a tight labor market for qualified personnel, such professional and technical support gains added importance as a way to improve the capacity of the states and communities in meeting public demands. The range of technical assistance provided is broad. It has included the making of surveys—for example, comprehensive river basin studies projecting requirements for such water and related land resources and needs as navigation, flood control, water supply, irrigation, water quality control, power, recreation, and fish and wildlife conservation. It has also included consultations on statistical data and engineering problems, and dissemination of research and research findings relevant for program development and in-service personnel training.

Such assistance is not confined only to agencies with grant-in-aid activity. For example, the Tennessee Valley Authority seeks to encourage industrial growth through better use of all resources of the region, including water supply, water transportation, and electricity. It does not provide matching grants or other forms of financial aid to states or communities, but it has undertaken to relate TVA projects to local planning efforts and to work closely with state planning agencies, providing professional consultation and technical assistance in cooperation with the agencies where needed.

No compilations have been made of the total spent by the national government in providing such professional consultation and technical aid. In 1966, however, for technical assistance alone to state and local health and health-related activities, it was estimated that $67.3 million had been spent.[10]

PLANNING AND PROGRAM COORDINATION

Surveys, subsequent planning in terms of the survey findings, and eventual programming in relation to planning have increasingly become preconditions to receipt of federal aid. Under the 1946 Hill-Burton program for hospital construction, for example, grant support was provided for projects which conformed to a statewide hospital plan. As additional health facilities were added to the list of eligible projects, the survey and planning provisions were also broadened. Provisions for highway aids, as of 1965, required the development of a comprehensive transportation planning process in urban areas. And mental health grants are being conditioned on community-wide assessments of mental health needs.

Another developing type of planning machinery looks at community facilities as a coordinated whole. Comprehensive community planning for urban development is being fostered by grant programs under the new U.S. Department of Housing and Urban Development (HUD). An even wider area of planning effort is being encouraged by the Appalachian and other regional economic development plans. From the outset, as from the first stages of the earlier area and district development program, these grants have been tied to an Overall Economic Development Program (OEDP). And the Community Action Program created by the original Economic Opportunity Act has established, as one of its conditions for granting federal support to local efforts, that a coordinated program must be outlined in a community's application proposal.

As the process of planning, programming, budgeting systems has been im-

---

[10] Selma J. Mushkin, *Health and Hospital Expenditures of State and Local Governments: 1970 Projections* (Chicago, Council of State Governments, May 1966).

plemented, a new direction has been given to planning provisions and requirements in federally aided programs. The Juvenile Delinquency and Control Bill, for example, sets forth—as a condition for approval of projects—an assessment of the relative costs and effectiveness of achieving rehabilitation of juvenile delinquents. Evaluation of programs and carrying out of jointly sponsored objective evaluation studies have been authorized by the Congress (see, for example, the Economic Opportunity Act of 1964), and comprehensive development planning is being defined in the terminology of PPBS directives.[11]

COMPLEMENTARY NATIONAL, STATE, AND INTERGOVERNMENTAL PROGRAMS

Grants-in-aid and other forms of federal assistance that include loans and taxation supports are only part of the intricately woven fabric through which the national government participates with state and local governments in meeting public demands for services. As the business of governments has grown, so has the variety of combinations of direct national action and intergovernmental cooperative action. Thus, the grant-in-aid structure cannot be considered in isolation. It is part of the complex of public production of services and income redistribution.

The meeting of public demands for new public services or better methods of producing them has required choices between direct nationally administered programs and programs administered by state or community. Those who decry the grant structure often fail to consider that Congress, in responding to public needs, has mainly two viable options: (1) direct national measures, or (2) some form of federal aid to states and cities. For the most part, Congress has opted for federal aids rather than direct national action for new public services. Even when national programs are launched—e.g., the rent subsidy program, or social insurance, or the OEO Jobs Corps—Congress has in no major instance called for a national take-over of responsibility for the provision of an existing public service, nor has congressional policy been aimed at reduction of state tax levies. The choices made often yield a combination of national, state, or local, and cooperative intergovernmental programs.

The following combinations may serve, at least partially, to suggest the intricate patterns that have emerged:

1. National programs, nationally financed and nationally administered, are complemented by a cooperative intergovernmentally financed but locally administered program.
2. National programs, nationally financed and primarily nationally administered, call upon states or localities to assist in the administrating by contractual arrangements for certain classes of public beneficiaries.
3. National programs, nationally financed and nationally administered, are called upon by states to assist in the administration of state activities.

The various income maintenance programs are perhaps the clearest instance of programs that are partly national in design, and partly state and local but federally aided. The social insurance program, small in its early years, was complemented clearly and deliberately by a federal-state cooperative program for assistance to the needy aged, needy blind, and needy mothers with young children in their care. While the two programs are administered independently, the levels of payment and the eligibility requirements of one program clearly affect those of the other. If old age and survivors' insurance payments are raised, the requirements for supplementary welfare assistance through public

---

[11] Bureau of the Budget Circular No. A-80, Jan. 31, 1967, and No. 68-2, July 18, 1967.

assistance programs are lessened. And if eligibility is broadened for insurance protection, the number of people qualifying for public assistance is reduced.

Similarly, the cooperative program of agricultural research financed through grants to state agricultural experiment stations complements the nationally administered Agricultural Research Service, which seeks improved methods of farm production, a broadened market for farm products, and control of plant and animal diseases and of pests. The national Forest Service also seeks to gain effective use of forest resources, partially by management of national forests and partially through cooperation between the national and state governments. The federal government and the states jointly provide financial aid for forest fire control and for tree planting. Technical assistance is given to woodland owners to encourage multiple use and management of their forest holdings. The research or management programs of the state experimental stations or state forests affect and in turn are affected by the national programs.

National programs are in some instances administered with the help of the states. For example, state vocational rehabilitation agencies administer, on a contract basis, determinations of eligibility for disability benefits under the national social insurance system. States, through their public health agencies, also administer certification of the vendors that are eligible, according to nationally defined standards, to participate in provision of health care to the aged under Medicare. Functions undertaken under such contracts may have as important an impact on state programs and quality of public services administered by the state as does a grant or a combination of grant programs.

In other instances, states turn to the national government for administrative support. Agreements have been executed by the Internal Revenue Service with a number of states for exchange of federal information on tax returns and tax audits. Similarly, state and local law enforcement officers rely on the FBI's national repository of identification data based on fingerprint records. Such functions carried out by the national government for states or communities offer an opportunity for technical assistance and personnel training that can do as much as, if not more than, a grant to improve a state's capacity to perform its public tasks.

In still other program areas the national government depends upon state or local services and facilities to meet its obligations to defined classes of beneficiaries. For example, state agencies providing welfare assistance and services to needy Cuban refugees are reimbursed by the national government. Similarly, states are reimbursed for unemployment benefits paid on behalf of the national government to federal employees and ex-servicemen.

POSSIBILITIES AHEAD

The recent widespread criticism of the pattern of federal grants-in-aid has included charges of excessive proliferation, too-high information costs, undue complexity, and serious lack of coordination. Nevertheless, Congress will undoubtedly continue to respond to demands from citizens and interest groups for federal support and encouragement of new public services. We may also expect that a large share of the public services administered by states and localities will be financed, directly or indirectly, out of tax revenues raised nationally. In a national economy within which industry and individuals move with considerable ease, the characteristic problems facing states and cities in raising revenue locally point to more sharing of federal revenues with those units of government. Federal taxation is more efficient, fairer in its distribution, and more in harmony with a closely interlocked national economic system. Urgent

Table 1–3. **ALTERNATIVE METHODS OF PROVIDING FEDERAL ASSISTANCE TO STATES AND LOCALITIES**

Types of Assistance	Basis of Federal Offering	Program Content Type	Purpose	Program-Related Conditions
LOANS				
Direct ⎱ Guaranteed ⎰	Project approval	Physical facilities, Public services	Cost reduction	Administrative, Financial, Statistical
TAX SUPPORTS				
Credits	Taxpayer returns	. . . . . .	Tax incentives	. . . . . .
Piggybacking	State or local tax levy	. . . . . .	Lowered administrative cost	. . . . . .
Shared revenues	Origins of tax	. . . . . .	Income effect	. . . . . .
GRANTS				
Conditional ⎱ Categorical grants, Block program grants, "Target" area grants ⎰	- - Formula, Project approval	Planning, Training of personnel, Demonstrations, Physical facilities, Public services, Income maintenance	Cost reduction, National min. standards, Benefit spillover offsets, Income effect	Administrative, Financial, Statistical, Program standards, Tax standards
Unconditional	Formula	. . . . . .	Income effect	. . . . . .

urban problems and the continuing acceleration of congestion will undoubtedly enforce this prospect.

The questions before the nation and the Congress are these:

1. Should we continue adapting and forging new grant-in-aid instruments for more narrow and more narrowly defined categorical programs?

2. Or should we seek more consolidation of grants for functional areas along the lines of the Partnership in Health program, which combined earlier grants for special disease categories and environmental health into a single formula grant for health?

3. To what extent should grant consolidations seek to identify the federal grant "carrot" for personnel training and program experimentation, development, and planning, as well as for production of specific new public products?

4. Should there be added to the federal grant-in-aid structure a general unconditional grant, and if such general support is provided, should it seek to safeguard the national concern with program standards, or should it become a substitute for the categorical assistance?

5. Should general support for a wide range of interrelated public services be provided along with federal grants for the implementation of PPB systems by states and localities and a build-up of staff capacity to carry out program analysis?

6. Optionally, should the national government forgo part of its revenue to subsidize tax-raising by states and localities through credits and further tax deductions?

The options for federal assistance are schematically arranged in Table 1-3 for the following general classes of alternatives: grants—conditional and unconditional; loans—direct and guaranteed; tax supports—credits, piggybacking, and shared revenues.

CHAPTER 2

The federal view of a grant-in-aid system

OVER THE YEARS the national government's rationale for grants-in-aid has continually shifted, but a common thread runs through the fabric of the grant structure: the notion of grants as a tool to promote, stimulate, and assist specific program activities. Some of the earliest grant programs purposed simply "to stimulate" and "to promote." A quick sampling of more recent grants reveals various wordings, but all with essentially the same intent: "to strengthen instruction"; "to assist in expanding and improving"; "to assist and encourage"; "to assist in the initiation, expansion, and improvement"; "to stimulate development."

In this chapter we ask: would it be practical to consider grant-in-aid programs as a system with more general objectives than those attributed to the grants that have been adopted piecemeal through the years? The answer to this question will obviously be conditioned by existing institutional arrangements and the political realities that underlie them. Therefore, we need to ask an additional and relevant question: how far should the federal government proceed in systematizing grants-in-aid, and what concepts should be applied in moving toward such a system? In addressing these questions, we are particularly interested in the implications of the development of planning, programming, budgeting systems (PPBS) by national, state, and local governments.

If we look beyond the specific statements of objectives for individual grants, what can be proposed as more general objectives of the grant-in-aid complex? Implicit in all grants is the general objective of modifying in some way the behavior of the grantee through the use of the grant as a "carrot." From among the numerous functions that have been proposed for a system of grants-in-aid, we have chosen four to be considered here. As discussed in separate sections below, these functions may be regarded as independent or as potentially complementing each other.

NATIONAL PROGRAM STANDARDS

One of the functions proposed would be the promotion of national standards for certain programs of concern to the nation as a whole. Basic to the proposal is the belief that the grant-in-aid mechanism is potentially an efficient way to promote national program *standards* while leaving program *development* and *administration* at the state and local levels.

The concept of "programs of national concern" is in itself somewhat vague. However, it may be most easily defined operationally—i.e., such programs are those which the national government chooses to foster. With this as a guideline, a review of existing grant-in-aid indicates that "programs of national concern" include at least three kinds of issues:

1. Activities affecting the nation's security and defense.
2. Activities at the local or state level which if carried out (or if not carried out) would have significant impact on jurisdictions outside the state of origin —for example, education, pollution control, transportation.
3. Services considered to be part of the birthright of citizens of this nation—for example, programs to ensure that all American citizens have adequate opportunity for individual growth and for a decent standard of living (based on income, health care, housing, and so on).

Many (if not most) domestic programs fall into both of the two latter categories. For example, the provision of at least a minimum level of education is of importance not only in regard to the opportunities made available for individual citizens but also because of the serious problems that lack of education in one state produces when undereducated individuals migrate from that state to cities in other states. Further, the assurance of adequate education is of importance to national security. (A CLOCKWORK ORANGE?)

The above definition in terms of the actions taken by the national government is of course not static. Congress, in passing legislation, is generally reacting to disparities between what the national consensus may deem desirable and what exists. For a number of programs that might well be defined as of national concern the independent decisions of states may produce results considered adequate without national government assistance. Consequently, we should expect an ever shifting scope for cooperative intergovernmental programs. As problems arise or are resolved and as the expectations of the populace change, the complex of programs of national concern will change.

Given, at any point in time, an accepted set of program areas for which there is national concern, there remains the very difficult task of defining appropriate program standards. Ideally, standards would be specified in terms of the end results of different courses of action: e.g., in pollution control, the quality of water and air; in dental health, the dental health status of the citizenry; in public safety, crime rates. Standards should be viewed as being dynamic rather than static; the thrust of program analysis in PPB systems is a continuing review in each program area of the nature of public problems and analysis of how much progress can be achieved at what cost. Program standards for any one time period should be set in the light of such information.

We are, however, faced with two problems in attempting to use this ideal approach: (1) the technical problem of relating the input of resources into a program (assuming resources are to be used in the most effective way) to the impact of the program on people, and (2) the intergovernmental relations problem of assuring that the input resources made available to the state through grants from the national government are in fact used in a reasonably effective way. The implementing of PPB systems at both the federal and state and local levels increasingly in the future should help in dealing with these problems. However, the administration of any grant-in-aid system will probably always be faced with the sensitive question of how tightly the national government should control the use of the grant.

Until there are effective ways of determining the relation of program inputs to outputs, and of controlling the use of inputs to achieve desired outputs, we will be (and are) forced to step back and describe program standards on the basis of inputs for purposes of designing grants-in-aid. For example, instead of specifying dental health program standards in terms of the dental health status of the citizenry, or even in terms of the amount of dental care service provided per individual, we may be forced to use such input measures as expenditures per capita for dental care.

Whatever the basis of their derivation, there will be program standards or targets which the federal government desires to promote in certain program areas. This first function of a system of grants-in-aid would then be one of producing the appropriate incentives to foster the achievement of these standards.

BENEFIT SPILLOVER

Another and somewhat different perspective on the function of a system of grants-in-aid has developed in recent years: its use to help correct distortions in expenditure decisions produced by benefit spillovers. The premise is that a state or local jurisdiction, when making a joint expenditure and taxation decision, acts exclusively in the interest of the citizens within its jurisdiction; thus, benefits that are external—that is, flowing to citizens of other jurisdictions—would be inadequately considered. By means of grants-in-aid the national government can provide a correction for these external benefits. Without such grants, states and localities make a set of independent suboptimal decisions on resource allocation that does not in the aggregate produce an optimal allocation of resources from the national point of view. This aggregate of suboptimal decisions can be viewed as a distortion in resource allocation.

The tidiness of the concept of grants-in-aid based on benefit spillovers as a part of an overall public expenditure theory gives it much weight. In general, public sector intervention becomes necessary to achieve economic efficiency in allocation of resources when benefits are collectively enjoyed as public goods or when there are large externalities that prevent individual purchases from being a good market signal. For example, an individual who chooses not to seek treatment for his tuberculosis may cause a spread of the disease to others unless the government intervenes to assure that the appropriate resources are devoted to controlling the disease. Negative benefits would accrue if private decisions alone were made on resource allocation. This type of conceptual framework applied across governmental or geographic lines essentially underlies the concepts of benefit spillovers on which this system of federal grants-in-aid has been formulated.

Implementation of a grant-in-aid system based on this concept would require a quantification of the benefits that accrue either positively or negatively.[1] One possible implication, as Jesse Burkhead has noted, is that we would need a "regional social diseconomies board" with authority to measure the spillover gains in welfare among states and to order compensatory federal funds in the amounts required to permit states to decide rationally on the allocation of resources.[2]

---

[1] In Chapter 3, a possible interpretation of the benefit spillover thesis is outlined that avoids this requirement, and in effect reduces the implementation of grants on a spillover basis to equivalency with the achievement of the minimum national standards objective.

[2] Jesse Burkhead, "Comment," in *Design of Regional Accounts,* Werner Hochwald, ed. (Johns Hopkins Press for Resources for the Future, Inc., 1961), p. 68.

A third function advocated for a grant-in-aid system is one that would work to attain greater "equalization" among the states. Actually, this function is usually thought of as complementary to other functions of a system.

The meaning of "equalization" as used in discussions of the role of grants-in-aid has not always been clear. For example, a casual analogy is frequently made between the distribution of income from wealthy to poor individuals and the distribution of revenues from higher income states to lower income states. However, this simple analogy can be very misleading, because the matter is much more complicated. The redistribution of income from the wealthy to the poor—say through progressive taxes and transfer payments—is a matter of "vertical equity," by which we mean the concept that a given government has of the appropriate way to give differential treatment to individuals who are judged not to be equals according to some specified set of criteria. Thus, the notion that higher income groups, through progressive taxation, should pay a relatively larger share of the cost of a public good (such as the common defense) is a value judgment taken in regard to vertical equity.

On the other hand, the concept that revenues should be taken from the higher income states and given to lower income states need not involve vertical equity considerations primarily. Only if all citizens in each state were to have incomes equal to the average per capita income in that state would this type of redistribution be a pure matter of vertical equity. When we have a case where the incomes in each state are in fact widely distributed, with a very substantial overlapping of the range of the distributions among the states, we become involved in "horizontal equity." By this we mean the concept that a given government has of the appropriate way to treat individuals who are judged to be equals by some specified set of criteria. Thus, the application of the same federal income tax rate to individuals in different states who are judged to be equals according to the criteria of income is a matter of horizontal equity.

Complete horizontal equity. The concept of complete horizontal equity in the provision of public goods and services in a federal system has been outlined by Buchanan.[3] As the key measure of horizontal equity, the fiscal dividend is introduced. For any individual, the fiscal dividend is the net difference between the dollar value of benefits received *from* public services and the dollars paid out *for* public services. According to Buchanan, horizontal equity would be achieved when the fiscal dividend for each individual in a peer group has been made equal to the fiscal dividend of every other person in that group. However, due to decisions regarding vertical equity, the fiscal dividend of individuals in one peer group is not necessarily equal to that of individuals in another group.

The differences in the distribution of income among the states mean that a common taxation policy applied in each state would yield different amounts of revenue per capita for public services. If the common tax policy is progressive, those states having a higher proportion of high-income individuals and a lower proportion of low-income individuals will obtain more revenues for public services. If all persons in a peer group, regardless of state residence, value public services to the same degree, we find that an individual in one state paying the same taxes as his peer in another state receives less in the way of benefits. In other words, the fiscal dividend of the peers is not equalized. In this situation, it

---

[3] James Buchanan, "Federalism and Fiscal Equity," *American Economic Review,* Vol. 40 (September 1950), pp. 583-99.

is proposed that the federal government use its uniform national tax mechanism to permit the elimination of these disparities in the fiscal dividend.

Equalization of public revenues. As a less heroic proposal, we could define the objective of equalization, not as an achievement of horizontal equity (as outlined by Buchanan), but rather as equalization of available public revenues. Rather than attempting to equalize fiscal dividends, the national government would limit its efforts to equalizing among the states the per capita revenues that would be derived from a uniform state taxation policy.

This concept of revenue equalization, it should be noted, implicitly assumes that the demand for public services is equal per capita or that the output of public sector goods required is equal per capita. Undoubtedly, such a proposal would encounter serious political objections, since it suffers from this deficiency.

Equalization of public services. The above equity difficulties might be alleviated if a less comprehensive function were stated. For example, it could be stated as an equalization of effort to attain a minimum level of services in a specific package of public programs that included education, health services, public safety services, recreational and cultural opportunities, transportation facilities, and so on. For each jurisdiction, the cost of such a minimum-level package would be determined, the local revenue base would be measured, and a set proportion of that base would be allocated to the cost of the package (presumably the smallest proportion that the most "fortunate" jurisdiction could devote to cover the cost). The federal government would then make up the difference for all jurisdictions whose specified proportion of the revenue base would not cover the cost.

The notion of equalizing effort (as measured by a proportion of revenue base) to achieve some minimum level of services is more palatable than that of equalizing available revenues. However, one must still face the very difficult practical problem of defining what should be a part of the package and at what level minimums should be set. To resolve this problem effectively (if it can be resolved politically at all) will require substantial effort in obtaining meaningful measures of need across a wide variety of programs for a wide variety of jurisdictions.

It should be noted that specific grant proposals have not been made to implement any of the above three concepts of equalization among the states. However, some partial steps in the direction of equalization have been advocated; these are discussed further in Chapter 9.

Equalization of effort to achieve national program standards. A much less ambitious and less comprehensive concept of equalization has been proposed (and incorporated to a degree) for implementation in the major categorical grants-in-aid. It might be described as follows. Certain problems (expressed either as explicit problems or as deficiencies in services) are considered to be national in character. The resolution of the explicit problems or the upgrading of the deficient services to minimum standards should not place a differential burden on taxpayers in different states. For example, the relative distribution of crippled children can to a large extent be considered an act of God. The fortuity that the number of crippled children in one state is larger than in another should not place a greater burden on the taxpayers of that state than on taxpayers in the other state. If we had a unitary nation, with uniform tax rates in toto, the distribution of the burden among the citizenry would be of a certain nature. One might argue, then, that the existence of a federal system ought not to change that burden.

This leads to a much more limited concept of equalization. If a national consensus exists in regard to the desirable level of services for a program area, such as services for crippled children, this can be viewed within the state as the "imposition" of an arbitrary external value judgment. Then, rather than talking of equalization of effort to achieve some equal level of utility as perceived by the states, we can speak of equalizing effort to meet a specifically defined standard for certain programs.

This leaves us with the problem of defining equal effort. Here, as with utility comparisons, we face the fundamental problem that relative effort can only be measured in terms of the utility forgone because of the effort made. In recognition of this problem, some arbitrary reference points can be specified. One would be that the incidence of the burden should be no different than the incidence which would exist if the nation were a unitary state rather than a federal state. This line of reasoning would call for equalization measures designed in such a way that the total amount paid by citizens in a given state would be no different than if the program were operated on the national level. This, however, leaves us with a technical problem, because the progressivity of taxes differs substantially among the states and the federal government. The resolution of this difficulty would be complicated.

A simpler reference point would be to define equalization of effort in terms of the fraction of a state's revenue base that must be devoted to implement the program standard. The measure would in effect ignore the differences in incidence of the burden produced by differences in progressivity of taxes. (We develop this concept of equalization in the discussion of grant design in Chapter 3.)

It should be clearly recognized that we do not have the concepts or tools that would permit us to define any method of achieving total equalization (as in Buchanan's concept). We are, however, able to slice away parts of the problem and, by introducing somewhat arbitrary constraints, to define ways of obtaining a rationale for some redistribution of revenues to achieve some very specific objectives.

LEVEL OF THE PUBLIC SECTOR

A fourth proposed function for a grant-in-aid system would promote a more desirable balance in the allocation of resources between the public and private sectors. The arguments in favor of using the national revenue-raising mechanism to improve this balance are several.

Fragmentation of local government. Our metropolitan areas contain the bulk of national population, income, and wealth. They also breed the largest domestic problems. There are huge disparities among local jurisdictions in the distribution of taxable resources, on the one hand, and public problems on the other. Fragmentation of government inhibits the achievement of a proper balance of these resources and problems. The national revenue system, however, is able to draw revenues from the relatively wealthy suburban communities in metropolitan areas and direct them to the areas in central cities where critical problems exist.

Interjurisdictional tax competition. The real or imagined threat of loss of industry and population, which appears to constrain state and local tax effort, is not a deterring factor in a national tax program. Federal tax rules and rates apply uniformly to all competitors in like circumstances. Even if the large disparities in problems and resources to meet the problems did not exist, state and local governments would have difficulty in drawing fully on their resource bases because of interjurisdictional competition.

A number of studies have been made of the effect of state taxation on industrial location. Although the findings are far from conclusive, the issue of constraint is seen to be present. In tax policy discussions, comparisons are repeatedly made between tax loads in one state and those in others, concerning all taxes or selected types—and especially those levied on industry. Whether the threat is real or imagined, the idea of tax competition acts as an inhibitor to public spending.

Linkage of expenditure decisions to taxation decisions. The majority of expenditure decisions reflect the result of the interplay between (1) the groups that urge more education for their children, cleaner rivers, more police protection, better libraries, and so on, and (2) the groups that would be called upon to pay the increased taxes, even if their members are not directly affected by the problems. In our system of government by consensus, if there is little opposition to an expenditure program, it will be adopted; if there is sizable opposition from any special interest group, it will fail of adoption. The closer government is to its citizens, the greater is the force of interaction among interest groups with the consequent built-in bias against new program developments. The reason for this characteristic of local government is clear: the smaller the jurisdiction that is spending and taxing, the more direct and obvious are the facts about who is to benefit and who is to pay. Consequently, it is argued that the national government can create a positive impetus to increases in spending in the public sector through provision of funds which in effect separate the decisions on taxation from those on expenditures.

This point is controversial. Others will argue that, in a democracy, the link between taxes and expenditures should be much tighter, that the implication of expenditure decisions for taxes should be made as clear as possible.

*   *   *   *

In this chapter we have outlined four major functions that might be promoted through the grant-in-aid system. In Chapter 3 we turn to the problem of grant-in-aid design when one or more of these functions is to be furthered.

CHAPTER 3

Grant-in-aid design

AS HAS BEEN NOTED EARLIER, grants-in-aid are a type of leverage the federal government has employed to modify the actions of state and local governments toward more consistency with national values. Generally speaking, the leverage produced by a given grant lowers the relative price of implementing a specific program, and this enhances the attractiveness to the state of carrying out programs at levels considered desirable by the federal government.[1]

Implicit in the grant-in-aid approach is the assumption that state or local officials attempt in some degree, at least, to act in the best interest of their governments—that is, a governor, a mayor, or a group of legislators will try to get the most for the state or the city from revenues potentially available. However, there are several reasons why this "action in accord with self-interest" does not hold completely. First, some decisions that are not in the best interest of the state or city, in the judgment of the primary state or city decision makers, are likely to be pushed through by narrow-interest groups; second, on some occasions, these same decision makers may take a view broader than the narrow self-interest of state or city in regard to programs; third, a governor and his staff or a mayor and his staff may lack the information necessary for an accurate judgment as to which course of action is in their jurisdiction's best interest.

As an example, consider a situation in which a state recognizes that it has a growing shortage of physicians. Suppose that an analysis (if made) would show that the majority of graduates from the state's medical schools do not remain in the state. Further, suppose a decision has been made to increase the size of the medical schools within the state as a response to the shortage of doctors. This decision to increase the capacity of the schools might reflect any one or more of the reasons cited above. The lobbying pressure for the medical schools may be strong; the governor (if an analysis has shown the departure of many medical graduates) may feel that the state has a responsibility to contribute to the national supply of doctors even though there is no direct return to the state from

---

[1] For simplicity of presentation in this chapter, the discussion of the design principles of grants-in-aid is limited to federal grants to one other level of government. Issues involved in assuring appropriate intrastate distribution of grants are discussed in Chapters 8 and 9.

the spillout of doctors; or finally, if analysis of graduates' destination has not been made, state officials may not realize that such a large fraction of graduates leave the state.[2]

The advent of Planning, Programming, Budgeting systems within the states may have a significant impact on the extent to which state officials are able to pursue program options that are in the state's best interest. If a substantial program analysis of the problem of meeting citizens' health service demands were carried out, it might reveal that a decision to increase the size of medical schools would be a very costly way to augment the number of resident physicians, compared to such other options as increasing the quality of postgraduate medical opportunities in the state or providing greater financial assistance to encourage state residents to take up the practice of medicine in the state. Analysis might even show that the approach of increasing the *number* of resident physicians is not as reasonable as turning to more *innovative ways of providing medical services*. Such knowledge in the hands of the governor and his staff might also be a useful tool to counteract special lobby groups.[3] To the extent that PPBS is implemented seriously in the states, one might expect the states to act more critically in regard to program options.

A MODEL OF THE EFFECTS OF GRANTS

In a discussion of criteria for the design of grants-in-aid, it is helpful to have a conceptual model of governmental behavior. The one we present here is based on the premise that governments act to some extent in their own interest, but not necessarily to the degree that decisions are generally made on the basis of hard quantitative analysis of costs and benefits.

The model draws upon price theory and treats the state or city as analagous to the rational consumer. The state (as represented by its decision makers) is considered to be rational in the following senses: (1) it has a consistent concept of the utility it would derive from the programs it might undertake:[4] (2) it moves to increase this utility, subject to the budget constraint under which it must operate.[5] To the extent that a state, as part of a PPB system, undertakes cost-effectiveness analysis of programs, one might expect its program decisions to be more consistent in approximating this behavior.

In this framework, the immediate effect of the offering of a particular grant-in-aid can be described in terms of an alteration to the budget constraint within which the state operates. For a matching grant, this comes about through a re-

---

[2] Of course the determining factor behind the decision may be something other than just the quantitative supply of doctors. It may be judged intuitively that a stronger medical training complex is required to attract the best students and medical researchers, even if a large proportion subsequently go elsewhere.

[3] There is nothing inherent in PPBS (or any system of rational planning) to prevent a state official from taking the "large" view. It may become evident, however, that the grant-in-aid package will operate more coherently as a system if state officials consider their decisions in terms of more easily predictable narrow state self-interest, leaving the corrections necessary for the national interest to the national government.

[4] There is no assurance of consistency, however, in the sense of the rational consumer when more than one individual has a voice in the ranking of program combinations. With majority rule and ordinal ranking, it is possible to find that combination a is preferred to combination b, which in turn is preferred to combination c, which in its turn is preferred to combination a, leading to an inconsistent ranking. For our purposes we here assume that one person, the governor, is dominant in the valuation of programs.

[5] This does not imply a rigid budget constraint for public programs. One of the "public programs" could be greater tax relief for state citizens.

duction in the apparent price of the particular program supported—the greater the federal share, the lower the apparent price. The lowering of the price of one program relative to all others has two effects: (1) a substitution effect in which a larger portion of that program is purchased relative to the others, and (2) an income effect leading to an increase in all programs arising from the increase in real income due to a lower average price level. For a general unrestricted grant, the effect appears as a general increase in available revenue, that is, the grant has only an income effect.

Grants can be categorized in different ways: for example, by the administrative procedures in their distribution—e.g., formula grants (grant allocation to recipients specified by statute) and project grants (allocated on a case-by-case basis)—or by the conditions attached to their use. For the moment we will categorize them according to the conditions attached to their use. Four types of interest are:

1. *Categorical (or conditional) matching grant, open-end.* A grant offering limited to use for a specified objective—requiring the recipient to match a fraction of the grant; no upper limit on the offering.

2. *Categorical (or conditional) matching grant, closed-end.* Same as above, except that there is an upper limit to the offering to each state.

3. *Categorical (or conditional) grant, no matching, closed-end.* A grant offering limited to use for a specified objective of determined magnitude for which no matching on the part of the recipient is required.

4. *General unconditional grant.* A grant offering which the recipient is free to use as he desires and which has no matching requirement.[6]

A schematic representation of the effects of these four types is shown in Figure 3-1. Diagrams a, b, c, and d indicate the apparent budget constraint a state would see before and after each grant offering. The scales on the axes on each diagram represent the magnitudes of particular public programs. In two dimensions we are limited to the display of two programs; as drawn, the horizontal axis represents a program of "national concern," the vertical axis, a program not of specific national concern. (We could also consider the vertical axis as representing the aggregate of all other programs.)

In principle, a utility value could be assigned to each program combination represented by each point between the X and Y axes.[7] This assignment could then be described as a utility surface with the altitude (in the third dimension) indicating the utility—the higher the altitude, the better the program combination. This altitude map can be shown in two dimensions as a contour map. Several illustrative contours have been sketched in on each diagram; in general, altitude increases as we move upward and to the right from the origin, point O. The goal of a rational decision maker in a state or city is to reach the highest utility possible, subject to the budget constraint.

The development of PPB systems ultimately could have a large effect on the degree to which state and local governments act in the rational manner implied above. Hopefully, program analysis will provide a better basis for estimating the actual impact of specific expenditures; consequently, the state and local

---

[6] The term "general unconditional grant" is sometimes also applied to grants with some conditions added, e.g., the grants may specify a required level of effort by the state or be allotted on the basis of tax effort.

[7] If we consider this to be the judgment of relative utility by a state's governor, these utility values could be ordinal—that is, the judgment would be made that one program combination has greater value, less value, or the same value as a second combination, without assigning absolute values of utility.

Figure 3-1.

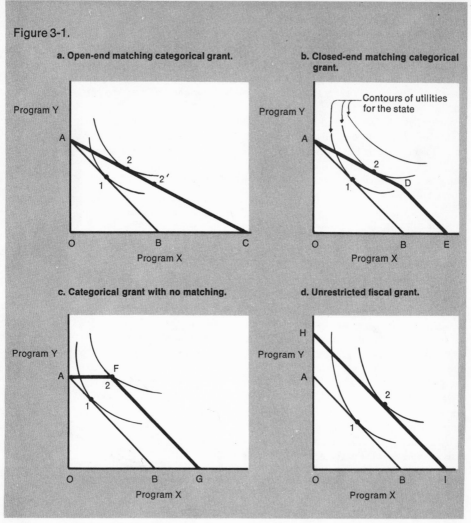

a. Open-end matching categorical grant.

b. Closed-end matching categorical grant.

c. Categorical grant with no matching.

d. Unrestricted fiscal grant.

officials will be making choices between programs more on the basis of trade-offs between program accomplishments and costs than has been the case in the past.

In all four diagrams, lines AB (the budget constraint without grants) represent the tradeoff options in the absence of any grant offerings; the slope of this line is the ratio of the unit price of program X to the unit price of program Y. (For simplicity, we assume that the program magnitudes are measured in constant cost increments.) In other words, the jurisdiction with its projected available revenue could purchase any combination of programs on the budget line AB (or it could purchase any combination represented by points below line AB and also reduce taxes).

An open-end categorical matching grant—shown with a 50-50 matching in Figure 3-1(a)—changes the apparent budget constraint to AC through an apparent reduction in the price of program X. Let us suppose that, in the absence of the grant, the jurisdiction would have carried out a program combination represented by point 1. In other words, in the judgment of the decision makers, point 1 represents the best program combination that can be purchased subject to the constraint AB. With the new tradeoff options produced by the matching grant, the rational ·decision maker (according to our definition) would opt for a different program combination which would include a larger level for program X.[8] In this way, the categorical matching should promote a higher level of implementation for the program of national concern. On the other hand, the level for program Y might be higher than it would have been in the absence of the grant as at point 2, or lower as at point 2′.[9]

The closed-end categorical matching grant is identical in effect to the open-end grant up to a level for program X where the allotment is exhausted, at which point the original tradeoff ratio comes into effect. This apparent budget constraint is represented by line ADE in Figure 3-1(b). At the program level corresponding to point D, the grant allotment would be exhausted. Up to the level of program X represented by point D, the changes in levels of X and Y could be determined by the combination of substitution and income effects. If a program combination were selected beyond point D, there is only an income effect and the matching grant acts as an unrestricted addition to income.

The categorical grant that requires no matching would produce an apparent budget constraint AFG as indicated in Figure 3-1(c). In this case, the increase in program X out to point F comes at no cost to the jurisdiction. Thus there should be a high likelihood that program X would be expanded at least to a level corresponding to point F. As in the case of the closed-end matching grant, there is some possibility that a program combination will be chosen beyond point F.

Finally, the unrestricted general grant has a pure income effect and merely shifts the budget constraint outward parallel to the original constraint, line HI in Figure 3-1(d). One would expect all programs to be increased in magnitude as if the total income were to increase due to other causes—the federal grant introduces no bias into the decision in this case.

Conceptually, one can view grants-in-aid as devices to change the nature of those tradeoffs that a jurisdiction sees as available to it in program development. Through such changes in tradeoffs, the national government can hope to influence the balance of program levels in the states and cities. The task of designing a grant-in-aid system can then be viewed as one of adjusting the apparent budget constraint of a state or city in a way that leads the state or city to develop programs of national concern while at the same time pursuing its own best interests.

We now proceed to a consideration of specific grant characteristics in the light of the four possible system functions as outlined in Chapter 2.

NATIONAL PROGRAM STANDARDS
In the design of a grant-in-aid system directed to fostering the achievement of standard levels of public services in programs of national concern, two major tasks must be faced. The first is to set appropriate standards for any given period of time; the second is to structure specific grant characteristics toward an acceptable likelihood that the standards defined will be achieved.

---

[8] A larger program X is selected for two reasons: (1) the relatively lower price of X makes it more attractive compared to Y (substitution effect), and (2) the lower average price for all programs gives the state greater real income (income effect).

[9] The uncertainly in the direction of change of program Y arises because now the substitution effect and income effect act against each other. These changes in the levels of X and Y can be described in terms of their price elasticities.

Setting program standards. How should one describe output when faced with the task of defining program standards for the purpose of grant-in-aid design? Many different levels of output could be examined. Consider, for example, the portions of Maternal and Child Health programs which are directed to the objective of reducing infant mortality and congenital defects. One might describe output (or impact) in terms of infant mortality rates and birth defect rates; these would be appropriate measures that reflect the impact of a complex of programs on a specific target population. Or one might back off to a lower-level measure for a program component, say family planning, and use, as output, program status as measured by the birth rate and family size for the target population. Stepping further back, one could describe the output of family planning in terms of the specific services provided—e.g., number and percent of women provided with guidance, or perhaps number of family planning centers established. Finally, one might use, as a crude proxy measure, the magnitude of the dollar input—e.g., the average number of dollars spent on family planning per poverty family.

Thus, in the maternal and child health example, we can see an array of measurable factors which might be considered as bases for setting standards. But how should one go about establishing a standard for any one time period?

We first examine an idealized procedure that would be consistent with the philosophy of a PPB system. We know that a problem exists in regard to the subject of maternal and child health—an undesirable disparity between the status of the subject in this nation and what seems to be achievable. The disparity is evident from at least two comparative measures: (1) the differing infant mortality and birth defect rates among various socioeconomic groups in the United States and (2) the difference between the average rates in this nation and those of other advanced nations.

The program analysis staff of the U.S. Department of Health, Education, and Welfare might be (and in fact was) charged with the responsibility of analyzing Maternal and Child Health programs, to seek information on the most effective ways to attack the problem.[10] The analysis would estimate what one might expect to accomplish in reduction of infant mortality rates and birth defect rates as a function of total cost for a broad array of program approaches. Ideally, the analysis would show the best combination of program approaches for any given commitment of total resources and would estimate the impacts of the approaches.

On the basis of this information *and* other relevant information and judgment, the responsible officials would decide what would be the most appropriate program package to pursue in the present time period.[11] In principle, the decision at this point is based, not on the level of federal outlays, but on total resource commitments required. Thus, a specific total resource commitment to a program combination made up of (1) prenatal care and improved nutrition for expectant mothers and (2) family planning services might be judged appropriate.

It would then be estimated that this total commitment of resources, if used in the way recommended, would change the infant mortality and birth defect rates for particular target populations by a certain amount. The federal government

---

[10] *Program Analysis: Maternal and Child Health Care Programs,* U.S. Department of Health, Education, and Welfare, Office of Program Coordination (October 1966).

[11] This would likely involve a complex interaction between the Congress and various levels of the Executive Branch.

would then have to try translating the hypothetically achievable into fact. It would be ideal to set standards for the program on the basis of such measures as mortality and defect rates, since these are the impacts of interest. Unfortunately, there are problems here.

The program analysis has developed an estimate of a causal chain, for example, in family planning from dollar inputs to resource inputs such as facilities and personnel, to services provided to people through these facilities, to the effect of these services on birth rate and family size, and finally to the effect of birth rates and family size on mortality and defect rates. As one proceeds along this chain, the uncertainty of the relations and the decrease in control between the links increases. In other words, it is much easier to specify that a given amount of dollars will in fact produce a certain set of facilities and personnel than it is to specify that those facilities and personnel will service a given group of people in a certain way, and that such services will produce a standard of maternal and child health.

At this point we run hard into a thorny question: how tightly must the programs be controlled by the federal government? The judgment that the nation as a whole should make a specific commitment of resources to maternal and child health was made in part on the basis of how much could be accomplished by that commitment. Because of the increasing uncertainties and existence of external factors as one traces cause and effect from inputs to health impacts, it is generally not feasible to set and control standards which are defined in terms of health impacts. If the program is defined and controlled broadly as maternal and infant care and one cannot meaningfully monitor and control health impact standards, there is no assurance that the resources will be put together at the state level in a way that reasonably corresponds to the program package which led to the decision to make the commitment in the first place. On the other hand, if programs are defined more tightly so that, for example, a certain fraction of maternal and infant care program funds are constrained to be used for family planning centers, assurance is greater that the desired program package will be implemented; however, this will entail a great increase in the complexity and rigidity of a grant-in-aid system.

There is no easy way out of this dilemma. Strengthening program analysis and planning at the state level should help to assure that funds which are not tightly controlled will be used well. However, this will not solve the problem. A continuing review of program objectives by the federal government will still be needed to ascertain to what extent the national interest requires narrow definition in any given program area.

During the immediate future, an in-depth analytical background will in most cases be lacking for deciding what commitments of resources should be directed to various objectives of national concern. Consequently, in the majority of program areas, judgments of appropriate standards must be made on the basis of gross inputs, e.g., expenditures per child for health or for general education. For the present, this factor in itself somewhat mitigates the problem of control of the use of resources. If, in fact, no one has adequate information on the best ways to allocate resources within a broad program area, the need for concern about controls vanishes.

In any case, the national government should have for any given time period an array of standards based on program inputs—in some cases very broadly defined and in others narrowly defined. These standards would articulate the priorities it would give at any one time to the range of programs considered to be of national concern. Over time, output standards could be substituted.

Design of grants. In principle, the standards set for the range of programs of national concern reflect the priorities attached by the Congress to advances in these areas in the light of estimated costs and the achievements expected. If the national government were to run these programs directly, presumably the allocation of federal dollars would correspond to these priorities.

Implementation of priority programs on the national level is complicated, however, by the nature of the federal system and the desire to have programs locally developed and administered. The grant-in-aid is intended to serve as a tool to induce the states to move toward implementing programs in accord with the priorities. Thus, by providing a carrot of the right magnitude, the federal government hopes to lead the states to the desired program resource allocations.

At the outset, we make two simplifying assumptions: (1) that the federal government has no difficulty in drawing revenues in the form of taxation; (2) that all states are identical. The first assumption can be interpreted to mean that the federal government need be concerned only with the most effective application of total revenues, whether federally raised or state and locally raised. The second is introduced to allow us to avoid, for now, questions of equalization among states and complications due to differences in social values among states.

Figure 3-2 depicts one program of national concern (program X) and a second program which represents the aggregate of all other state programs (program Y). We are supposing that, in the absence of federal support, a state with budget constraint AB would elect a program combination (X_o, Y_o). We assume that a program standard X_s $(X_s > X_o)$ has been established for program X.

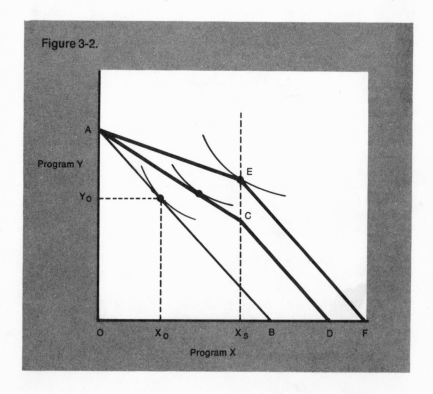

Figure 3-2.

Program Y

Program X

How should a grant-in-aid be designed to promote achievement of the level X_s? We expect the state to increase the level of a program if the program's price is reduced. The magnitude of the increase will depend on the nature of the decision process in the jurisdiction and on underlying program information. For example, if the jurisdiction routinely makes use of cost/effectiveness analysis in its program decisions, the prior program level presumably would have been based in part on criteria concerning the payoff from the program relative to its cost. The response to the grant offering would then depend on how the change in the program cost affects the decision criteria. Uncertainty will be substantial, and the task of estimating state response to grants will not be easy in any case.

Two different grant options are shown in Figure 3-2. Both are closed-end grants at the standard program level X_s, since the federal government has not committed itself to promoting levels above the standard. (In fact, if attention is to be focused on the achievement of a set of national standards, open-end grants are undesirable in that they would lead some states, presumably the wealthier, to draw upon federal resources to expand programs above the standards. Considering the objectives stated, one would assert that these resources could better be used in other program areas.) As illustrated in Figure 3-2, the grant producing an apparent budget constraint ACD provides insufficient incentive for the state to achieve the minimum standard level. On the other hand, the grant corresponding to the budget constraint AEF would induce the state to reach the standard level.

The design of a grant to achieve the stated level requires some estimate of the response of the state to various price reductions. The appropriate criteria for the grant design are:

1. For establishing the matching conditions, a federal proportion should be defined that just induces the state to move to program level X_s.
2. The allotment to the state for that program should be set by determining, at the established matching ratio, the total federal share for implementation of program level X_s. The setting of total input dollars for achievement of program level X_s requires that need factors be built in. For example, if the program standard for general education is set in terms of per child expenditures, the cost of the program obviously requires an estimate of the school age population.

Clearly, information will be inadequate to determine accurately what the matching ratio should ideally be. However, regardless of accuracy, this is a judgment that *must* be made.

Federal dollars versus total dollars. If we now remove the assumption that federal dollars are easy to obtain, we are confronted with a serious problem regarding allocation. Suppose two programs serve the same objective and have commensurable outputs. Analysis might show that the maximum progress toward the objective with a certain total commitment would be obtained with a 60 percent and 40 percent allocation of total funds to the two programs, respectively. However, in estimating responsiveness of the state to the two options, it might be found that a very small inducement would be needed to lead the state to increase the level for the second program, whereas a very large inducement would be required to increase the level for the first. If federal dollars are hard to come by, it would be likely that the largest improvement in progress toward the objective that could be induced through the use of limited federal revenues would lead to a resource allocation which deviates substantially from the 60/40 mix that analysis indicates as the best package.

This difficulty may not occur so frequently between program areas in which outputs are commensurable, where in fact there will be measures that allow objective assessments of the relative effectiveness of different program packages. Rather, it would seem more likely to appear as a biasing factor between very different programs. That is, it may be relatively much easier to induce states to spend for the construction of physical things than for increases in, say, welfare programs. The extent to which the maximization of bang-for-the-buck in federal dollars does not conform to maximization of bang-for-the-buck in total dollars may be an inescapable cost of federalism. In any event, the designers of grants-in-aid must be conscious of the fact that this disparity exists.

A somewhat different perspective on the problem might result if the federal government were to abandon the goal of promoting total priorities in favor of the less ambitious goal of promoting certain *minimum* standards. In this view, federal dollars would be used first to gain implementation of minimum standard levels in the most effective way, which might be substantially below the levels corresponding to the standards reflecting the priorities for total resource allocation. The cost of federalism would then tend to be reflected more in the abandonment of federal concern for program implementation above the minimum standard levels.

Whichever way the standards are defined, the criteria for the design of any one grant would be formally the same. The total grant-in-aid system considerations, when more than one grant is involved, are discussed in greater detail in Chapter 6.

Interstate variations. If we now remove the second assumption—that all states are identical—we introduce a new array of problems. It is an observed fact that not all states will respond to a given matching grant in the same way. This is due to such factors as different social preferences in the different states, variations in perception of the problem, and differences in fiscal capacities. At a given matching ratio, a wealthy and progressive state is likely to respond more strongly than a poor and conservative state.

Several approaches could be taken in the light of this phenomenon. For example, all states could be proffered the same matching ratio for a given grant, with the realistic expectation that not all will achieve the standard level and that for some the inducement to meet the level will be much stronger than it needs to be. Other approaches could be adopted that would differentiate among states on a variety of bases; two of these—equalization among states, and efficiency in the use of federal dollars—are discussed in separate sections below.

Equalization in categorical grants-in-aid. One of the major factors that affects the response of states to matching grants is the substantial variation of the revenue base among the states. Since states with low income will in general have more difficulty in meeting their share of a matching grant than states with high income, it is argued that grant design should take recognition of the differences in revenue base from state to state. This approach can be rationalized on the ground of efficiency as well as of fairness.

The Advisory Commission on Intergovernmental Relations has formulated a set of objectives for grants-in-aid that, in addition to being directed to achievement of national standards, incorporates a partial measure of equalization. This is stated as "a uniform fiscal effort on the part of each state to support such a minimum program [a program of specified national minimum standards]." [12]

[12] Advisory Commission on Intergovernmental Relations, *The Role of Equalization in Federal Grants* (January 1964), p. 49.

In other words, the partial equalization advocated by the Commission is concerned only with an equalization of fiscal effort by the states in meeting the very specific program standards considered to be of national importance, and does not include the concept of equalization of state income or even of equalization of available public revenues. Any movement toward the latter two goals is purely incidental to the more specific objectives stated.

An attempt to meet the Commission's specific concept of equalization also involves an attempt to estimate how much effort different states are required to exert to implement the program standard. But this is not in fact measurable, for true effort can only be measured in terms of what other things the citizens of a given state must forgo in carrying out the program standard and of the actual disutility they suffer from giving up these other things, whether they be private goods or public goods. We do not know how to compare utility among different groups of people. Thus, fundamentally, we do not know how to equalize effort.

However, the fact that equality of effort cannot (at least at present) be measured does not prevent us from doing something in the way of equalization. It is likely that general agreement can be reached about using certain "proxy" measures of fiscal effort. For example, one might accept percentage of total income devoted to a program as a commensurable indicator of effort. Or one might use the percentage of the revenue yield of a standard package of taxes applied in a state as an indicator.

Thus, as one approach, we might estimate that the states would be willing to devote a certain percentage of their revenues to achievement of a specific nationally defined standard. Then, for example, the matching provisions would be set as follows: the federal government would provide a share of each dollar spent (up to the total cost for implementing the standard in the state) in the proportion fixed by the ratio of the difference between the total cost to implement the standard and a specified percentage of the standard tax yield to the total cost for the program. (Note that the state is not necessarily required to implement a particular set of taxes. The theoretical yield of a standard tax package is used only for the purpose of determining the federal share in matching.) It follows that the allotment would be the difference between the total cost for the program and the specified percentage of the tax yield.[13]

The variable matching designed to achieve a uniform effort in moving to the national standard program level is somewhat similar to variable matching as defined by the Hill-Burton allotment percentage.[14] However, there is a significant difference in that the Hill-Burton federal percentage includes a factor to correct for variations in fiscal capacity (as measured by per capita income) but does not include a factor to correct for variations in total cost for implement-

---

[13] In symbols, if p is the percentage of yield of the standard tax package to be devoted to the program, C_i the total cost to implement the program standard in the ith state, and t_i the yield of the standard tax package in the ith state, then for the ith state:

$$\text{federal percentage of matching} = 100 \, \frac{C_i - pt_i}{C_i}$$

$$\text{allotment} = C_i - pt_i$$

$$\text{total federal outlay to all states} = \Sigma \, C_i - pt_i.$$

[14] *Grants-in-Aid and Other Financial Assistance Programs Administered by the U.S. Department of Health, Education, and Welfare, 1967 Edition* (Government Printing Office, 1967), p. 201.

ing the standard program.[15] Only if total cost to implement the program standard is directly proportional to population does the Hill-Burton formula become equivalent to the formula defined in this paper. This could be a rather important difference.

One further comment is appropriate. If *input measures* (e.g., expenditures per child, expenditures per capita) are used as program standards instead of *output measures,* it would be preferable if some weighting factor took account of the deviations among the states in input-output relationships.[16]

The design of a grant-in-aid intended to equalize state effort to meet nationally defined standards should meet the following criteria:

1. The total program cost for which federal sharing is provided should be determined on the basis of the defined standard and need. If standards are defined in terms of input measures, the total program cost should be adjusted for price level.
2. The federal proportion in the matching conditions should be set in the aggregate so that all states are likely to move to the standard level. The matching conditions should be variable, including both fiscal capacity and total need measures so that each state would make the same effort in reaching the standard level.
3. The allotment to each state is determined by the above two factors and would be the difference between the total cost to implement the standard program and the percent of fiscal capacity that has been defined as the appropriate state share.

In Chapter 4, we examine the inducements provided by selected formula grants in the light of the equalization objectives outlined in this section.

Efficiency in grants-in-aid. As noted earlier, the type of equalization presented above could be pursued on at least two grounds. The first is a notion of fairness about the burden that ought to be carried by various states in meeting goals set in the light of the national good (as discussed above). The second has to do with efficiency.

The concept of efficiency in grants-in-aid directed to the achievement of national program standards discussed here is that presented by Rafuse.[17] It can be described as follows. Given that national standards for program service levels have been determined, the most efficient grant-in-aid system is the one that induces the states to achieve these standards at the least direct cost to the federal government.

---

[15] The Hill-Burton allotment percentage is $100 - 50 \dfrac{Y_i}{Y}$, where Y_i is per capita income in the ith state and Y average per capita income in the United States. The formula defined in this paper can be written as

$$\text{federal percentage} = 100 \frac{C_i - pt_i}{C_i} = 100 - \frac{100 \, pt_i}{C_i}.$$

If we assume that $t_i = ax_iY_i$ where x_i is the population in the ith state (i.e., yield is proportional to total income), and define p such that $100pa = \dfrac{50}{Y}$,

we have:

$$\text{federal percentage} = 100 - 50 \cdot \frac{Y_i}{Y} \cdot \frac{x_i}{C_i}.$$

[16] Cf. Robert W. Rafuse, Jr., "The Efficiency of Conditional Grants-in-Aid," in *Revenue Sharing and Its Alternatives: What Future for Fiscal Federalism?,* Vol. II, Prepared for the Subcommittee on Fiscal Policy of the Joint Economic Committee, July 1967 (Government Printing Office, 1967), p. 1058.

[17] *Ibid.,* p. 1053.

Clearly, to determine the grant characteristics that would induce this achievement would be a very difficult task. The sort of firm information on which estimates of state response need to be based is insufficient. Further, there is a basic difficulty in tailoring grants individually: a state, when aware of the process, could employ strategy to increase the federal share to its program. The procedure of setting matching ratios on the basis of a state's responsiveness provides a disincentive for the state to develop programs—i.e., by holding back, the state could hope to obtain a larger federal share.

However, such gamesmanship may be avoided by certain further partial steps toward efficiency. Research may be able to ascertain that the relative preferences of states in certain program areas can be estimated on the basis of objective factors not open to easy manipulation by the states. Rafuse suggests, for instance, as a hypothetical example, a study of the development of high-quality laboratory facilities in secondary schools:

> A careful study of the provision of laboratory facilities would be undertaken with a view to identifying the factors that are the most important determinants of the policies of school districts with respect to such facilities. Such a study might establish that the demand for laboratory facilities is directly related to the following factors: the average personal income of the community per school-age child, the proportion of the adult population with a college degree, and the size of the school district. On the basis of this information it would be possible to define a grant formula that would make the Federal matching share a specific inverse function of the three variables. The result would be no more than a crude approximation to the theoretically desirable formula, since the true demands of school districts can only be estimated from historical data. It would, however, be a considerable improvement over methods presently in use, which are not really designed to produce information about demands, and which result in formulas that rely exclusively upon such gross variables as population and personal income for virtually every program.[18]

There is some potential, then, in the idea that greater efficiency in the use of federal dollars to achieve specific program standards can be attained through research on the demand for services and the design of grants on the basis of the findings. (Research on determinants of public expenditures is reviewed in the Appendix following the last chapter of this study.)

It should be pointed out, however, that if the objectives for achievement of national standards are viewed as complementary to another objective—i.e., increasing the total public share in the economy—the concern for the kind of efficiency discussed here lessens. If the federal revenue tax system is being utilized to provide added revenues to the states and localities, efficiency in use of *total* funds—federal, state, and local—emerges as more significant than efficiency in use of *federal* dollars. From the national viewpoint, whether this additional revenue comes in the form of a conditional grant or an unconditional fiscal grant is not necessarily critical.

BENEFIT SPILLOVERS

A fundamental problem in resource allocation arises in a nonunitary government: some of the governmental units with narrow jurisdictions may make taxing and expenditure decisions that are not comprehensive enough to be in accord with the total good. One taxing jurisdiction may be responsible for funding and operating a program that produces some benefits for individuals outside the jurisdiction. An example of such a program was suggested earlier in this chapter, in regard to a hypothetical state that operates a medical school from which most graduates leave the state. In this situation, the citizens of the state paying for the school would not reap all of the benefits.

---

[18] *Ibid.*, p. 1057.

Let us assume that this state carries out rigorous cost-benefit analysis of its medical school operation. It is very possible that the state decision makers, upon seeing the results of analysis, would develop the medical education program only up to the point at which the marginal benefits received by the state equal the marginal cost to the state. However, to the extent that the graduates remain in this nation, it is clear that the marginal benefits to the nation as a whole are greater than those to the state. Consequently, the state, by terminating program development at the level which *it* views as optimum, carries out a program that is below optimum from the *national* point of view. We may then argue that the most comprehensive taxing jurisdiction, the national government, must apply corrective action to induce overall optimal resource allocation. One approach for correction is the use of grants-in-aid. George Break has specified four criteria for these grants:

1. They should be categorical or conditional.
2. They should be matching grants with both the grantor and the grantee governments sharing in the cost of the supported programs.
3. The grantor government, since it is paying for benefits received, is entitled to ask that its funds be used efficiently and to exercise some controls over the grantee's operation of all supported programs.
4. They should be open-end rather than closed-end.[19]

Grants designed to balance benefit spillovers should be categorical, since the spillovers are program related. They should be matching grants, with the provisions set so that, for each program increment or project considered, the federal government's share of the marginal costs would equal the ratio of the marginal benefits that spill out to the total marginal benefits derived from the incremental expenditure. Under these conditions, the state that implements a program to the level at which marginal cost to the state equals marginal benefit for the state also reaches the level at which total marginal cost equals total marginal benefits for the nation as a whole. (An Addendum at the end of this chapter presents an analytical formulation of several options for federal cost sharing.) Thus, program optimization by the state would be consistent with program optimization for the nation. Ideally, the grants would be open-end since, if the matching conditions are properly set and the states behave rationally, the system is self-regulating in a way that is consistent with optimal resource allocation.

The idea of using grants to correct for benefit spillovers is attractive. The process permits one to place the problem of intergovernmental finances in the same context as general public expenditure theory. It should be recognized, however, that the notion of *rationalizing* (as opposed to *designing*) grants-in-aid has been based on this concept for some time. For example, the proposal that federal grants should be supplied for construction of highways that serve interstate transport has long been accepted—basically on the benefit spillover thesis. The new thrust of the benefit spillover proposal is one of *designing* grant provisions on quantitative measures of the interjurisdictional spillovers. It is to this point that our discussion is directed.

Two entirely different operational grant design concepts can be drawn from the formalism of benefit spillover correction outlined above. The first (as implied by the newer literature on the subject) seems to lead to a highly sophisticated quantitative system for designing grants. Quite aside from the technical

---

[19] George F. Break, *Intergovernmental Fiscal Relations in the United States* (Brookings Institution, January 1967), Chap. 3, section on "Optimizing Grants."

difficulties involved, this approach rests, in our view, on a rather shaky conceptual basis.[20]

The reasonableness of *designing* the matching provision of categorial grants on the basis of quantitative estimates of benefit spillovers rests on two interrelated key assumptions: (1) that governments act in a highly rational manner in comparing costs and benefits of programs, and (2) that the benefit derived from a program is a measurable objective entity.

The first assumption. Studies have been made (the most important was in the area of local education expenditures) which allow the interpretation that jurisdictions do behave as if they take account of benefit spillovers in their decisions on program level.[21] Even if these studies were conclusive, however, there would still be problems. The notion of correction for benefit spillovers is directed toward the goal of "optimality" of resource allocation. To implement a system then requires, not only that expenditures be a known function of the degree of spillovers, but also that they bear an ascertainable relation to an "optimum" level in the absence of spillovers (or when corrections for spillovers are made). There is no empirical evidence one way or the other on this matter (or, as is discussed later in the chapter, on whether this is even a meaningful question).

The second assumption. This is closely related to the first assumption's problems as outlined in the paragraph above. That is, what are benefits and what do we mean by "optimality" of resource allocation? We are involved in evaluating the benefit derived from programs as seen by at least two different sovereign bodies made up of different populations. How are benefits to be calculated? Who does the computation and is there any independently defined quantity that we can call a "benefit"? For example, a given local community may take particular pride in its library system and consequently develop it to a much higher level than libraries in surrounding communities. At the same time, other services may be at relatively lower levels. Suppose there are no spillovers. Who is to say which of the communities has the more optimal resource allocation? If there are benefit spillouts, who is to assign the quantitative measures of these to be comparable with internal benefits?

The task of designing grants on a quantitative basis to correct for benefit spillovers is particularly beset with difficulties when the programs involved are closely related to local value-judgments and social mores. This would be the case when the programs deal with value-judgments regarding equity, minimum standards of services, or the opportunities that are considered to be the birthright of citizens of this nation.

On the other hand, it must be conceded that universally acceptable commensurable benefit measures could be derived for some programs—e.g., those whose effects are primarily economic. For such programs, there would then remain the technical problem (which is not trivial) of measuring benefit flows over space and time to determine the appropriate corrective factors. If this measurement can be accomplished, benefit spillover grants could be implemented for that subset of grants.

A second interpretation, which avoids the problems discussed above, can be

---

[20] It should be noted that the following discussion is the interpretation that we and certain other writers have made of the meaning of the benefit spillover argument as expressed in the literature. If we are incorrect in this interpretation, the subsequent critique may be unfair.

[21] Burton A. Weisbrod, *External Benefits of Public Education* (Princeton University, Industrial Relations Section, 1964).

made of the implications of the benefit spillover thesis as a basis of grant design. It treats the question of optimality of resource allocation on a phenomenological basis. That is, we assert, by definition, that the actual expenditure decisions made by a jurisdiction are optimal for that jurisdiction, regardless of the process through which it perceives benefits and costs.[22] Thus, (1) optimality is defined and (2) any assumptions about a particular rational process on the part of the jurisdictions are avoided. Unfortunately, this interpretation eliminates anything new in the benefit spillover approach—as compared, for example, to the concept of promoting national minimum standards.

Let us say that the national government approaches the problem of grant design as follows. Looking at a given program in a particular state or city, it would ask: what benefits would be perceived externally if the jurisdiction were to move from program level A to program level B? The benefit measure to be used at a particular point in time would be the maximum amount of funds the national government would be willing to devote to this change. The next question would be: what benefits would the jurisdiction perceive by moving level A to level B? The measure of benefits would be the maximum amount of funds the local jurisdiction would be willing to devote to this change. The total benefits, then, could be *defined* as the sum of these two amounts, and the share of the actual cost that the federal government would offer is (as noted earlier) equal to the ratio of the marginal benefits that spill out to the total marginal benefits that derive from the incremental expenditure. If the total cost is prorated in this way and is less than the benefits as measured by willingness to pay, the program change would be implemented. The process would be continued up to the point that national benefits and national costs and local benefits and local costs are equated. In our phenomenological approach, this would then be a total optimization of resource allocation.

This interpretation would also permit the promotion of minimum national standards through the benefit spillover approach. In this situation, the benefits perceived by the nation, as measured by willingness to pay, would be equal to the total cost of achieving the standard. Whether the federal government would in fact pay that amount would depend on the incremental benefits that the state or locality may perceive in moving up to the minimum standard level.

Thus, we see that the latter interpretation avoids the problems mentioned earlier. There are no particular assumptions made about rationality of decision making on the part of grantees. The only analytical problems are those of estimating how much a state or locality is willing to pay for a given change in service, and how much the national government is willing to pay for the same change, and then prorating the cost appropriately. It should be apparent, however, that this interpretation reduces the benefit spillover approach essentially to the approach that was outlined for the use of the grant-in-aid "carrot" to achieve national program standards.

Consequently, we find ourselves taking the position either that the benefit spillover approach is generally beset with serious conceptual and technical difficulties—or that there is really nothing new or unique about it.

Demonstration and research grants. There is one type of grant-in-aid for which the benefit spillover approach is particularly relevant—those grants dealing

---

[22] The assertion that actual decisions are by definition optimal is not the same thing as saying that there is no basis for program changes. In any jurisdiction, there are always forces that do not believe the current decisions are optimal. As the strength and position of these forces change, and as external events occur, there will be continuing pressures to question decisions and push for change.

with demonstration and evaluation of new program approaches and research on public problems. The demonstration of the effectiveness of an innovative approach to a problem produces benefits that accrue predominantly to jurisdictions other than the ones conducting the project. (The same is true of research projects.) The case can be made that a given state should not be asked to take the risk of funding unproven projects that, if successful, will be of national benefit.

In consonance with the benefit spillover rationale, project grants designed for demonstration, evaluation, or research purposes should be totally federally funded, or nearly so. As Figure 3-1(c) illustrated, the 100 percent federal grant would allow the state to undertake the project without distorting its normal budget constraint. However, if the primary objective is to learn about program impact and effectiveness, the demonstrations should be subject to a research design to ensure that their findings are of widespread value.

INTERSTATE EQUALIZATION

We have already discussed the question of interstate equalization in regard to the achievement of externally proposed program goals.[23] We concluded there that partial equalization, in the sense of equalizing the proportion of fiscal capacity that a state must devote to achieving the program standards, can be built into formula grants.

Horizontal equity. There remains, however, the possible broader objective of further equalization among the states. As outlined in Chapter 2, greater equalization among states is directed toward the goal of horizontal equity, which is concerned with equal treatment of equals in a federal system.

The most appropriate grant for achieving greater horizontal equity is the unrestricted fiscal grant. Since no specific program goals are sought, the redistribution of revenues should produce no artificial relative price changes which would bias state and local expenditure decisions. If the objective is one of attaining total horizontal equity as defined by Buchanan (see our Chapter 2, above, footnote 3), the grant allocation would be determined by measuring the fiscal dividends of the citizenry and shifting federal funds to allow equalization of the fiscal dividends for peer groups.

Two major problems exist in regard to this role for grants-in-aid. First, as Scott has emphasized, there is no way to assure that the redistribution of revenues to units of government at the state level will in fact lead to equalization of fiscal dividends.[24] Each state's share of an unconditional grant may be computed in a way to make equalization of the fiscal dividend possible, but not assured. Second, and more fundamental, we have no meaningful way of measuring the fiscal dividend of a given individual in terms commensurable with that of other inidviduals. Here we are faced with the basic conceptual problem of welfare economics, that of comparing interpersonal utilities.

On the other hand, if the goal is the less ambitious one of equalizing available public revenues among the states (see Chapter 2, section on "Equalization of public revenues"), the undertaking by the national government might be variously defined, but essentially it involves raising the revenues per inhabitant in each state so that the total from federal and state sources combined would be equal. The national government's grant would be determined as a residual of

---

[23] See subsection "Equalization in categorical grants-in-aid," above.

[24] Anthony Scott, "The Economic Goals of Federal Finance," *Public Finance,* Vol. 19 (No. 3, 1964), pp. 241-88.

the uniform per capita amount and the per capita amount each state could raise, either by imposing equal tax burdens on each group of taxpayers in similar economic circumstances or by imposing equal effective tax rates on a uniformly defined tax structure. Full equalization would mean raising all the states to the level of the highest. Partial equalization within a lesser grant sum would mean raising the low states up to the next highest level that the grant monies would permit on a sequential basis. That is, the state with the lowest revenue would be raised to the next highest and these two states to the level of the next highest, and so on, until all available grant funds were exhausted.

As noted earlier, this goal of equalizing public revenues is likely to be politically unacceptable, since it ignores differences in need and demand for public services among the states.

A number of formulas for a general fiscal grant that produce some redistributtion of revenues among states can be developed. (This is discussed in Chapter 9.) There are, however, no clear criteria for establishing how far one should proceed in this type of redistribution.

We have no operational basis for deciding whether Rhode Island is poorer or wealthier than Nebraska when all of the factors (e.g., fiscal capacity and need and demand) are considered that conceptually should be included in assessing horizontal equity. This would be only an academic question if there were general agreement that certain states are in fact "poorer" than others; however, such agreement does not exist. Some will argue that the southeastern states are "poor" due to low income. Others argue just as strongly that the northeastern states with relatively high income are relatively "poor" due to the high demand for public services. (Chapter 5 elaborates the points noted in this paragraph.)

Minimum level of public services. In principle we could measure for each state the resource requirements to implement appropriate packages of programs for different population groups (e.g., urban-rural) to various different levels. Then general fiscal grants could be designed at each level that would equalize the effort made by the citizens of the states if they were to implement that level in the same way that effort would be equalized in relation to achievement of national program standards. Rather than making the grant conditional with a matching requirement of expenditures in the selected program package, the amount received by a state could be weighted by tax effort and program cost indices. The amount allotted to a given state would be computed as though one were designing a broad categorical grant for state programs, with built-in equalization similar to the arrangements for the earlier categorical grants. However, to avoid the imposition of national standards in state programs, the money could be spent by the state as it desired, with the only matching required being that implied by the tax effort index as a weighting factor. There is, of course, no assurance that the states would spend the money in a way that accords with the procedure for determining the states' share.

In defining packages of public services for estimating fiscal requirements, it is not possible to include all potential public programs. Thus, one must designate which programs are to be included. As noted earlier, there would probably be agreement on some, such as education, health facilities, garbage removal, and transportation services. But what about museums, parks, or public theaters? One could argue that these are the very things that make life tolerable in highly urbanized areas. In general, there is no objective basis for selecting the set of potential public services to be included. If this approach were to be pursued seriously, a substantial effort would be required to decide on a national basis what "the minimum level of public service" should be defined to cover.

PUBLIC/PRIVATE SECTOR BALANCE

The use of the federal tax system to alter the balance of spending between the public and private sectors has been increasingly advocated. Moreover, additional federal grants-in-aid can achieve this purpose. If no specific program goals are sought, the unconditional grant may be the most appropriate mechanism for this purpose.[25] In a sense, the general fiscal grant could be considered as a conditional grant for one broad program—"spending in the public sector."

There remains the problem of how unconditional grants should be distributed if equalization objectives are not sought. In principle, the revenues should be returned to the place of origin; this, however, is administratively quite difficult. Most proposals for unconditional grants have called for allocations to the states based on relative population, largely because this would be simple to administer. (Discussed further in Chapter 9.)

Since the additional federal grants-in-aid are intended to increase spending in the public sector, provisions should be considered to ensure that the funds are not used to substitute for current state or local spending. The addition of tax effort provisions would, in effect, make the additional grant a matching grant for spending in the public sector. A threshold tax effort index level might be used to help ensure that none of the federal funds are substituted for state and locally raised funds.

SYSTEMS OF GRANTS-IN-AID

Two patterns for structuring a system of federal grants-in-aid are summarized here to illustrate the concept of a package of grants-in-aid designed to serve multiple objectives.

The first pattern. In this system, categorical matching grants would be designed to achieve optimal resource allocation for society as a whole, as the fifty states make independent allocations of revenues for public programs.[26] The categorical grants would be limited to those program areas in which there are significant benefit spillouts from the implementing jurisdiction. As outlined earlier, matching provisions would be set to provide appropriate compensation to the state for the benefit spillouts.[27] Ideally, such grants would match from a zero expenditure level in the specific program category and would be open-end, allowing the state complete freedom to decide on how much of the federal grant monies it wishes to make use of at the specified matching ratio.

Experimental projects constitute a specific area that would continue to receive substantial support on the basis of benefit spillovers. However, to obtain precise estimates of the expected value of such spillovers would probably not be feasible. Rather, federal agencies will be forced to operate on a pragmatic basis in determining the incentives necessary to promote new approaches to public problems.

An unconditional fiscal grant could be designed to serve a number of purposes in this system. First, it could be used to improve the balance of resource

---

[25] It should be noted that tax credits, as opposed to grants-in-aid, have been advocated for this purpose (see Chapter 10).

[26] The system outlined here is essentially in accord with that proposed by George Break; see footnote 19, above.

[27] The term "matching grant" is used quite generally here to denote any federal compensation to a state that is a function of the level of program operation selected by the state in one or more particular areas. Strictly speaking, the matching ratio should not be constant but should vary as a function of program size. In practice, it is likely that a single matching ratio would be set that would approximate the ideal matching formula.

allocation between the private and public sectors in the states. Second, it could serve as a means for facilitating the achievement of greater uniformity in public service levels among states through the inclusion of some equalizing features. Third, it could be designed to permit the federal government to provide leverage for economic stabilization.

Theoretically, this system presents a neat solution to the problems of a grant-in-aid system. Categorical aids are limited to correcting for resource allocation decisions that are impaired by benefit spillovers, and an unconditional grant is implemented to serve central fiscal-economic purposes.

The second pattern. In this system, the position is taken that national distribution goals have traditionally been pursued through programs administered at the local level. However, since these programs affect the national birthright of each citizen, there is a need to incorporate a mechanism into the grant-in-aid system to assure this birthright.

Categorical matching grants in this system perform a dual function. First, they would be designed to provide a high assurance that national standards reflecting a national consensus are paramount. In this vein, national support for state planning and personnel development may be viewed as a special case of assuring a minimum state performance consistent with national values. Second, the categorical grants would be designed to overcome the uneconomic decisions on resource allocation resulting from benefit spillovers.

If it is believed that there should be a high degree of horizontal equity in meeting nationally defined standards, then equalization measures should be incorporated in the design of the matching grant. A recommendation along this line for public welfare programs was made in the 1966 Report of the Advisory Council on Public Welfare; under the proposal, the federal government would:

> Specify national standards for adequate and equitable financial assistance and social services and for program administration.
>
> Specify each State's share of the costs of the comprehensive program under the national standards. The State share would be expressed as a percent of total personal income payments in the State; the percents would vary among States as necessary to ensure reasonable and equitable fiscal effort among all States.
>
> Assume full financial responsibility for the difference in cost of the comprehensive program in each State.[28]

To achieve a high assurance that states throughout the nation will move to the desired program levels, the total federal share would have to be set at a sufficiently high level.

Two options are possible in the specification of matching requirements. One of them might require, as implied in the Advisory Council's recommendations, that the state implement the national standard before it receives any federal aid. Alternatively, matching might be offered from a zero expenditure level with the federal matching set to provide the appropriate federal share at the standard level.

The equalization categorical matching grant would be closed-end at the national program standard level. Beyond that level, however, there would be an open-end matching grant designed to compensate for benefit spillovers if they should be significant. For those program categories in which national standards have not been set, but where the benefit spillovers are significant, open-end matching grants would be provided as in the first pattern of a grant system

---

[28] Advisory Council on Public Welfare, *"Having the Power, We have the Duty,"* Report to the Secretary of Health, Education, and Welfare (Government Printing Office, 1966), p. 34.

described earlier. As before, there would be substantial grant support for the high-spillover demonstration and innovation projects.

However, in our second system of grants, the general fiscal grant would play a somewhat different role. It could serve the following five functions.

1. As before, the general fiscal grant would help achieve a better balance between the private and public sectors. It would provide a source of revenues responsive to national economic growth that would not be affected by interjurisdictional tax competition or by pressure groups who benefit by lower taxes and a smaller public sector.

2. The general fiscal grant would tend to reduce the likelihood that specific categorical grants might distort state and local budgets, i.e., that the "carrot" provided by a categorical grant might induce the state to forgo other public expenditures.[29] The pure income effect of an unrestricted grant can act to offset the net negative substitution effect of a given matching grant on other programs.

3. The general fiscal grant provides flexible revenues to permit a state or locality to fill the inevitable gaps between specific categorical grants and to tailor the specific grants to local needs.

4. One may (or may not) assign the general fiscal grant the function of further redistributing federal revenues among states and localities—a further redistribution sought because of the comparative equity and efficiency of national revenue sources.

5. The general fiscal grant can serve as an additional tool to promote economic stabilization.

This second pattern of a system of grants-in-aid is more complex than the first in that it tries to serve both allocation and distribution functions within the categorical aid programs. However, it seems to be more in accord with developments and apparent preferences in the ongoing system of grants.

---

[29] See Chapter 6, section on "Budget Distortion and Grant Substitution."

ADDENDUM TO CHAPTER 3

Alternative rules of federal share in matching

THERE ARE NUMEROUS OPTIONS for setting the federal share in grants-in-aid directed toward correcting the distortions produced by benefit spillovers. In this addendum, we examine three options, all of which under the assumptions of the benefit spillover theory lead to "optimal" program levels as seen both from the state and national viewpoints. The difference in the effects of these three options shows up in a variation in the federal share in the total program cost.

We use the following notation for the ith program level increment:

$$\triangle B_i^{st} \text{—benefits to the state}$$

$$\triangle C_i^{st} \text{—cost to the state}$$

$$\triangle B_i^{ext} \text{—benefit spillout}$$

$$\triangle C_i^{fed} \text{—federal share of the costs}$$

$$\triangle B_i^{tot} = \triangle B_i^{st} + \triangle B_i^{ext} \text{—total benefits}$$

$$\triangle C_i^{tot} = \triangle C_i^{st} + \triangle C_i^{fed} \text{—total costs}$$

In the benefit spillover theory, the state is assumed to implement programs in increments in sequence from 1 to n, where n is determined by the condition that:

$$\frac{\triangle B_n^{st}}{\triangle C_n^{st}} = 1 \tag{1}$$

We now consider three cost-sharing options.

1. Proportional sharing. The federal share for the ith increment in this case is set as described earlier in this chapter (in the third paragraph of the section "Benefit Spillovers"). This rule may be written algebraically as:

$$\triangle C_i^{fed} = \frac{\triangle B_i^{ext}}{\triangle B_i^{tot}} \cdot \triangle C_i^{tot} \tag{2}$$

To demonstrate that [with a federal share given by (2)] state action in accord with condition (1) leads to optimal decisions for the nation as a whole, we first write (1) as:

$$\frac{\triangle B_n^{st}}{\triangle C_n^{st}} = \frac{\triangle B_n^{tot} - \triangle B_n^{ext}}{\triangle C_n^{tot} - \triangle C_n^{fed}} = 1 \tag{3}$$

Substitution of (2) with $i = n$ into (3) gives:

$$\frac{\triangle B_n^{tot} - \triangle B_n^{ext}}{\triangle C_n^{tot} - \dfrac{\triangle B_n^{ext}}{\triangle B_n^{tot}} \cdot \triangle C_n^{tot}} = 1 \tag{4}$$

Multiplying numerator and denominator of (4) by $\triangle B_n^{tot} / \triangle C_n^{tot}$ gives:

$$\frac{\dfrac{\triangle B_n^{tot}}{\triangle C_n^{tot}} \cdot \triangle B_n^{tot} - \triangle B_n^{ext}}{\dfrac{\triangle B_n^{tot}}{\triangle C_n^{tot}} \cdot \triangle C_n^{tot} - \triangle B_n^{ext}} = 1 \tag{5}$$

which reduces to:

$$\frac{\triangle B_n^{tot}}{\triangle C_n^{tot}} = 1 \tag{6}$$

Thus we see that the marginal benefits are equated to the marginal costs for the nation as well as for the state.

2. Federal payments equal value of benefit spillout. In the second option, the federal government would pay (for an incremental program change) an amount to the state equal in value to the measured benefit spillout. Thus:

$$\triangle C_i^{fed} = \triangle B_i^{ext} \tag{7}$$

Substituting this into (3) with $i = n$ gives:

$$\frac{\triangle B_n^{st}}{\triangle C_n^{st}} = \frac{\triangle B_n^{tot} - \triangle B_n^{ext}}{\triangle C_n^{tot} - \triangle B_n^{ext}} = 1 \tag{8}$$

But this may be written as:

$$\triangle B_n^{tot} - \triangle B_n^{ext} = \triangle C_n^{tot} - \triangle B_n^{ext} \tag{9}$$

or,

$$\frac{\triangle B_n^{tot}}{\triangle C_n^{tot}} = 1 \tag{10}$$

Again we obtain simultaneous equating of marginal costs and marginal benefits for state and nation.

3. Federal payments equal the difference of total cost and dollar value of state benefits. The third option provides that the federal share be set so that the state pays "full value" for the marginal benefits it receives from a change in program level. Thus for option three:

$$\triangle C_i^{fed} = \triangle C_i^{tot} - \triangle B_i^{st} \tag{11}$$

With the insertion of this expression into equation (3) for all i, we immediately see that the ratio $\triangle B_i^{st} / \triangle C_i^{st}$ is identically equal to unity for all levels to which the federal share is offered.[1] The state thus automatically operates at an optimal level as seen from its own perspective. However, this does require an added

---

[1] As specified, the formula calls for a tax on the state when $\triangle B_i^{st}$ is greater than $\triangle C_i^{tot}$. We assume in that range that no tax would be imposed; the federal share is always positive or zero. If the phenomenon of diminishing returns operates, as it should, at some point the total marginal costs will become and remain larger than the marginal benefits to the state.

condition to ensure optimality from the national view. The federal share must be offered only up to an increment n at which,

$$\frac{\triangle B_n^{ext}}{\triangle C_n^{fed}} = 1 \tag{12}$$

Substituting (11) for $i = n$ into (12) and writing $\triangle B_n^{st} = \triangle B_n^{tot} - \triangle B_n^{ext}$ gives:

$$\frac{\triangle B_n^{ext}}{\triangle C_n^{tot} - \triangle B_n^{tot} + \triangle B_n^{ext}} = 1 \tag{13}$$

which is seen to reduce to:

$$\frac{\triangle B_n^{tot}}{\triangle C_n^{tot}} = 1 \tag{14}$$

Each of the three cost-sharing options described above leads to a simultaneous equating of marginal benefits to marginal costs for state and nation. Option two would be the most costly to the federal government, with options one and three representing lower federal costs in descending order.

It should be clear that option three actually is the equivalent of the approach described earlier in this chapter (in the subsection "Design of grants") for the implementation of grants-in-aid to promote certain standards of performance. There the problem of designing the grant (at lowest cost to the federal government) was reduced to one of estimating what would be "just enough" incentive to induce the state to move to the desired level. In the terminology of costs and benefits, this is the same as setting the federal share so that the state will pay "full value" for the marginal benefits it receives from the program increment.

CHAPTER 4

Structure of major Health, Education, and Welfare formula grants to states and localities

IN THE PRECEDING CHAPTER, we outlined some of the principles of design for grant-in-aid systems in the light of broad functions that might be served. The discussion emphasized one component of the system: categorial grants-in-aid directed toward fostering adequate performance in programs of national concern. Requirements that would meet the objective of equalizing state effort to reach common performance levels in those programs were included in the discussion of design.

We then found ourselves particularly interested in what the correspondence might be between the principles of design criteria suggested in Chapter 3 and the actual designs of existing individual grants. We therefore chose for review the major categorical grants administered by the Department of Health, Education, and Welfare, as a sample group that exhibited a considerable range of structural formulas for grants.[1]

Analysis in this chapter is limited to the so-called formula grants, that is, grants which are allocated among the states on the basis of established criteria and may or may not require matching funds from the grantee. Our discussion includes the grants going directly to state governments and also those that may go directly to local governments or other organizations in those cases where there is an allotment of funds within the state boundary.

GRANT ALLOTMENT

In regard to allocation of the maximum amount of grant money that a state (or organizations within a state) can draw upon, we can classify grants in two ways: (1) the allocation (or allotment) is based on a *measure of need for the service* among the states; (2) the allocation is based on a *measure of need and a*

---

[1] *Grants-in-aid and Other Financial Assistance Programs Administered by the U.S. Department of Health, Education, and Welfare, 1967 edition* (Government Printing Office, 1967).

Table 4–1. **MAJOR HEALTH, EDUCATION, AND WELFARE GRANTS
CLASSIFIED BY TYPE OF ALLOTMENT FORMULA**

Allotment formula types	1967 Appropriation (in thousands)
GRANTS WITH FISCAL CAPACITY MEASURES IN ALLOTMENT FORMULA	
Community Mental Health Center Construction	$ 50,000
Mentally Retarded Facilities Construction	15,000
Child Welfare Services	46,000
Hospital Facilities Construction	270,000
Comprehensive Public Health Services	62,500[a]
Services for Crippled Children, Fund B	25,000
Maternal and Child Health Services, Fund B	25,000
Strengthening Instruction in Sciences, et al.	88,200
Strengthening Instruction in the Humanities	500
Higher Education Facilities, Community Colleges and Technical Institutes	101,000
Improvement of Undergraduate Instruction	14,500
Basic Support for Vocational Rehabilitation	236,000[b]
Public Assistance	4,170,000
GRANTS WITHOUT FISCAL CAPACITY MEASURES IN ALLOTMENT FORMULA	
Services for Crippled Children, Fund A	$ 25,000
Maternal and Child Health, Fund A	25,000
Library Services and Construction	76,000
Educational Improvement for the Handicapped	2,425
ESEA Title I	1,053,410
ESEA Title II	102,000
ESEA Title III	135,000
ESEA Title V	22,000
Land Grant Colleges	14,500
Adult Basic Education	30,000
National Teacher Corps	11,328
National Defense Student Loan	193,115
Higher Education Facilities, Other Undergraduate Institutions	354,000
Guidance, Counseling, and Testing	24,500
Vocational Education	273,377
Educational Opportunity Grants	112,000
College Work Study	134,000
Mental Retardation, Implementation	2,750
Innovation in Vocational Rehabilitation	3,000
Aging-Community Planning	6,000
Community Services and Continuing Education	10,000

[a] 1968 authorization.

[b] Estimated.

[c] For Public Assistance Grants there is not an allotment in the usual sense, since the amount for which a state is eligible is determined by the number of eligible recipients and the level of payments per recipient. We have, however, included the grants under this heading because the measures of fiscal capacity are used in determining matching ratios.

SOURCE: *Grants-in-Aid and Other Financial Assistance Programs Administered by the U.S. Department of Health, Education, and Welfare, 1967 Edition.*

measure of fiscal capacity among the states.[2] Table 4-1 shows the major HEW formula grants grouped into these two classifications.

The measures of relative need differ among the formulas. In most of the HEW programs, a crude measure of need is employed, usually the relative size of the population in the state, or of some specific target group within the state. For example, the need measure for the George-Barden Act (Vocational Education) is the relative number in the farm population for agricultural education; in the total population for distributive education; in the rural population for home economics; and in the nonfarm population for trade and industrial education. In one major HEW program, Title I of the Elementary and Secondary Education Act of 1965, a more sophisticated measure of need weights the target population on the basis of the average expenditure per child in the state. Since the Title I funds are targeted directly to school districts having deprived children, this weighting has the effect of defining "need" more in accord with the "accepted" level of program support in the state.

Several different measures of fiscal capacity are used in the allotment formulas. The most common is the so-called Hill-Burton federal percentage ($100 - 50\, Y_i/Y$), where Y_i and Y are the average per capita income of the respective state and the United States.

MATCHING REQUIREMENTS

Matching requirements in obtaining program funds also vary from grant to grant. And although some of the newer grants require no matching at all, the largest number still do require matching. Furthermore, most of the latter are uniform matching grants—that is, for each program, the matching percent required of the grantee is the same for all states; however, from grant to grant the matching percentages required of a given state do vary. Finally, several of the formulas are characterized by variable matching for a particular grant, that is, the required matching percentage varies from state to state, depending on some measure of the fiscal capacities of the states. Table 4-2 classifies the major HEW formula grants according to the three types mentioned above and indicates the share in matching—or the range of the federal share for variable matching grants.

TYPES OF FORMULAS

In this section we discuss specific illustrations of the types of grants described briefly above.

Allotment on basis of program need, no matching. The most common form of the allotment formula for grants allocated on the basis of "program need" is:

$$A_i = a_o + a_1 \frac{P_i}{P_t} \qquad (1)$$

where A_i is the allotment to the state, a_o and a_1 are constants, P_i is the size of the relevant target population group in the ith state, and P_t is the size of the total target population group within the United States. This formula assumes that need is proportional to the size of the clientele group, with an allowance for fixed administrative costs. For some of the grants of this type, the constant a_o is zero, i.e., the allotment is strictly proportional to the target population.

---

[2] Later in this chapter this distinction is shown to be somewhat ambiguous. The categorization in Table 4–1 is made on the basis of whether a measure of fiscal capacity (e.g., per capita income) is included explicitly in the allotment formula.

Table 4–2. **MAJOR HEALTH, EDUCATION, AND WELFARE GRANTS CLASSIFIED BY TYPE OF MATCHING REQUIREMENT**

Matching types	Federal matching percentage
UNIFORM MATCHING GRANTS	
Higher Education Facilities	
Other Undergraduate Institutions	33⅓ %
Community Colleges and Technical Institutions	40
Services for Crippled Children, Fund A	50
Maternal and Child Health, Fund A	50
Strengthening Instruction in Sciences, et al.	50
Strengthening Instruction in Humanities	50
Improvement of Undergraduate Instruction [a]	50
Guidance, Counseling, and Testing	50
Vocational Education	50
Community Services and Continuing Education	50
Aging-Community Planning 1st year	75
Aging-Community Planning 2nd year	60
Aging-Community Planning 3rd year	50
Basic Support for Vocational Rehabilitation	75
College Work-Study	75
Mental Retardation: Program Implementation	75
Innovation in Vocational Rehabilitation first 3 years	90
Innovation in Vocational Rehabilitation last 2 years	75
Adult Basic Education	90
National Defense Student Loan	90
National Teacher Corps	90
Educational Opportunity Grants [b]	
VARIABLE MATCHING GRANTS	
Community Mental Health Center Construction	33⅓ - 66⅔ %
Mentally Retarded Facilities Construction	33⅓ - 66⅔
Child Welfare Services	33⅓ - 66⅔
Hospital Facilities Construction	33⅓ - 66⅔
Comprehensive Public Health Services	33⅓ - 66⅔
Library Services and Construction	
Titles I, II, IV-A, IV-B	33 - 66
Public Assistance [c]	
GRANTS REQUIRING NO MATCHING	
Services for Crippled Children, Fund B	100%
Maternal and Child Health, Fund B	100
Educational Improvement for the Handicapped	100
ESEA Titles I, II, III, V	100
Land Grant Colleges	100

[a] Exceptions made in hardship cases.

[b] States must maintain effort.

[c] Complex formulas for different ranges of programs.

SOURCE: See Table 4–1.

When an unmatched formula grant is allocated on the basis of relative populations of target groups, the act of appropriation by Congress implicitly sets the "program standard" for that fiscal year. In this case, the program standard is specified in terms of dollar input—the magnitude of expenditures per capita for the target population.

This, quite clearly, is a very crude measure to be used as a proxy for allocating grant funds to encourage uniform program accomplishment. It assumes that cost factors for resource inputs (e.g., labor, equipment, facilities) are uniform among the potential recipients. Further, it assumes (even if cost factors were uniform) that the same level of expenditure per capita produces essentially the same effect among different states and localities. However, this type of measure is simple and relatively easy to implement; consequently, it has been used in the majority of HEW formula grants as a basis for determining grant allocations.

As noted earlier, a more sophisticated measure of need was used in Title I of the ESEA of 1965 to determine the amount of funds to be provided to a local school district (through the state agency):

$$A_{ij} = P_j \cdot \frac{E_i}{2} \text{ or } P_j \cdot \frac{E_{us}}{2} \tag{2}$$

whichever is larger, where A_{ij} is the magnitude of the grant to the jth school district in the ith state, P_j is the population of "deprived" children in the jth school district, E_i is the average per child expenditure for elementary and secondary education in the ith state, and E_{us} is the average per child expenditure for elementary and secondary education in the United States.

Formula (2) differs in two distinct ways from formula (1): the program level in the sense of specific level of operation in a given local district is *not* determined directly by the appropriation act (however, the coverage of the program can be affected by the appropriation), and the amount going to a given local district is a function, not only of the size of the target population in that district, but also of the historical expenditure pattern in the state (or in the United States as a whole). In other words, a weighting factor has been introduced in the estimation of need which takes account of the milieu within which the program operates. This factor can be interpreted as a partial correction to the problem of variation in cost factors, but, more important, it tends to define requirements for program development for the educationally deprived in a given local district in terms of the standard of support for education in the surrounding area—that is, the state or the nation as a whole.

To interpret this weighting factor as a reward for effort appears inappropriate. First, the absolute level of expenditures per capita is not a good indicator of effort in the absence of measures of the resource base or the demand for services. Second, the use of statewide averages as a measure to reward effort is not very meaningful for a grant that is delivered to specific school districts with average or above average numbers of deprived children.

For the grants discussed in this section, no matching is required from the state or the localities within the state. Consequently, equal fiscal effort (that is, no fiscal effort) is required of the grantee. Included in this grouping of grants are: the Elementary and Secondary Education Act (Titles I, II, III, and V), Land Grant Colleges, Education Improvement for the Handicapped, and Training for Education of Handicapped Children (that portion of the grant going to state agencies).

If one is willing to consider the per capita expenditure measure (weighted or unweighted) as an acceptable measure of program performance level, then grants within the grouping meet the criteria for grants designed to permit equal fiscal effort in the aggregate among the states to achieve a uniform level of program accomplishment. The standard for program accomplishment in a given year is set by the Congress, either implicitly through the appropriation, or, as in the case of ESEA Title I, directly. The fiscal effort required on the part of the states to reach the specified program level is zero and therefore equalized. It should be noted that the standard program level itself is a function of the past fiscal effort in the state in the case of ESEA, Title I. This creates an implicit matching incentive effect on expenditures in the longer run. This effect, however, does not enter into the question of equalization of effort to achieve the program standard as it is defined in the current year. Finally, the absence of matching requirements also leads to a high assurance that the program standard will be achieved.

Allotment on basis of program need, uniform matching. The largest number of HEW grants fall under this heading. The criteria for allocating funds among the states are essentially the same as for the group of grants discussed above, i.e., the allotment formula corresponds to formula (1).

The grants discussed here, however, do require that the grantees provide some degree of matching funds. In the case of uniform matching, all recipients of a grant from a given formula are required to provide the same amount of matching funds per federal dollar received. The degree of required matching for major grants does vary from program to program, as Table 4-2 shows. Grants with uniform matching requirements are not designed to equalize fiscal effort among the states, nor were they intended to do so.

Allotment on the basis of program need and per capita income, uniform matching. In moving toward greater consideration of the differences in the fiscal capacity of the states to deal with the problems that they face, steps were taken to incorporate "equalization" factors into the grant-in-aid formulas. One simple notion of equalization appears to have been that "the states with lower fiscal capacity should receive a relatively larger share of the federal grant."

One formula often interpreted as being directed toward greater equalization is the type that incorporates measures of need and fiscal capacity in the allotment but retains uniform matching. The Public Health Service used this type in the formula grants for disease control; subsequently, this was replaced by the Comprehensive Public Health grant that incorporates a measure of fiscal capacity in the matching formula. The formula has also been used in grants for strengthening instruction in science and the humanities, for higher education facilities in community colleges and technical institutes, for improvement of undergraduate instruction, and for a recent simplification of basic support for Vocational Rehabilitation, which at one time had a variable matching provision.

We might now try to assess the implications of such a design for a grant. We consider first a basic support grant. For example, the allotment to a state for basic support of Vocational Rehabilitation is:

$$A_i = a_1 \frac{P_i\left(1.0-0.5^{Y_i}/Y\right)^2}{\sum_j P_j\left(1.0-0.5^{Y_j}/Y\right)^2} \tag{3}$$

where A_i is the allotment to the ith state, a_1 is a constant depending on the size of the appropriation, P_i is the population of the ith state, Y_i the per capita income of the ith state, and Y the U.S. per capita income. The matching percentage provided by the federal government is the same for all states; in fiscal year 1967 it was 75 percent.

We assume for the moment that population *is* an adequate measure of program need. For discussion, we also assume that two states with the same population have identical populations of persons needing vocational rehabilitation and that the size of this target group is a known fraction of the total popula-

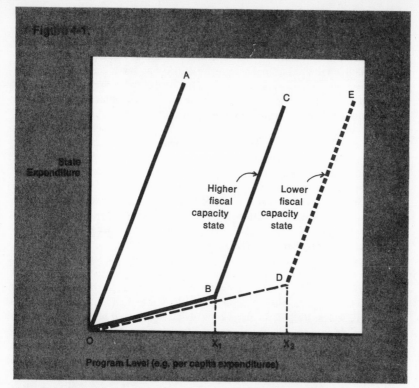

Figure 4-1.

tion. Further, we assume that conditions of treatment and prices are such that the expenditure per capita is a reasonable indicator of program performance level. In this case we could then say that an expenditure of X_1 per capita in each state represents the same standard of performance in dealing with the problem in each state. On the other hand, in the case of an expenditure X_2 per capita in one state and X_1 per capita in the other, where $X_2 > X_1$, the first state can be said to have a higher level of performance in meeting the problem.[3]

Let us now examine what a grant design that has fiscal capacity measures in the allotment, but not in matching, implies in terms of relative effort to meet certain standards of performance. Figure 4-1 displays graphically the relation between expenditures of state-raised revenues and program performance level for the two hypothetical states described above. In the figure we assume that the states have different fiscal capacities and that the grant allocation formula contains these measures, while the matching formula does not. The expenditure/performance relationship for both states in the absence of a matching grant is indicated by line OA; that for the higher fiscal capacity state with the grant offering by OBC; and that for the lower fiscal capacity state by ODE.

We note that the matching grant reduces the amount of state monies required to achieve a given level of performance in each case. Since the matching is uniform, the amount of state-raised revenues as a function of performance up to a program level X_1 is identical for the two states. From level X_1 to X_2, the lower

---

[a] For the conditions described, it is a matter of indifference to the argument whether a greater expenditure means (1) that the level of service for those rehabilitees in the program is higher, or (2) that more persons are included in the program at the same level of service.

fiscal capacity state, since it receives a larger allotment per capita—see formula (3) above—continues to be eligible for matching funds. It is immediately clear that this type of grant is not designed to achieve a standard level of performance with a uniform effort by the state. Up to the level X_1, the lower fiscal capacity state is required to make a greater effort than the higher fiscal capacity state, since the actual expenditures required of the states are identical. What the grant does is to provide incentive for the lower fiscal capacity state to move to a *higher* level of performance rather than to provide greater equalization of effort to attain a common level of performance. The objective of equalization of effort to achieve common levels of performance is only reached if the higher fiscal capacity state elects to carry its program level up to X_2 also. Consequently, this type of grant works toward equalization of effort only if we assume that *all* states carry program performance at least to the level implied by the allotment to that state with the lowest fiscal capacity. In fact, if we view the matching grants in terms of incentives, this type of grant implies that lower fiscal capacity states should make a greater relative effort and achieve higher standards of performance than do the higher fiscal capacity states.

An entirely different interpretation can be placed on the significance of the uniform matching grants that incorporate fiscal capacity measures in the allotment formulas. In this interpretation, the case could be made that these are not intended to be equalization grants at all, in the sense of equalizing fiscal efforts among the states. Rather, the fiscal capacity measure could be interpreted as an additional proxy measure of program need. This seems to be a plausible interpretation of the formula grant for strengthening instruction in the sciences and other critical subjects.[4] It could be argued that those states with higher fiscal capacities historically procured more of the equipment and facilities necessary to support teaching of the sciences. Consequently, at this point in time, their program need per student is less than that of the states with lower fiscal capacities. To the extent that historical practice is correlated with fiscal capacity, one could argue that fiscal capacity is a reasonable proxy measure to use as a weighting factor for program need. However, if this interpretation is accepted, the use of a fiscal capacity measure as a program need measure should be transitional, and should be modified as the historical gap is closed.

In summary, it is apparent that at least two different interpretations can be placed on the formal objectives of grants incorporating fiscal capacity measures in the allocation formula but not in the matching requirements. If these grants are intended to be equalizing in effort by the states, it should be recognized that they are not designed to equalize effort to achieve common standards of performance. Rather they would tend to induce among the states differing relative efforts to meet differing standards of performance. On the other hand, if a measure of fiscal capacity is intended as a proxy measure of need, the grants should be considered on the same footing as other nonequalizing grants, e.g., those for Vocational Education. However, if the latter interpretation is accepted, then a continuing review of the relevance of fiscal capacity as a measure of program need is called for.

Allotment on the basis of program need, variable matching on the basis of per capita income. The grants under Titles I, II, IVA, and IVB of the Library Serv-

---

[4] It would also seem to be a plausible interpretation to be applied to the allotment of Fund B of the Maternal and Child Health and the Services for Crippled Children grants, which, however, require no matching.

Figure 4-2.

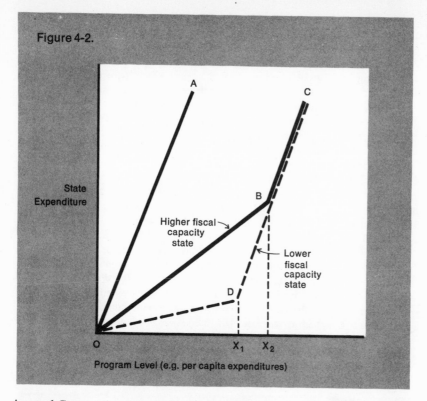

ices and Construction Act are of this type. The allotment for this grant to the ith state is:

$$A_i = a_o + a_i \frac{P_i}{P_t} \qquad (4)$$

The federal share in matching to the ith state is:

$$F_i = 1.0 - 0.5^{Y_i}/Y \qquad (5)$$

Let us assume, as in the discussion of basic support for Vocational Rehabilitation, that program need is indicated by relative population and program performance level by per capita expenditures. Now, if we examine graphically the relationship between expenditures of state revenues and program level for the two hypothetical states (identical except for per capita income) we find somewhat the reverse situation as for basic support of Vocational Rehabilitation.

Figure 4-2 displays this situation, with line OA showing the relationship in both states in the absence of the federal grant, line OBC that for the higher fiscal capacity state with the grant, and line ODC that for the lower fiscal capacity state. To the extent that the factor (1.0-0.5 Y_i/Y) equalizes effort between the states per total dollar spent for the program, we observe a grant which equalizes effort up to a program level (per capital expenditure) X_1, the point at which the lower fiscal capacity state exhausts its allotment. However, we now have a situation in which the state with a higher fiscal capacity continues to receive a subsidy up to a higher program level X_2, whereas the lower fiscal capacity state receives no further subsidy. In fact, if both states were to imple-

63

ment the program to the same degree to a level at or above X_2, they both would make the same total expenditures (since their total allotments would be identical).

Consequently, we find (*if* we assume per capita expenditure is the appropriate measure for library services) that the grant which incorporates fiscal capacity measures in matching, but not in the allotment, provides incentives for the lower per capita income states to move to lower program standards than higher per capita income states. However, up to the lowest implied program standard, there would be an equalizing effect.

As in the last type of grant formula discussed, a different interpretation can be attached to the form of the grant discussed here. It could be argued, particularly for the Library Services grant, that per capita expenditures are not an adequate indicator of program performance level in the sense of meeting need. We should recognize that need is not a simple, absolute measure; rather, it is in part defined by the demand that the local population expresses for the service. Thus, a case could be made that the demand for library services is less in some states than in others and, further, that demand may be positively correlated with per capita income. Then, in the reverse of the argument on strengthening instruction in the sciences, one could assert that the *absence* of a fiscal capacity measure in the allotment for the Library Services grant is an implicit weighting factor in the measure of program need. One could then argue that the grant *is* designed as one intended to equalize effort to achieve a uniform program performance level where now performance is measured, not only in terms of absolute expenditures, but also by the magnitude of the demand for the service.

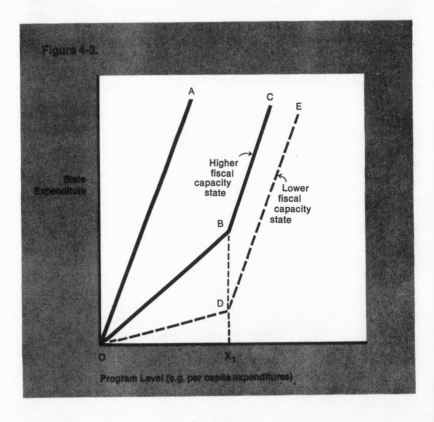

Figure 4-3.

Allotment on the basis of program need and per capita income, matching on the basis of per capita income. We now turn to the more complicated grants, which incorporate fiscal capacity measures in both the allotment and the matching formulas. These include Child Welfare Services, Construction of Facilities for Community Mental Health Centers and Mentally Retarded, Hill-Burton, Comprehensive Public Health Services, and Public Assistance. The simplest of them is for Child Welfare Services. The allotment and federal share in matching for the ith state are:

$$A_i = a_0 + a_1 \frac{P_i(1.0 - 0.5 Y_i/Y)}{\sum_j P_j(1.0 - 0.5 Y_j/Y)} \tag{6}$$

and

$$F_i = 1.0 - 0.5 Y_i/Y \tag{7}$$

where P_i is the number of children under age 21 in the ith state.

Again, if we accept expenditures per child under 21 as an adequate measure of program performance level and the factor F_i as an adequate correction to equalize state effort per total dollar expenditure, we find that the Child Welfare Services grant is designed to induce equal effort to achieve a uniform performance level among the states.[5] Figure 4-3 shows the relation between state expenditure and program performance level for the two hypothetical states described earlier. Here we see that the subsidy is offered up to a common performance level X_1 and that the lower fiscal capacity state carries a smaller fraction of the expenditure than the state with the higher fiscal capacity.

The Hill-Burton hospital facilities construction grant is slightly more complicated than the Child Welfare Services grant in that it incorporates the square of the federal percentage in the allotment. The allotment formula is:

$$A_i = a_1 \frac{P_i(1.0 - 0.5 Y_i/Y)^2}{\sum_j P_j(1.0 - 0.5 Y_j/Y)^2} \tag{8}$$

The description of the grant states explicitly that the second use of the factor $(1.0 - 0.5\ Y_i/Y)$ is intended as a measure of program need.[6] If this is accepted as an appropriate weighting factor to be applied to the population need measure, the Hill-Burton formula is formally consistent with the Child Welfare Services grant and is designed to induce an equal effort to achieve a uniform program performance level among the states.

The remainder of the grants in this grouping contain more complicated and mixed formulas which cannot be categorized easily in regard to the extent to which they meet the criteria for grants designed to equalize effort to achieve uniform program performance levels.

---

[5] As discussed in Chapter 3, if we define equalization of effort as an equalizing among the states of the percent of total income devoted to achieving the common program performance level, the definition of the federal share in terms of per capita income may deviate from our concept of equalization. It was shown in Chapter 3 that only in the case where the cost of implementing the uniform program performance level is in the same proportion to state population for all of the states is the concept of equalization met. In the Child Welfare Services grant, this would mean that the population under age 21 would have to be a constant proportion of state population for all states.

[6] *Grants-in-Aid and Other Financial Assistance Programs, op. cit.*, p. 201.

The classification of formula grant types considered in this chapter can be summarized briefly as follows.

1. Grants with allotment on the basis of program need measures, no matching. To the extent that the measures of need in terms of population are adequate, these grants can be interpreted as equalizing grants directed toward uniform program performance levels.
2. Grants with allotment on the basis of program need measures, uniform matching. These are not purported to be equalizing but rather are intended to provide undifferentiated support for uniform program performance levels.
3. Grants with per capita income measures in the allotment formula, uniform matching. These grants could be interpreted as intended to be equalizing, but not properly designed to equalize effort to achieve uniform program performance levels; or as *not* intended to be equalizing, but rather that the use of per capita income in the allotment is intended to serve as a program-need weighting factor.
4. Grants with allotment on the basis of program need, which incorporate per capita income measures in the matching provisions. These equalize effort per total dollar expended, but do not provide inducements for the states to move to uniform program performance levels as measured by per capita expenditures.
5. Grants containing per capita income measures both in allotment and in matching provisions. The simplest of these meet the formal criteria for grants intended to equalize effort to achieve uniform program performance levels; the remainder are too complicated to be categorized neatly in regard to their effects on fiscal effort and program performance level.

The variance in the functions implied by the structure of the formula grants within the U.S. Department of Health, Education, and Welfare is abundantly clear. If the grants-in-aid are to be viewed as a consistent system, then effort should be made to modify the grant formulas to the extent feasible. It does not make sense in a system view to have some of the grants designed for equalization and others not. Further, if equalization is sought, there should be a uniform concept of what is meant by equalization. We have seen that the intention toward equalization is ambiguous in some of the grants. And it is obvious that a systematic and continuing review should be made of the range of grants to verify whether the matching provisions reflect the priorities for the programs.

If the concept of equalization of effort to achieve uniform performance levels in programs of national concern is to be fostered, two aspects of continuing research on grants-in-aid appear to be vital. The first of these is to obtain better measures of program need. The implementation of PPB systems at national, state, and local levels can be of great importance in achieving this. Second, there is the need to obtain more meaningful measures of fiscal capacity and fiscal effort among jurisdictions. Chapter 5 addresses these problems in greater depth.

RESPONSE OF THE STATES TO HEW FORMULA GRANTS

How have the states responded to the formula grants offered by HEW over the years? This question is an essential starting point for estimating changes that might be, or ought to be, made in the grant formulas.

Table 4-3 lists the matching experience of states for fiscal year 1966, showing by grant the distribution of eligible jurisdictions according to the percent of available funds matched. It indicates clearly that the response to the grants has been very strong, with relatively few states not responding to the grants to the extent possible. Only four grants stand out as exceptions—Community Mental Health Center Construction, Construction of Facilities for Mentally Retarded, basic support for Vocational Rehabilitation, and Vocational Rehabilitation in-

Table 4–3. **MATCHING EXPERIENCE OF THE STATES, FISCAL YEAR 1966, FORMULA GRANTS ADMINISTERED BY THE U.S. DEPARTMENT OF HEALTH, EDUCATION, AND WELFARE**

Grant	Number of states not making full use of allotments by percent of availability matched				
	0-24	25-49	50-74	75-99	Total
ESEA Titles I, II, III and V [a]					
Adult Basic Education	0	0	0	0	0
Community Service and Continuing Education	4	0	1	2	7
Educational Opportunity Grants	0	0	0	0	0
College Work-Study	0	0	0	0	0
Improvement in Undergraduate Instruction					
TV Equipment	2	1	1	0	4
Other Equipment	1	0	1	5	7
National Defense Student Loan	0	0	0	0	0
Strengthening Instruction in Sciences, et al.	0	0	0	0	0
Strengthening Instruction in Humanities	0	0	0	0	0
Guidance, Counseling, and Testing	0	0	0	0	0
Higher Education Facilities					
Community Colleges and Technical Institutions	0	0	0	0	0
Other Undergraduate Institutions	0	0	0	0	0
National Teacher Corps [b]					
Library Services (Title I)	0	0	0	0	0
Library Construction	0	0	0	0	0
Land Grant Colleges [a]					
Vocational Rehabilitation—basic support	0	0	3	30	33
Vocational Rehabilitation—innovation	13	6	6	11	36
Hospital Facilities Construction	1	3	1	3	8
Mental Retardation—implementation	3	0	0	5	8
Community Mental Health Center Construction	42	9	0	0	51
Comprehensive Public Health Services	0	0	0	0	0
Maternal and Child Health Services	0	1	0	5	6
Services for Crippled Children	1	0	1	3	5
Child Welfare Services	0	0	0	3	3
Public Assistance	0	0	0	0	0
Aging-Community Planning [b]					
Vocational Education					
Vocational Education Act of 1963	0	0	0	0	0
George-Barden and Supplemental Acts	0	0	0	0	0
Smith-Hughes	0	0	0	0	0
Education Improvement for the Handicapped [a]					
Mentally Retarded Facilities Construction	27	8	3	3	41

[a] No matching required.

[b] Figures not available.

SOURCE: Unpublished data from the U.S. Department of Health, Education, and Welfare.

novation. The lack of response to the first two can perhaps be explained by the lack of a local establishment to put up the matching funds, but for the latter two the explanation is more difficult, especially since the federal matching is a favorable 75 percent.

When we look at the response by state (Table 4-4), no particular patterns emerge as stronger than others. Of the twenty-eight grants listed in Table 4-3, no state has made full use of all; on the other hand, no state has allowed more

Table 4-4. **NUMBER OF HEALTH, EDUCATION, AND WELFARE GRANTS WITH ALLOTMENTS NOT FULLY USED, BY STATE, FISCAL YEAR 1966**

		Number of grants with allocations not fully used (for grants listed in Table 4-3) (by percent of available funds matched)					Number of grants with allocations not fully used (grants in Table 4-3, excluding Community Mental Health Construction, Mentally Retarded Facilities Construction, Vocational Rehabilitation—basic support, Vocational Rehabilitation—innovation) (by percent of available funds matched)				
		0-24	25-49	50-74	75-99	Total	0-24	25-49	50-74	75-99	Total
NEW ENGLAND	Maine	2	1	1	0	4	0	0	0	0	0
	New Hampshire	1	1	2	2	6	1	0	1	1	3
	Vermont	2	2	1	0	5	0	1	0	0	1
	Massachusetts	2	1	1	0	4	0	0	0	0	0
	Rhode Island	0	1	1	1	3	0	0	0	0	0
	Connecticut	1	2	0	0	3	0	1	0	0	1
MIDEAST	New York	1	0	0	3	4	0	0	0	0	0
	New Jersey	1	0	2	2	5	0	0	2	1	3
	Pennsylvania	2	0	1	0	3	1	0	0	0	1
	Delaware	0	1	0	1	2	0	0	0	0	0
	Maryland	2	1	0	1	4	0	0	0	0	0
	Dist. of Columbia	1	0	0	1	2	0	0	0	1	1
GREAT LAKES	Michigan	2	1	0	1	4	0	0	0	0	0
	Ohio	2	0	0	1	3	0	0	0	0	0
	Indiana	3	0	0	1	4	1	0	0	0	1
	Illinois	2	0	0	2	4	0	0	0	0	0
	Wisconsin	1	1	0	1	3	0	0	0	0	0
PLAINS	Minnesota	1	1	1	1	4	0	0	0	0	0
	Iowa	1	1	0	2	4	0	0	0	1	1
	Missouri	1	0	0	3	4	0	0	0	1	1
	North Dakota	2	1	0	1	4	0	0	0	0	0
	South Dakota	3	1	0	1	5	1	1	0	1	3
	Nebraska	2	0	0	2	4	0	0	0	2	2
	Kansas	2	0	0	3	5	0	0	0	2	2
SOUTHEAST	Virginia	2	1	0	2	5	0	0	0	1	1
	West Virginia	1	1	0	0	2	0	0	0	0	0
	Kentucky	2	0	0	1	3	0	0	0	0	0
	Tennessee	3	1	0	2	6	1	1	0	1	3
	North Carolina	2	1	0	2	5	0	0	0	1	1
	South Carolina	1	0	0	4	5	0	0	0	1	1
	Georgia	1	0	0	1	2	0	0	0	0	0
	Florida	1	1	0	1	3	0	0	0	0	0
	Alabama	2	1	0	1	4	0	1	0	0	1
	Mississippi	3	1	0	3	7	1	0	0	2	3
	Louisiana	1	0	2	0	3	0	0	0	0	0
	Arkansas	2	0	1	1	4	0	0	1	0	1
SOUTHWEST	Oklahoma	2	0	0	1	3	0	0	0	0	0
	Texas	2	0	0	3	5	0	0	0	2	2
	New Mexico	1	1	1	1	4	0	0	0	0	0
	Arizona	2	1	0	1	4	1	0	0	1	2
ROCKY MOUNTAIN	Montana	3	0	0	2	5	1	0	0	1	2
	Idaho	2	0	1	3	6	0	0	0	2	2
	Wyoming	2	0	1	2	5	0	0	0	1	1
	Colorado	3	0	0	1	4	0	0	0	0	0
	Utah	4	0	0	1	5	1	0	0	0	1
FAR WEST	Washington	1	1	0	2	4	0	0	0	0	0
	Oregon	3	0	0	0	3	0	0	0	0	0
	Nevada	2	1	0	2	5	2	0	0	2	4
	California	1	0	0	2	3	0	0	0	1	1
	Alaska	5	0	1	0	6	2	0	1	0	3
	Hawaii	2	1	0	1	4	0	0	0	0	0

SOURCE: Unpublished data from U.S. Department of Health, Education, and Welfare.

than seven, and only six states more than five, of the grant allocations to go unused. If we exclude the four grants mentioned above as exceptions, we see a tighter grouping. Nearly half of the states have used up their allocations in the twenty-four remaining grants, and only one state has allowed more than three allotments to go unused.

This would seem to indicate, in the aggregate, that in the formula grants considered here the matching provisions have provided sufficient incentive, and perhaps too much. If our conjecture is correct that the lack of response to the two community facilities construction grants has been due to lack of established local interest groups to mobilize resources, there would seem to be a strong argument for a substantial increase in the federal percentage of matching (perhaps with smaller allotments) in the early years of this grant program. Of the two Vocational Rehabilitation grants, the innovation grant is so small as to be an insignificant issue. The more interesting question centers on the partial response to the basic support for Vocational Rehabilitation. Analysis of the reasons for this problem appears to be warranted at this time, to ascertain what modifications in the grant should be made to encourage greater response.[7]

---

[7] It should be noted (see Table 4–3) that while many states have not taken full advantage of basic support for Vocational Rehabilitation, all have made use of a substantial portion ($\geq$ 67 percent) of the allotment.

CHAPTER 5

Measuring need and
fiscal capacity

TRADITIONAL GRANT-IN-AID DESIGNS called for allocation of federal funds among states either on the basis of population or as a flat sum per state. Population was essentially used as a proxy for measuring relative "need." The proxy gained acceptance in part because equal per capita amounts suggest a "fair share" for each state, but also because needs were assumed to be about the same everywhere. Combined with 50-50 sharing, this type of need measure results in grant offerings that can yield uniform per capita expenditures within the narrowly interpreted limits of the cooperative program. But states did not take up grant offerings uniformly; in the aggregate, more federal grant money went to states with incomes above the United States average—states that had more ready access to matching funds because of their relative superiority in economic and fiscal resources.[1] Correction for this disparity led to adoption of equalization-type formulas and even earlier to allocations of federal funds on the basis of "financial need" without matching requirements.[2] During the latter part of the 1940's and in the 1950's, formulas were increasingly adopted by the Congress to equalize both the level of public services and the state fiscal burdens required to finance those equal services. Design of an equalization formula required measurement of fiscal capacity or of a standard of tax effort for the aided program.

Indexes of "need" and "fiscal capacity" have been the subject of much research.[3] Nevertheless, a further review of the indexes is indicated. The purpose

---

[1] See V. O. Key, Jr., *The Matching Requirements in Federal Grant Legislation in Relation to Variations in State Fiscal Ability*, Social Security Board, Bureau of Research and Statistics, Memorandum No. 46 (Government Printing Office, February 1942).

[2] Committee on Economic Security, *Social Security in America*, Social Security Board Publication No. 20 (Government Printing Office, 1937).

[3] See, for example, M. O. Clement, "Fiscal Equity and Federal Grants-in-Aid," *Southern Economic Journal*, Vol. 29 (April 1963); Thomas D. Hopkins, "Income Distribution in Grants-in-Aid Equity Analysis," *National Tax Journal*, Vol. 18 (June 1965); Richard A. Rossmiller, "The Equalization Objective in State Support Programs: An Analysis of Measures, Need, and Ability," *Ibid.*, Vol. 18 (December 1965); Bruce F. Davie and Joseph T. White, "Equalization Alternatives in Grant-in-Aid Programs: Allotment Formulas and Measures of Fiscal Capacity," *Ibid.*, Vol. 20 (June 1967).

would be threefold: (1) to improve the measurements used in those programs for which the more traditional equalizing grant approach is still appropriate; (2) to achieve measures that could be applied as part of the design of objective formulas for grants that are now made on a case-by-case or project basis because existing indexes are not appropriate to the program purpose; (3) to help improve allocations under any unconditional fiscal grant.

Different indexes of "need" and "fiscal capacity" may be called for by the different purposes. For grants that seek to achieve a minimum public service level throughout the nation, better definition of the minimum level and quantification in accord with this definition may be sufficient. Case-by-case grants, however, do not have as their purpose such standard minimum levels. Rather, they are intended to permit those states and communities that perceive "a problem" and are prepared to meet it (given federal financial assistance) to do so. The indexes suitable for a general unconditional grant will differ, depending on the objectives toward which this aid is to be applied. If the grant is intended to meet "blight in the cities," one set of measures may be appropriate; if it is directed generally to augment public sector resources, another set may be involved; and if revenue equalization is intended, still a third set of indexes may be required.

This chapter presents in a summary way new directions for measuring "need" and relative fiscal capacity.[4] It draws on our experimental research undertaken over the period 1963-65 to develop new approaches to measuring program requirements relative to fiscal capacity. It also suggests an agenda for additional research.

PUBLIC SERVICE NEEDS

The familiar indexes applied in grant allocations assume a uniformity among states in minimum public service needs or standards. Yet the facts are otherwise: there is diversity among states in both the demand for and the supply of public services. On the demand side, standards and desire for public services reflect the diverse industrial compositions of the states and the unevenness of urbanization. There are also regional variations in the preferences about the public-private mix of responsibility for higher education, hospitals, housing, and so forth.

On the supply side, differences exist in the prices of inputs and in the resources required for comparable service per recipient (taking account of economies of scale and varied technologies). The inputs needed to achieve the desired output may differ between states, and the price of the inputs may vary more (or less) than the price changes implicit in differences in personal incomes. To make a viable community, for example, population density may compel provision of a range of engineering-type services such as water supplies, sewers, and solid waste disposal. Moreover, since the efficiency of government expenditure is not the same from one jurisdiction to the next, the quality of public services may vary, even if prices and cost per unit input are assumed to be constant.

As indicated in Chapter 3, a number of grants have sought achievement of some national minimum standard. The purpose, however, is the achievement of

[4] See Selma Mushkin, "Public Investment and Consumption: The Outlook in States and Localities," Joint Economic Committee, *Revenue Sharing and Its Alternatives: What Future for Fiscal Federalism?* Vol. III (Government Printing Office, 1967), pp. 1229-48; Selma Mushkin and Gabrielle Lupo, "State and Local Finances Projections: Another Dimension?" *Southern Economic Journal*, Vol. 33 (January 1967).

minimum program results and outputs; thus, variations among states in supply should be considered. In practice, a "minimum standard" is typically formulated in terms of dollars spent per person, with no attention given to varied prices, inputs, or technological determinants of expenditures to achieve standard outputs. Variations in demand are necessarily disregarded, except in determining the grant price at which the state may be induced to achieve the desired national standard.

As the national government moves forward in its implementation of a Planning, Programming, Budgeting system, output indexes will come to be defined more clearly. Along with such measurement, we may anticipate that program standards in cooperative intergovernmental programs will be redefined in terms of product.

Even now, when the measurement of program benefits in intergovernmental programs is still partial and approximate, congressional debate on grant appropriations is centering on the public product gained. The recent debate on the appropriation for grants under Title I of the Elementary and Secondary Education Act is indicative. "Learning" that is produced through education is not a single product but a variety of products. For simplicity of measurement, however, "reading skill at grade level" has been adopted as the program standard. And the congressional debate has centered on this reading product. Thus, this single criteria is being used to assess a complex of learning products for which, in principle, minimum standards can be set.

Such public products as transportation and communication, public safety, water supplies, good health, and learning are achieved by a variety of means or programs. The "public" content is necessarily different in congested urban areas from what it is in isolated farm areas. While these differences in public service requirements are now widely recognized (for example, the differences in solid or liquid waste disposal in cities and on farms), allocations of federal funds by formula among states apply uniform measures of need that fail to reflect such differences. The traditional grant-in-aid political rule—"something for every state"—stands in the way of correction that might produce a somewhat closer relationship between the product desired and federal assistance. Further, one might argue with good reason that income measures of financial need should also be adjusted to reflect the differences in "real" enjoyment or want satisfaction that the dollar income permits. Income is now adjusted for certain imputed items such as rental value of owner-occupied dwellings; it could be adjusted further to impute a value to the availability of clean spring water, or of clean air, or for the negative value of polluted air or of heavy chlorination of reused water. Congestion produces public product needs that have no comparable product requirements in less congested places. And the volume or quality of the public product needed varies from place to place within urban communities.

Differences among states in the proportion of dependent groups in the population—young persons and old—are large enough to impair the usefulness of total population as an index of need, and especially so when measuring fiscal capacity relative to need. Income distributions vary among the states, but even more importantly the significance of these dollar distributions for the daily life of the "poor" is disparate.

We are a long way from having social and economic indicators that can help measure public service outputs and the benefits from the production and distribution of those public products. Steps are being taken by the U.S. Department of Health, Education, and Welfare to formulate such indexes. In February 1967, Senator Walter F. Mondale of Minnesota, in recognition of the gaps in information, introduced legislation ("The Full Opportunity and Social Accounting Act") that would, among other things, "devise a system of social indicators, help develop program priorities, evaluate the effectiveness and impact of our efforts at all levels of government." [5]

Formulation of minimum standards waits on the development of appropriate social indexes. At this time, moreover, the program inputs that can achieve even such proxy minimum standards as "reading skills" are not clearly known, nor have the price differentials and other interstate differences that affect the expenditure for the required inputs been quantified.

Expenditure requirements in states cannot be identified through averages. There are wide variations among states and within them. The nation, on the average, is now urban-placed and urban-minded and is undertaking to cope with central-city problems. Interstate population shifts have resulted in additional numbers of persons in states whose standards for all public services are relatively high. For example, the share of the school-age population that now lives in states with relatively high educational expenditure per child in average daily attendance is larger than it was earlier. A larger share of dwellings is served by sewerage and water systems. And a larger share of welfare recipients now lives in states where the poor receive assistance at levels that at least approximate concepts of minimum budgetary needs of the more prosperous states.

Expenditures are further increased, and strains placed on the traditional public programs of the central cities, by the lower standards for public services of the agricultural areas where in-migrants to cities originate. The migrants are often poorly equipped, through prior public education and public health investments, for living and working in complex urban areas. These underinvestments in distant places are converted into public costs in the higher income regions for literacy education, job retraining, public health services, public welfare payments, and expenditures associated with juvenile delinquency, crime, and deteriorating neighborhoods.

It is true that sparsity of population, as well as density, creates its own costs of plant and of minimal administrative organization. For certain classes of services and facilities the historical patterns of income variation have resulted in more, rather than less, dependence on the public sector in the lower-income rural states.[6] However, out-migration of population in some of the more rural states has facilitated an increase in income that permits an expansion in public services.

The national response to the public service requirements of the industrial states has been to design a case-by-case approach to federal aid. Traditional formulas for allocation and especially for equalization aids did not meet the perceived variations in public output required and its budgetary impact. The case-by-case grants are intended to facilitate and encourage the implementation of certain state and local public services as quickly as possible in accord with the local voter-consumer preferences for those services. The project-grant route used offerings of federal financial support that set aside the existing measure of "need."

FISCAL CAPACITY

Two differing concepts of capacity to which expenditures can be related have been identified by past research on measuring fiscal capacity. In the first, eco-

---

[5] *Congressional Record,* Vol. 113, No. 17, Feb. 6, 1967, p. S1534.

[6] For example, the South, with its relatively low per capita income, looks to public institutions for a major share of hospital care.

nomic variation among states or localities is defined by income flows, and capacity for satisfaction of public and private wants is assessed by these flows. In the second, a potential tax yield is derived for a uniformly defined tax structure that reflects the restraints on state and local taxation. The selection of a capacity measure to assess the relative ability of the states to tax for the financing of expenditure requirements will influence the findings for different regions of the United States relative to each other.

Various income flows approximating the relative capacity to raise revenues in the states have been used in the past to emphasize the differences between income received at place of residence and income produced at place of productive activity. Furthermore, adjustments have been proposed to reflect the drain of federal taxes on income available for state and local taxation and to make more comparable the methods of counting income in farm and urban areas. Measures of income flow have been corrected to take account of differences in the distribution of the income and to allow for minimum family living needs.

More recently, the concept of a composite income index of capacity has been advanced that would combine into a single index the several types of income flows out of which taxes are paid. The problem of weighting these several income flows, which has long stood in the way of obtaining a composite income index, was resolved by an objective type of weighting scheme that follows the classification system used in national economic accounts. Under this scheme of weights, each of the categories of state and local taxation is assigned to its appropriate income-flow measure. Or, more specifically, personal direct levies are assigned to personal income, business levies to income produced, and corporate net income taxes to corporate income. Weighting personal income, income produced, and corporate net income by the proportion of state and local taxes paid out of each of the three types of income yields a composite income index of capacity that takes account of the different stages at which taxes are imposed on income.

In a 1962 staff report to the Advisory Commission on Intergovernmental Relations a uniform tax system concept was used.[7] This concept had been outlined initially by John K. Norton (1926) and developed in later studies by Mabel Newcomer (1935) and Leslie L. Chism (1936), both of which aimed at deriving a measure of the tax capacity of the states that would reflect the various taxing devices through which the states and localities could raise funds.[8]

The Advisory Commission's staff study placed heavy emphasis on property taxes, with almost 45 percent of the yield from this source. Such an emphasis derives from the selection of a standard tax system that is representative of prevailing tax practices. The criterion of "prevailing" taxes imposed by state and local governments was defined in accord with exclusions from taxes and exemptions from tax where more than half of the nation's population lives. The rate of each tax in the representative system was set at such a level that, when the rate was applied to the tax base in all states, it yielded the same amount of revenue as the states collectively derived from this type of tax in 1960.

---

[7] Advisory Commission on Intergovernmental Relations: A Staff Report, *Measures of State and Local Fiscal Capacity and Tax Effort* (Government Printing Office, October 1962).

[8] Leslie L. Chism, *The Economic Ability of the States to Finance Public Schools* (Teachers College, Columbia University, 1936); Mabel Newcomer, *An Index of the Taxpaying Ability of State and Local Governments* (Teachers College, Columbia University, 1935); John K. Norton, *The Ability of the States to Support Education* (National Education Association, 1926).

The Advisory Commission's staff report asked:

What causes the relative capacities of the States measured by the yield of the representative tax system to differ so much from their relative capacities measured by personal income? In particular, why do the relative capacities of the Plains, Rocky Mountain, and Southwestern States appear so much higher under the representative tax system than under personal income? And why do the relative capacities of the New England and Mideastern States appear so much lower?

Very briefly, the answer is this: The Plains, Rocky Mountain, and Southwestern States have higher than average ratios of taxable property to personal income, and of taxable sales to personal income, while the New England and Mideastern States have lower than average ratios. Hence, the Plains, Rocky Mountain, and Southwestern States rank higher on both property tax yield and on nonproperty tax yield of the representative tax system than they do on personal income, while the opposite is true of New England and the Mideast.[9]

Other criteria may be applied in developing the yield of a uniform or standard tax system for all the states. Clearly, measuring fiscal capacity of the states and localities by calculating what the yields of a representative tax system would be in each of the states is only one of several approaches. The possibilities are many, because there is no obvious or unique solution to the problem of specifying a standard or uniform structure and its exemptions and exclusions, and of setting the rates on the several taxes included. However, a tax structure (within the standard system) that calls for a larger share of income taxation and a smaller proportion of total yields from property taxation would bring the capacity index closer to the personal income count.

Fiscal capacity indexes, when applied in existing grants-in-aid, are converted either to per capita figures to yield an array of measures of state capacity relative to "need," or to indexes of tax or program effort representing variations in use of the available capacity to finance all public services or a specifically defined public service.

Possibilities of applying an alternative index, one that would show emerging expenditure requirements relative to fiscal capacity, stimulated our research on a measure termed "capacity requirements".

CAPACITY REQUIREMENTS DEFINED

The capacity requirement index is computed as the proportion of fiscal capacity in the state that would finance expenditures not met by federal aids or by public charges and fees, as follows:

$$CR = \frac{E - (F + G)}{C}$$

with E representing expenditure requirement; F, fees and charges; G, federal grants-in-aid; and C, fiscal capacity. (As already indicated, there are alternative measures of fiscal capacity that may be selected for use in this index.)

The capacity requirements index is a way of anticipating likely expenditure effort relative to fiscal capacity in a state. Expenditures are netted of federal aids, since, in the aggregate, existing grant distributions result in higher federal payments relative to own revenues in the low-income states. These relatively larger payments reflect the existing equalization provisions of some grant programs. The federal aid amounts already flowing into a state constitute an addition to its capacity to finance desired expenditures or, alternatively, serve to reduce the magnitude of expenditures to be financed from own funds.[10]

---

[9] Advisory Commission on Intergovernmental Relations: A Staff Report, *op. cit.,* p. 56.

[10] Given the nature of our federal system, aided expenditures are not undertaken *unless* desired and valued by the state or local government.

When requirements are shown relative to personal income, they measure about the same tax loads on income as does the more familiar tax effort index (defined as tax collections as a percentage of income of all residents of the state) except that the capacity requirement index is modified to reflect public debt borrowings as well as taxes.[11] Differences in consumer-voter preferences about public service are reflected in the tax effort index as they are in the capacity requirements index.

How are interstate differences in expenditure requirements to be measured for this purpose? As suggested earlier, the indexes generally applied in federal grant-in-aid formulas assume expenditure requirements to be uniform per person. Alternatively, for some purposes, it may be assumed that interstate differences in expenditures are a reasonable proxy for differences in requirements or differences in preferences. In this view, the taxes voted in each state represent a response to insistent demand pressures. Other measures could be adopted, including expenditure estimates based on defined standards of public product outputs or on projected expenditure demands.

The capacity requirements index, like the conventional tax effort index, does not measure an isolated fiscal phenomenon. It reflects a composite of factors affecting the consumer-voters' decisions on the desired allocation of resources for the satisfaction of wants. Differences in the proportion of dependent age groups in the population (for example), and in unemployment, housing, and highway requirements are reflected, at least partially, in the relative emphasis placed on different functions and on the tax loads assumed for their financing. Preferences and requirements for the various functions and activities of government differ, as do the standards for those functions and activities. Similar capacity requirements indexes for two states may not mirror the same types of fiscal phenomena. In one state, consumer preferences for higher standards may raise the amount of taxes the citizens are willing to pay; in another, the same tax increase may be undertaken to finance, not higher standards of service, but maintenance of program levels for an expanding population.

Expenditures for the purpose of measuring capacity requirements are defined to include (1) those expenditures classified as "general" by the Governments Division of the U.S. Bureau of the Census; (2) government contributions to retirement programs that are not counted as part of general expenditures; and (3) governmental subsidies for utility operations (transit, water systems, gas, electric utilities). Charges and fees are those classified by the Census Bureau as associated with general expenditures, and include such revenues as tuition and fees charged by public institutions of higher education and patient fees charged by public hospitals. Federal aids represent federal payments to state and local governments, including grants-in-aid and payments for contractual services.

Traditionally, states are viewed as fiscally poor and fiscally rich, depending upon their relative income. When expenditures of the states and regions are arrayed (after deduction of charges associated with the expenditures and of the categorical aids provided by the federal government for their financing) the "unfinanced" portion of the expenditures would, in this view, vary inversely with income. One current view, however, holds that pressures on tax resources are greater in many high-income states than in many low-income states. Fragments of experience to this effect underlie a modified national grant policy, and the viewpoint has been empirically verified by findings on a capacity requirements index. The capacity requirements index is higher in the West and in the

---

[11] Net positive profits of utilities and of liquor stores in liquor-monopoly states are included along with taxes.

northern states on the Eastern Seaboard than in the South and the Midwest (Table 5-1).

RESEARCH STUDY AND FINDINGS

As an approach to measuring capacity requirements, state and local expenditures were projected to 1970 from a base of fiscal year 1962.[12] Revenues were also estimated within the overall framework of a national economic model in a highly disaggregative methodology, and the traditional capacity index was used to derive a capacity requirements ratio.[13]

More sharply variant, with the same regional patterns, are the per capita amounts of required taxation (and borrowing) projected for 1970. The projected capacity requirements are about two-thirds higher in New England and the Mideast than they are in the Southeast. About 20 percent of the 1970 population of the United States will live in the two states—California and New York—that require the highest taxes (or borrowing) per capita to finance their expenditures in excess of charges and federal aids. This amount ($510) is just twice as high as the average per capita tax ($255) required for the 20 percent of the population living in the states with the lowest per capita income.

Table 5–1. **PERSONAL INCOME AND CAPACITY REQUIREMENTS INDEX, FISCAL YEAR 1962 AND CALENDAR YEAR 1970 (PROJECTED)**

Region	Per capita personal income		Average annual per-cent increase in personal income	Index of capacity requirements as percent of U.S. average	
	1962	1970	1962 - 1970	1962	1970
UNITED STATES	$2,368	$3,207	5.4%	100.0%	100.0%
New England	2,618	3,580	5.1	98.9	104.5
Mideast	2,728	3,729	5.2	101.4	102.5
Great Lakes	2,521	3,346	5.2	94.4	92.2
Plains	2,241	3,068	4.8	97.4	94.5
Southeast	1,749	2,416	5.5	97.9	95.6
Southwest	2,023	2,657	5.2	90.7	93.9
Rocky Mountain	2,284	3,029	5.3	102.2	104.6
Far West	2,811	3,743	6.6	114.5	113.8

SOURCES: 1970 estimates from State-Local Finances Project, The George Washington University; 1962 figures computed from U.S. Bureau of the Census, Governments Division, and U.S. Department of Commerce, Office of Business Economics, data.

But the per capita income difference, as projected, is in the ratio of about eight to five (1.62).

This state-by-state quantification, reversing traditional notions about which states are fiscally poor and which fiscally rich, is not altogether surprising. It reflects the expenditure impacts of differences in population density and urbanization and also mirrors the differential effects of population growth on demands

---

[12] Selma Mushkin and Gabrielle Lupo, "Project '70: Projecting the State-Local Sector," *Review of Economics and Statistics*, Vol. 49 (May 1967).

[13] Data availability restricted the comparisons to a set using personal income as the index of fiscal capacity. No other capacity measure is projected to 1970 on assumptions consistent with the results of the study (referred to in footnote 12), which were used here in assessing interstate variations in capacity requirements.

for new public facilities. More importantly, it shows the regional differences in inputs required per standard unit of output as well as variations in consumer-voter attitudes toward standards of public services and toward allocation of responsibility between public and private sectors. And it nets out the estimated federal grant-in-aid distributions.

The findings, moreover, are similar to those obtained for earlier years, using an index of the interstate variations in taxes as a percent of income, the more familiar tax effort index. The tax effort in recent years has been higher in such centers of population concentration as California and New York than in the Midwest and the Southern states. It has also been moving up more rapidly in California and New York than in many other places—especially in the South.

Wider disparities with alternative capacity measures. The impact on relative requirements for fiscal capacity of variation in the capacity measure chosen can be examined, using 1962 data. A comparison of the 1970 projections with 1961-62 experience indicates that the general research findings are *not* a consequence of the special characteristics of the 1970 economic model or of the projection procedures through which they were derived. Capacity requirement indexes relative to personal income are in about the same relative array in the historical past as in the projected future.

The 1962 fiscal data on state and local government operations, derived in the Census of Governments, 1962, show about the same pattern of requirements as a percentage of personal income as do the 1970 projections with the higher requirement index in the Western and the North Atlantic states and the lowest indexes in the Southwestern and Great Lakes states.Within regions, the projected capacity requirements index shows about the same variations among states for 1970 as for the base year of the study, 1961-62 (see Table 5-2). For the states in the Great Lakes region, for example, and the neighboring state of Minnesota, the pattern of capacity requirements, while divergent among states, is projected as about the same for 1970 as it was in the base year 1961-62. On the one hand are Indiana, Illinois, and Ohio, with relatively low levels of public services for the region, and on the other, Wisconsin, Minnesota, and Michigan, with their higher public service standards, as comparisons of expenditures for selected public program areas would suggest.

Examination of the differences in the relative capacity position of the states indicates that it is in the New England states, where capacity requirements are shown to be above the national average, that the use of either income produced or composite income as a capacity measure would raise the requirement index further. In the Southwest, the change in capacity measure would lower the capacity requirements further. These regions are identified because they show the largest variations between an income-produced measure of fiscal capacity and a personal-income measure. In New England, the personal-income ranking is higher than the income-produced ranking, owing to the large share of personal-income attributable dividends and interest in that region. In the Southwest, where absentee ownership of mineral-producing properties is a significant characteristic of the region's economy, the ranking on the basis of income produced is substantially higher than that on the basis of personal income (see Table 5-3).

Thus, a substitution of income produced (or a composite-income index) for personal income in measuring fiscal capacity and assessing the relative strain of state and local expenditure requirements on that capacity widens rather than reduces the differences between the high-requirement states and the low.

But this widening is minor compared with the changes that result from sub-

Table 5–2. **REQUIREMENTS AS PERCENT OF CAPACITY AND PER CAPITA, CALENDAR YEAR 1970, PROJECTED, AND REQUIREMENTS AS PERCENT OF CAPACITY, FISCAL YEARS 1957 AND 1962**

State and region	1970			1962		1957	
	Capacity requirements (percent)	Capacity requirements as percent of U.S. average	Requirements per capita	Capacity requirements (percent)	Capacity requirements as percent of U.S. average	Capacity requirements (percent)	Capacity requirements as percent of U.S. average
United States	11.2%	100.0%	$359	10.6%	100.0%	9.6%	100.0%
New England	11.7	104.5	418	10.5	98.9	10.9	113.8
Maine	12.0	107.1	345	12.3	115.9	9.8	102.6
New Hampshire	11.1	99.1	344	9.6	90.5	10.6	110.4
Vermont	13.4	119.6	368	11.9	112.2	12.2	126.6
Massachusetts	12.5	111.6	452	10.7	100.8	11.6	120.5
Rhode Island	12.1	108.0	367	10.3	96.4	8.8	91.6
Connecticut	10.1	90.2	419	10.0	93.5	10.6	110.0
Mideast	11.7	104.5	435	10.8	101.4	9.5	98.5
New York	13.1	117.0	521	12.3	115.9	10.9	113.8
New Jersey	10.6	94.6	402	8.8	83.2	8.0	83.8
Pennsylvania	10.4	92.9	341	9.6	90.6	8.1	84.2
Delaware	8.4	75.0	358	8.9	83.8	6.6	69.2
Maryland	9.9	88.4	355	10.0	94.3	9.7	101.5
Dist. of Columbia	13.1	117.0	568	9.5	89.3	7.1	74.3
Great Lakes	10.2	91.1	342	10.0	94.4	8.8	91.4
Michigan	11.0	98.2	351	11.6	108.6	10.0	104.1
Ohio	9.4	83.9	304	9.1	85.9	8.2	85.6
Indiana	10.3	92.0	323	9.5	89.7	8.4	87.2
Illinois	9.8	87.5	374	9.2	86.5	8.0	83.0
Wisconsin	12.1	108.0	370	12.4	116.2	10.5	109.8
Plains	10.5	93.7	324	10.4	97.4	10.2	106.3
Minnesota	12.2	108.9	377	12.2	114.3	11.3	117.3
Iowa	10.8	96.4	327	11.2	105.0	10.7	111.7
Missouri	9.1	81.2	299	8.5	79.7	7.8	81.4
North Dakota	12.7	113.4	340	12.4	116.4	12.2	127.6
South Dakota	10.4	92.9	272	11.0	103.5	11.8	122.6
Nebraska	9.4	83.9	293	9.0	84.8	9.8	101.7
Kansas	10.8	96.4	314	10.3	96.5	12.2	127.3
Southeast	10.7	95.5	257	10.4	97.9	9.4	98.2
Virginia	9.3	83.0	242	9.4	88.3	8.4	87.9
West Virginia	11.5	102.7	306	10.6	100.0	8.2	85.0
Kentucky	11.1	99.1	264	12.4	116.9	8.1	84.6
Tennessee	10.5	93.7	248	10.1	95.0	9.7	101.4
North Carolina	10.3	92.0	245	9.7	91.5	8.7	90.4
South Carolina	9.6	85.7	211	9.0	84.7	9.5	99.0
Georgia	11.1	99.1	269	9.8	92.2	9.3	97.2
Florida	9.9	88.4	273	10.4	97.4	10.3	107.2
Alabama	10.8	96.4	248	9.7	91.4	9.2	95.4
Mississippi	12.9	115.2	235	13.1	122.8	10.2	106.1
Louisiana	13.2	117.9	313	13.1	123.1	12.2	126.8
Arkansas	10.2	91.1	204	8.8	83.1	8.8	91.6
Southwest	10.4	92.9	276	9.6	90.7	9.1	94.9
Oklahoma	10.6	94.6	269	10.0	94.0	10.5	109.3
Texas	9.9	88.4	264	9.3	87.1	8.5	88.8
New Mexico	10.2	91.1	268	9.0	84.9	8.8	91.1
Arizona	12.7	113.4	358	12.4	116.1	11.6	120.9
Rocky Mountain	11.5	102.7	349	10.9	102.2	10.4	107.8
Montana	11.9	106.2	332	10.4	97.8	10.4	107.9
Idaho	12.0	107.1	299	10.1	95.0	9.7	100.9
Wyoming	9.9	88.4	325	10.6	99.2	9.1	94.9
Colorado	11.3	100.9	377	10.9	102.4	11.0	114.3
Utah	12.2	108.9	347	11.2	105.7	10.0	104.0
Far West	12.6	112.5	472	12.2	114.5	10.6	110.2
Washington	11.2	100.0	359	11.7	110.3	11.3	117.6
Oregon	11.5	102.7	369	11.4	107.6	10.1	105.1
Nevada	11.3	100.9	448	11.4	107.1	9.8	102.0
California	12.9	115.2	499	12.3	115.6	10.5	109.6
Alaska	9.9	88.4	386	7.6	71.1	5.7	59.5
Hawaii	13.6	121.4	429	13.2	123.6	12.2	127.5

SOURCES: Fiscal years 1962 and 1957 computed from U.S. Bureau of the Census, Governments Division, data; 1970 projections from State-Local Finances Project, The George Washington University.

stituting the yield of a standard tax system for any income measure of capacity. The relative requirements in relation to capacity were larger in 1962 for the states on the North Atlantic seaboard, particularly those in the populous Mideast and lower New England. These states can be counted as even poorer fiscally, while the Plains, Southwest, and Rocky Mountain states are counted as relatively well off in regard to the strain imposed by their fiscs on their capacity. The relative ranking of the Great Lakes and the Far West states changes little.[14]

Table 5–3. **CAPACITY REQUIREMENTS AS PERCENT OF U.S. AVERAGE, USING ALTERNATIVE CAPACITY MEASURES**

	Capacity measure		
Region	Personal income	Income produced [a]	Representative tax system yield [b]
UNITED STATES	100.0%	100.0%	100.0%
New England	98.9	100.9	112.8
Mideast	101.4	101.1	117.6
Great Lakes	94.4	94.5	96.2
Plains	97.4	96.7	85.1
Southeast	97.9	94.7	93.6
Southwest	90.7	86.2	69.3
Rocky Mountain	102.2	100.8	83.0
Far West	114.5	122.2	112.1

[a] Based on distribution of gross product originating in 1962 and personal income in 1963, as estimated (in 1964 dollars) in National Planning Association, *State Projections to 1975* (Regional Economic Projection Series, Report No. 65-11, 1965).

[b] Based on distribution of yield of representative tax systems in 1960 and personal income in 1960, as estimated in Advisory Commission on Intergovernmental Relations: A Staff Report, *Measures of State and Local Fiscal Capacity and Tax Effort* (October 1962) and (personal income) in *Survey of Current Business* (August 1964).

Projections understate expenditure variations. In using the 1970 projections to assess capacity requirements, two characteristics of the projections must be borne in mind. First, it was assumed that the quality (or output per recipient) and scope (or proportion of potential recipients actually receiving the service) of services provided within each state to the public would in no instance decline but that existing interstate differences would, by and large, persist. Second, increases in quality and scope of service in each function for each state were projected as responses to nationally recognized needs, as evidenced by federal grant-in-aid enactments. In the past, federal aid has stimulated the introduction of new public services and expansion of existing services; for the period ahead, it was assumed that the new aids would also encourage improvements in the program areas for which assistance was provided.

The projections of expenditures were scaled to likely program developments, function by function, within the framework of economic and demographic assumptions. There was no intention to estimate expenditures to achieve a "desirable or standard public service level." In accord with this design of the study, the regional variations in expenditures per capita that existed in the past and in the base years were projected to persist through 1970. Similarly, variations

---

[14] Advisory Commission on Intergovernmental Relations: A Staff Report, *op. cit.,* p. 56.

were projected to continue for the separate states and for the separate functions. Underlying these projections of variations in expenditure levels is a concept of voter-consumer demand—a concept in both the public and private sectors that is intrinsically nonequalitarian. To consider more equality in public expenditures per capita, among regions, a different type of expenditure measurement must be formulated. It should be based, not on concepts of choice by the recipient or demand, but on program standards or standard public service packages.

The projections were built up on the assumption that, for each program or activity, approximately the same response would be made by each state to the new federal grant-in-aid offering. Thus, a uniform response to the national policy directions was embodied in the projections; for example, the projections assume that the new federally aided medical assistance program for children and other needy groups would be adopted by all states. Neither the manner of response of a given state to the nationwide program movements, nor potential new programs not initiated with federal assistance were projected or forecast. Likely state-initiated improvements in the quality of public services to fill deficiencies relative to the national standard so as to meet generally recognized demands for higher quality were included only as a response to national aids.

The assumption of an almost uniform response on the part of the states and jurisdictions within the states to federally aided programs leads to understatement of the extensions of program and of the extensions in quality and scope in those states where citizen concern is greatest; in others it leads to overstatement of the extensions in quality and scope. In general, the capacity requirements are understated for the states in which the requirements are already high, and overstated for those with relatively lower requirements. Thus the procedures and assumptions regarding changes in quality and scope for 1970 public service expenditures, as projected, dampen the differences between the high-capacity and the low-capacity requirement states, as does the choice of the capacity index itself.

The research findings point to consideration of a capacity requirements index (computed from historic data) in some of the grants now offered to states as a substitute for per capita personal income. More importantly, such an index begins to meet the perceived problems that have led to a case-by-case approach to grants-in-aid. We are concerned here especially with measurements that can be applied in federal grants-in-aid in lieu of the administrative judgments that are now used to allocate project funds so as to carry out the intent of the distribution of those grants. And we are concerned with measurements that can be applied in allocating additional federal revenues to the states through unconditional or consolidated categorical aids.

For the purpose of allocating additional federal funds still another index appears appropriate—an index of the increments or growth in capacity requirements.

INCREMENTAL CAPACITY REQUIREMENTS

Changes in the capacity requirements reflect the relative growth in expenditure requirements and in the economy of each state. These changes from one period to another indicate whether requirements are growing at the same rate as income is, or faster or slower. For those states with the fastest growth in requirements, additional federal grants would help reduce tax pressures that keep expenditures from expanding when required.

The incremental capacity requirement (ICR) is shown as a change in capacity requirements, that is, the incremental share of fiscal capacity that would have to be devoted to taxes if these expenditure requirements were to be financed:

$$\text{ICR}^t = \text{CR}^t - \text{CR}^o \text{ or } \frac{E^t - (F^t + G^t)}{C^t} - \frac{E^o - (F^o + G^o)}{C^o}$$

where t=t year and o=base year. (All other symbols are as previously defined in the section on "Capacity Requirements Defined," above.)

Looking at the historical past, expenditure requirements for the nation as a whole rose between fiscal 1957 and fiscal 1962 faster than income. In 1962, 1 percent more of the (higher) income was required to meet expenditures in excess of charges and grants than in 1957. This direction of change is projected to continue to 1970. The share of 1970 personal income in the states required to finance public service requirements and facilities is projected as 0.6 percentage points larger than the share needed in fiscal 1962, despite the large estimated growth in federal grants. This projected increase points to borrowing or higher tax collections in the amount of the increase—$4 billion—at the assumed $668 billion personal income level. When the rise in incremental requirements is projected for all regions of the nation, the rate of increase for New England, the Mideast, the Southwest, and the Rocky Mountain regions is found to be higher than the national average.

Table 5– 4. **INCREASES IN REQUIREMENTS AS PERCENT OF CAPACITY AND GROWTH IN CAPACITY**

Region	Percentage points rise in capacity requirements		Average annual percent increase in capacity (personal income) fiscal 1962 to calendar 1970
	Fiscal years 1957 to 1962	Fiscal 1962 to calendar 1970	
UNITED STATES	1.0	0.6	5.4%
New England	−0.4	1.2	5.1
Mideast	1.3	0.9	5.2
Great Lakes	1.3	0.2	5.2
Plains	0.2	0.1	4.8
Southeast	1.0	0.3	5.5
Southwest	0.5	0.7	5.2
Rocky Mountain	0.5	0.6	5.3
Far West	1.6	0.4	6.6

SOURCES: 1970 estimates from State-Local Finances Project, The George Washington University; 1957 and 1962 computed from U.S. Bureau of the Census, Governments Division.

When we turn from the regional picture to the changes in state capacity requirements, we find greater diversity, with fourteen states scattered among all regions (except the Southwest) projected to decrease their requirements. Eleven are projected to increase their capacity requirements as a percent of personal income by two or more times the nationwide average increase. A similar diversity among states is suggested by comparison of the capacity requirement changes over the period 1957-62, when for five states, including three in the Southeast and two on the North Atlantic seaboard, the capacity requirements increased more than twice as rapidly as the national average. In twenty one states the increase was half or less than half the national average

Table 5–5. **TAX REVENUE AS PERCENT OF PERSONAL INCOME, FISCAL YEAR 1957 AND AVERAGE FOR FISCAL YEARS 1964-66** [a] *(in percent)*

State & Region	Tax effort 1957	Tax effort 1964-66	Percentage points rise	Percentage of U.S. average 1957	Percentage of U.S. average 1964-66
United States	8.5%	10.1%	1.6	100.0%	100.0%
New England	8.7	9.8	1.1	102.4	97.4
Maine	9.0	10.7	1.7	105.9	105.7
New Hampshire	8.1	8.9	0.8	95.3	88.2
Vermont	10.7	12.2	1.5	125.9	120.6
Massachusetts	9.4	10.3	0.9	110.6	102.0
Rhode Island	7.7	9.7	2.0	90.6	96.0
Connecticut	7.4	8.8	1.4	87.1	87.4
Mideast	8.3	10.3	2.0	97.6	101.4
New York	9.4	11.8	2.4	110.6	117.0
New Jersey	7.0	8.6	1.6	82.4	85.1
Pennsylvania	7.8	9.1	1.3	91.8	90.1
Delaware	5.2	9.1	3.9	61.2	90.4
Maryland	7.5	9.1	1.6	88.2	90.1
District of Columbia	7.0	8.0	1.0	82.4	79.4
Great Lakes	7.6	9.3	1.7	89.4	92.2
Michigan	8.4	10.1	1.7	98.8	99.6
Ohio	6.9	8.4	1.5	81.2	82.8
Indiana	7.1	9.5	2.4	83.5	94.4
Illinois	7.4	8.6	1.2	87.1	85.3
Wisconsin	9.6	12.0	2.4	112.9	119.1
Plains	9.0	10.4	1.4	105.9	103.0
Minnesota	10.1	11.8	1.7	118.8	117.2
Iowa	10.1	11.1	1.0	118.8	109.6
Missouri	7.0	8.8	1.8	82.4	86.7
North Dakota	12.1	11.5	−0.6	142.4	113.8
South Dakota	11.4	12.0	0.6	134.1	119.3
Nebraska	8.2	9.1	0.9	96.5	89.7
Kansas	9.4	10.8	1.4	110.6	107.1
Southeast	8.6	9.5	0.9	101.2	94.3
Virginia	7.9	8.3	0.4	92.9	81.9
West Virginia	7.7	9.9	2.2	90.6	97.9
Kentucky	7.7	9.0	1.3	90.6	88.7
Tennessee	8.5	9.2	0.7	100.0	91.5
North Carolina	8.4	9.6	1.2	98.8	95.0
South Carolina	8.9	9.2	0.3	104.7	91.0
Georgia	8.6	9.2	0.6	101.2	90.8
Florida	9.1	10.1	1.0	107.1	100.2
Alabama	7.7	9.1	1.4	90.6	90.5
Mississippi	10.9	10.9	0	128.2	107.9
Louisiana	10.4	11.2	0.8	122.4	111.0
Arkansas	8.7	9.3	0.6	102.4	91.8
Southwest	8.3	9.7	1.4	97.6	96.2
Oklahoma	9.4	10.0	0.6	110.6	99.0
Texas	7.9	9.2	1.3	92.9	90.9
New Mexico	9.4	11.4	2.0	110.6	112.9
Arizona	9.4	11.9	2.5	110.6	118.0
Rocky Mountain	9.7	11.4	1.7	114.1	112.5
Montana	9.9	11.4	1.5	116.5	112.9
Idaho	9.3	11.2	1.9	109.4	110.7
Wyoming	9.7	11.6	1.9	114.1	114.6
Colorado	9.8	11.5	1.7	115.3	113.4
Utah	9.6	11.2	1.6	112.9	110.8
Far West	9.6	11.6	2.0	112.9	114.9
Washington	8.9	10.6	1.7	104.7	105.1
Oregon	10.2	10.4	0.2	120.0	103.1
Nevada	9.3	10.2	1.9	109.4	101.0
California	9.6	11.9	2.3	112.9	117.7
Alaska	5.5	8.1	2.6	64.7	80.5
Hawaii	9.4	11.2	1.8	110.6	110.8

[a] The 1964-66 tax effort is computed for the three-year interval, fiscal year 1964 through fiscal year 1966.

SOURCES: U.S. Bureau of the Census, Governments Division; and U.S. Department of Commerce, Office of Business Economics.

increase in percentage of income and in ten of these states capacity requirements declined.

To discover whether these directions and divergencies are confirmed by the most recent "hard" data, we turned to tax effort measures in lieu of capacity requirements (Table 5-5). Of the states that enlarged their tax effort between 1957 and 1966 by 2 or more percentage points of income, further large increases are implicit in the large incremental capacity requirements projected for nine of them. Furthermore, almost 20 percent of the nation's population in 1966 lived in the two states (California and New York) that have increased their tax effort from 1957 to 1966 by 2.3 and 2.8 percentage points respectively, close to twice the increase in the national average. Both of these states in 1957 and in 1966 made an effort that was more than 10 percent above the nationwide average, and they are projected to have the highest expenditure requirements per capita in 1970, except for the District of Columbia.

At the other extreme, the same proportion of the 1966 population lived in twelve Southern states, comprising the Southeast region (exclusive of Florida); these states increased their tax effort from fiscal 1957 to 1966 by only 1 percentage point on the average, an increase 40 percent below the national average, from 101 percent in 1957 to 94 percent in 1966. For 1970, these states are projected to have capacity requirements of 10.8 percent, and incremental requirements from 1962 to 1970 of 0.4 percentage points, three-fourths of the national average.

Changes in capacity requirements depend on (1) the growth of fiscal capacity or personal income, (2) the growth of expenditure requirements, and (3) the initial value of the ratio of expenditure requirements to personal income. This is not surprising. If personal income is growing at a relatively slow rate, then, unless expenditure requirements also grow at a lower than average rate, the increment in capacity requirements will be relatively large. A relatively rapid increase in personal income will tend by a reverse mechanism to be associated with a less than average increment in capacity requirements.

REQUIRED TAX INCREASES

At the margin, the decision on expenditures is whether or not to spend, when doing so would necessitate tax rate increases or introduction of new taxes. An index of the increases in taxes required by the growth in expenditures, state by state, (or locality by locality) is one variation of the measure presented earlier. Building on the research that has been done, we can assess relative changes in effective tax rates, for individual levies and for a weighted average of these levies. Taking yields as a percentage of a tax base (defined in a standard way), these effective tax rates permit comparisons among jurisdictions of tax decisions that have been taken to enlarge public services. Such an index could be applied in rewarding, by additional grant support, those jurisdictions which make the difficult decision to increase taxes. The selection of an index based on tax increments depends upon whether a reward system, to gain expanded state and local taxation for support of a higher volume of public goods, seems a desirable way to enlarge the public sector.

Use of an index of tax increments to "reward" states and localities has the deficiency of any index that ignores the record of performance in back years. Those states, for example, that taxed themselves at relatively high effective rates but made no change would receive relatively less than states that had poor showings for a prior period but were moving quickly to up their public service levels by adding new taxes or increasing tax rates. The usefulness of the incremental approach, however, may be illustrated by the potential application of the index to state grant programs. Central cities in many places would receive added grants as rewards for their raising of property taxes and introducing income or sales taxes; rewards would be relatively high in the cities compared with their suburban fringes.

Past tax performance provides one approach to an index; future rate change provides another. By developing projections of incremental tax requirements a different purpose would be served. An index of required tax increases based on such projections would furnish a basis for anticipatory grants to help alleviate comparative fiscal strains and facilitate the projected expenditure growth. Drawing on the projections of Project '70, comparative figures are shown of required tax increases for a future period. Embodied in the capacity requirements for 1970, as estimated for each state, are likely expenditure patterns and projected economic and demographic changes. These same changes will lead to automatically increasing tax collections but not necessarily to yields matching the expenditure increases. This difference between future revenues from existing taxes and future expenditures indicates required additional financing through new taxes, higher rates (or broader coverage) of existing taxes, or borrowing.

How serious is this need for additional tax yields in any one state compared to another? As a measure of feasibility and of potential fiscal crises, this "unfinanced" portion of required capacity is related to the projected tax yields of the existing revenue structures. The expression of incremental yield requirements, as a percent of projected yields, indicates the magnitude, for each state, of the revenue changes necessary to finance expenditures. The variation among states in this measure is understated by the expenditure projections used. The projections take no account of likely divergence in new program levels from "average," and they dampen the differences between the high- and the low-expenditure states. The required tax increases are understated in those states where capacity requirements and voter concern are high; for some states where incremental tax requirements are negative, this surplus is understated.

Alternative approaches could be used in measuring the taxing structure through which revenues are raised; each approach would seek to answer a different question about incremental taxation. One such alternative is to assume a uniform taxing structure across the fifty states, whereby the same effective rates of taxation are applied to the value of the same tax bases in each jurisdiction, with the differences reflecting differences in economic characteristics of the states. Another is to assume uniformity of responsiveness to economic growth of the differing tax structures within the various states, assuming actual initial levels of tax collections.[15] Still another approach is to project yields of existing tax structures as of some particular date, assuming constant effective tax rates. State and local tax collections would be projected under existing tax law and rates to show the amounts that would be raised if no further tax action were taken; this estimate would be compared with revenues required.

Two illustrations are given in Table 5-6 of the estimate of required tax increases between a base period and a future year. The years 1961-62 and 1970 are used for this illustration.

Just as expenditure projections were scaled to likely program developments and continuing present interstate variations, so too the taxes were projected for 1970 as close to likely future reality as possible. The required tax increases

---

[15] The measure of incremental capacity requirements is identical with a measure of required incremental tax yields assuming a uniform, unitary, personal income elasticity of state and local tax revenues.

Table 5–6. **REQUIRED PERCENTAGE TAX INCREASES, CALENDAR 1970 PROJECTED, HIGH AND LOW REVENUE ESTIMATES**

State and region	Required tax increases, high revenue estimate		Required tax increases low revenue estimate	
	Increase	Percent of U.S. average	Increase	Percent of U.S. average
United States	4.8%	100.0%	13.0%	100.0%
New England	12.1	252.1	20.6	158.5
Maine	3.6	75.0	13.0	100.0
New Hampshire	6.9	143.7	16.7	128.5
Vermont	8.2	170.8	19.8	152.3
Massachusetts	12.2	254.2	20.0	153.8
Rhode Island	23.5	489.6	32.9	253.1
Connecticut	13.2	275.0	21.8	167.7
Mideast	8.0	166.7	15.0	115.4
New York	4.2	87.5	9.6	73.8
New Jersey	13.1	272.9	23.3	179.2
Pennsylvania	10.8	225.0	18.4	141.5
Delaware	6.0	125.0	11.3	86.9
Maryland	9.6	200.0	17.9	137.7
District of Columbia	44.7	931.2	57.5	442.3
Great Lakes	4.0	83.3	11.6	89.2
Michigan	3.1	64.6	10.2	78.5
Ohio	5.7	118.7	14.1	108.5
Indiana	7.1	147.9	13.4	103.1
Illinois	4.5	93.7	12.7	97.7
Wisconsin	−1.6	−33.3	4.7	36.2
Plains	−4.0	−83.3	3.6	27.7
Minnesota	−13.9	−289.6	−6.7	−51.5
Iowa	1.7	35.4	8.8	67.7
Missouri	1.6	33.3	9.6	73.8
North Dakota	16.7	347.9	25.2	193.8
South Dakota	−6.9	−143.7	2.1	16.2
Nebraska	6.1	127.1	14.3	110.0
Kansas	−8.0	−166.7	−1.4	−10.8
Southeast	2.1	43.7	12.8	98.5
Virginia	7.1	147.9	16.4	126.2
West Virginia	15.8	329.2	29.2	224.6
Kentucky	12.5	260.4	23.1	177.7
Tennessee	6.5	135.4	16.8	129.2
North Carolina	−1.2	−25.0	7.3	56.2
South Carolina	−1.5	−31.2	7.4	56.9
Georgia	11.0	229.2	20.6	158.5
Florida	−11.8	−245.8	−3.5	−26.9
Alabama	8.2	170.8	19.6	150.8
Mississippi	14.7	−306.2	25.7	−197.7
Louisiana	7.6	158.3	17.1	131.5
Arkansas	−1.8	−37.5	10.0	76.9
Southwest	2.9	60.4	12.4	95.4
Oklahoma	−1.7	−35.4	9.0	69.2
Texas	5.9	122.9	14.9	114.6
New Mexico	−6.6	−137.5	4.6	35.4
Arizona	0.5	10.4	10.0	76.9
Rocky Mountain	−0.6	−12.5	8.7	66.9
Montana	0.6	12.5	10.4	80.0
Idaho	−8.9	−185.4	−1.1	−13.1
Wyoming	−3.6	−75.0	10.8	83.1
Colorado	3.2	66.7	12.2	93.8
Utah	−2.7	−56.2	6.2	47.7
Far West	5.5	114.6	14.4	110.8
Washington	−1.5	−31.2	5.7	43.8
Oregon	4.9	102.1	13.9	106.9
Nevada	17.2	358.3	25.8	198.5
California	6.1	127.1	15.3	117.7
Alaska	6.2	129.2	24.9	191.5
Hawaii	10.4	216.7	17.6	135.4

SOURCE: State-Local Finances Project, The George Washington University.

(RTI) are shown as the percentage increase in tax collections implied by financing of expenditures:

$$RTI_t = \frac{E_t - (F_t + G_t + T_t)}{T_t}$$

where T^t represents tax receipts from the tax structure as enacted May 1, 1965, in each state. The tax revenues, like expenditures, were projected from a base of fiscal 1962 data, with "taxes" defined in accord with the classification of taxes by the Governments Division of the U.S. Bureau of the Census. The only deviation from this classification is inclusion of (1) net liquor store profits in the liquor-monopoly states as a "tax" and (2) the net positive profits from local utility operations that become available for general expenditure purposes.

The pattern, by state, of required tax increases is the result of the interplay of several variables. Together, these variables determine the level of estimated future fiscal adequacy or inadequacy.[16]

The tax effort made in 1962 is the base line from which the increments are counted. It is from this base of taxing practices, which finance low, moderate, or high levels of public service provisions in the states, that the tax yields in 1970 are estimated. The higher the proportion in the past of personal income in the state collected by the state and localities in taxes, the higher it is likely to be in 1970, and the lower the required additional taxes will be, if other things are equal.

In combination with initial year tax effort, the taxing structures of the states and localities affect the sensitivity of the taxes to economic growth. The automatic responsiveness of the revenues of state and local taxes to increases in income is measurable by the income elasticity of tax yields of a particular tax structure, exclusive of rate and structure changes.[17] Such implicit personal income elasticities of estimated tax collections (from taxes in effect in fiscal 1962) were derived. Since the elasticity coefficients measure revenue responsiveness to economic growth, the rate of growth of personal income must be taken together with the elasticity. Where the state's revenue structure is elastic, the faster personal income grows, the more tax collections will automatically increase relative to fiscal capacity. Where the revenue structure is inelastic, then the slower the rate of personal income growth, the higher will tax collections remain relative to fiscal capacity.

---

[16] Algebraically, required tax increases in year t, RTI_t, is defined as

$\frac{E_t - (F_t + G_t + T_t)}{T_t}$. Let revenues in year t from tax changes made between years o and k

be A_k; then, since $CR_t = E_t - (E_t + G_t)$, $C_t = C_o(1 + r_c)^t$, and $T_t = T_o(1 + r_t)^t$, we can

substitute to get $RTI_t = \dfrac{CR_t}{\dfrac{T_o[1 + r_t]^t}{C_o[1 + r_c]^t} + \dfrac{A_k}{C_t}} - 1$. Defining E, the personal income elasticity of

yields of a given tax structure, as $\dfrac{r_t}{r_c}$, we can approximate RTI_t by $\dfrac{CR_t}{\dfrac{T_o[1 + (E-1)r_c]^t}{C_o} + \dfrac{A_k}{C_t}} - 1$,

where T_o/C_o is the tax effort in the base year, and A_k/C_t is tax effort in year t resulting from tax structure changes between years o and k.

[17] The income elasticity coefficient is the ratio of the per annum growth rate of the revenues from a given tax structure to the per annum growth rate of personal income in the state. If the coefficient is greater than 1, the tax structure is elastic, and revenues increase more than income with economic growth (tax effort and, probably, capacity-use automatically increase). If the coefficient is less than 1, the structure is inelastic, and tax revenues increase, but less rapidly than does personal income (tax effort automatically declines).

AGENDA FOR RESEARCH

The agenda for research needed to improve and develop better indexes of public services and fiscal capacity is long. We attempt to set forth only a part of it here.

A large-scale effort is required to formulate public service requirements in output terms and to develop such standards as could be applied in grant formulas. A number of questions about the research must be answered initially. What products should it be addressed to? For which groups of persons? In how large numbers? In what places? With what resources? At what costs? We do know that research is needed on price differentials among and within states for the different resource inputs for public products, and that far more extensive study and experimentation is required on inputs that can add to public service outputs.

Additional research is indicated to apply need indexes and fiscal capacity measures in an anticipatory way rather than after the fact. Indexes related to the future in each state depend on projections of future revenues, expenditure requirements, and economic changes. Yet very few state governments are presently familiar with expenditure patterns and expenditure developments in their local governments, and not many more concern themselves with advance fiscal projection for the full gamut of their own state programs.

One answer is to undertake projection as an on-going process, so that the forecasts can be continually revised and updated in the light of new developments, rather than in the one-shot fashion in which our Project '70 study, described earlier, was of necessity conducted. (Suggestions concerning the effect of changing the economic growth rate of the model on the projections of Project '70 were made in 1967, in a brief note in the *Southern Economic Journal*.[18] However, the discussion there addresses itself to national totals only.)

A more general research approach is the predictive model of the national economy, with state and local government constituting an endogenous sector. Traditionally, state and local purchases of goods and services and government transfer payments have been viewed as exogenous variables in the interdependent economic system. For operational application in grant policies, however, these purchases and transfers need to be analyzed so as to introduce them endogeneously. Little research has been done in this area, but beginnings have been made, including some work on endogenous relationships for federal and state transfer payments in econometric models for the entire economic system. State-local expenditure determinant studies have been coming forth as doctoral dissertations in ever increasing numbers.[19] Most of these, however, have been cross-sectional analyses, using states as units, and cannot be applied for predictive purposes within the framework of an economic model for the nation and the states. Studies across time for the states can be so applied.

Definition and quantification of the linkages between public and private sectors in each state, and between the national economy and the economy of each state, are needed for development of predictive models yielding the type of estimates presented in this paper as illustrative. Such a research effort has many purposes, and one by-product would be the projections of emerging expenditure developments in the states in relation to the capacity of the states. Research is,

---

[18] Selma J. Mushkin and Gabrielle C. Lupo, "State and Local Finances Projections: Another Dimension?", *Southern Economic Journal*, Vol. 33 (January 1967).

[19] See references in the Appendix following the last chapter of this volume.

in fact, in process on projection models for the economy of the states in relation to national economic growth.[20]

To be acceptable for policy purposes, such predictive models as are developed must be easily understood and reasonably accurate. The accuracy of the research will be the test of its productiveness; demonstrations of accuracy will permit and encourage application of the findings. The present tools for measurement of capacity and effort are not sufficient as policy instruments. *Ad hoc* solutions, such as project grants, are not adequate and, in fact, have given rise to a number of problems. These problems (and some proposals for their solution) are summarized in Chapter 7.

It is clear that we need predictive models not only for state and local government purchases of goods and services and transfer payments, but also for revenue receipts.[21] Income elasticity studies of state and local taxes have yielded some results applicable for the indexes outlined, but much more needs to be done in testing and improving these methods. Hardly any research has been devoted to the companion problems of charges and fee revenues, and to analysis of their movements relative to outlays for the programs with which they are associated. A reasonable projection procedure for dealing with federal aids, which by their character must remain in part exogenous to the economic system, begs for study, not only as a part of some capacity index, but also to make advance fiscal planning feasible for states and localities. Far more can be done to assess the links between endogenous variables in the economy and those aids. The two largest existing grants, for example, are related to other important facets of the economic structure—highway aids to gasoline consumption and public assistance grants to transfer payments—and these relationships can be put to valuable predictive use.

The pattern of studies we have undertaken here, in an attempt to generalize the disaggregative methodology, points to the exploration of models of growth changes for each of the following segments of state-local expenditures: personal services, construction, transfer payments, and procurement. This exploration is now under way. But if operational indexes are to be achieved, vastly more—and more comprehensive—research will be required, including the items on the agenda for research we have so briefly outlined above.

---

[20] Since 1953, the University of Michigan Research Seminar on Quantitative Economics, directed by Professor Daniel B. Suits, has been using a series of models to make annual short-range forecasts and long-range projections of regional economies.

[21] For a summary of work to date on revenue estimation for states and localities, see Eugene P. McLoone, Gabrielle C. Lupo, and Selma J. Mushkin, *Long-Range Revenue Estimation* (State-Local Finances Project, The George Washington University, October 1967).

CHAPTER 6

Priorities: national, state, local

IN THIS CHAPTER WE EXAMINE THE ISSUE OF PRIORITIES, from both the national and the state and local points of view. In particular, the following questions are considered in the three main sections that follow:

1. What are some of the factors that must be taken into account to ensure that grants-in-aid reflect national priorities?
2. What is the significance of the charge that grants-in-aid distort state and local budgets?
3. What is the evidence that budget distortion or (its opposite) substitution does result from the current grant programs?

CONSISTENCY OF FEDERAL PRIORITIES

If we assume that a grant-in-aid acts as a "carrot" through effective reduction in the price of the favored program relative to others, we are forced to examine the design of a particular grant within the context of the total system. It is apparent that a program of national concern competes not only with other local programs but also with other programs of national concern. This problem of competition among national programs is likely to become more acute as the federal intergovernmental revenues and the corresponding required state or local matching funds in the aggregate become a larger fraction of state and local revenues.

For example, referring back to Chapter 4, we may ask whether the national government really places higher priority on the full range of programs for which the HEW grants have been picked up strongly by the states than it does on Vocational Rehabilitation. Or whether, at the local level, the progress in the Community Mental Health Center program is in line with other programs being fostered at the local level. Of course, if funds are available, the carrot may be made more attractive through adding federal dollars to those programs that are lagging. A more reasonable approach, however, would be to review the entire grant package to see whether the allocation of federal dollars, the state or local response, and the federal priorities are in line with each other. This kind of central review ought to be conducted on a continuing basis, to ensure that, as problems come and go, there will be a corresponding modification in the grants-in-aid intended to deal with the problems.

The consistency of the federal priorities has a counterpart consideration, namely, the necessity of assessing the aggregate fiscal impact on each state implied by the total federal grant-in-aid package. If the standards set for national programs are met, what does this imply in terms of the total federal dollars going to a state relative to its own resources? What is the aggregate of matching funds that the state would need to tie to the federal grants? How do these funds compare with state-raised revenues and unrestricted federal revenues? How much in the way of incremental state funds do new grants require? These questions are particularly important in regard to the effect of categorical grants on the ability of the state to plan adequately and to tailor the federal programs to specific circumstances in the state.

A key element in the problem of designing grants to reflect national priorities is the matter of so-called budget distortion at the state and local level. It is to this topic that we now turn.

BUDGET DISTORTION

The federal categorical grant is frequently criticized on the grounds that it distorts state and community budgets, but the concept of distortion has remained vague. We therefore offer two alternative formal definitions here.

1. Distortion of the first kind may be defined as the deviation of the expenditure pattern of the jurisdiction from what it would have been if the federal grant allotment were to have only an income effect.
2. Distortion of the second kind may be defined as any reduction in the expenditure for any jurisdictional program below the level that would have existed in the absence of the federal grant program (this definition is assumed to hold only for "noninferior" programs).[1]

The basic premise of the first definition is that tax dollars collected within a state's boundaries to be used for domestic programs within the state belong to the state and should be expended as it sees fit. Thus, any effort by the national government to insert different priorities for these programs is, by definition, distortionary. This concept leads to one of two positions: (1) the federal government should not collect taxes to be used to support internal domestic programs (at least not through categorical grants-in-aid), or (2) the grants provided by the federal government should be in the form of unconditional fiscal grants which, having only an income effect, do not perturb state priorities for public programs.

While some state officials may condemn the imbalance (in their view) produced by categorical grants, the thesis that values arrived at by national consensus are relevant and should be fostered in the American concept of federalism is ingrained and probably accepted in principle by most state officials. The rationale presented for the importance of grants from the most comprehensive government to other levels is quite compelling.

The federal government does bear a large responsibility, however, for ensuring that the grants it offers comprise a balanced package. Grants should not be implemented in a way that leaves serious gaps in programs. The Advisory Council on Public Welfare in its 1966 report to the Secretary of Health, Education, and Welfare made a large point of this problem of gaps that exist for no adequate reason:

Large numbers of those in desperate need, including many children, are excluded even from this level of aid [public assistance] by arbitrary eligibility requirements unrelated

---

[1] We define an "inferior" program as one whose magnitude would be decreased as the public revenues available to the jurisdiction are increased.

to need such as those based on age, family situation, degree of disability, alleged employ-ability, low earnings, unrealistic requirements for family contribution, durational residence requirements, and absence of provisions for emergency assistance.[a]

The federal government must face the problem of gaps not only in welfare, but in all program areas it seeks to promote. The attractiveness of the notion of consolidation of narrow categorical grants into broad functional grants arises in large part from the anticipated reduction of the impact of this kind of distortion. (This matter is discussed in depth in Chapter 8.)

The second, and more limited, definition of distortion is fully consistent with the view that the federal government does have a role in encouraging programs of national concern. The definition holds that federal grants would be considered distortionary only when constructed in a way that causes states and localities to forgo program expenditures which would have been made in the absence of the federal grants. Consequently, even though federal grants might change the balance of local program expenditures, they would not be regarded as distortionary so long as no state or local program is reduced in absolute terms.

The effects that the design of a specific grant may have on the matter of distortion are shown schematically in Figure 6-1. In a simplified case in which only one program is aided by a closed-end matching grant, the aggregate of other programs (including tax relief) in the state is plotted on the Y axis, and the aided program on the X axis. In the absence of a federal grant, the budget line would be AB and the program combination (X_0, Y_0). The federal government has taken the position that the appropriate standard level for program X is X_s, which is larger than X_0. Three different closed-end matching grants are shown. Grant ACD has the lowest federal matching. If the price elasticity for program X is sufficiently high, the state might be induced to move to level X_s at point C. In so doing, however, it must reduce the expenditures for the aggregate of other programs, cutting back their level from Y_0 to Y_1. This produces distortion of the second kind as defined above. (If the reduction in the level of Y were to come entirely from increased state taxes, one might prefer not to label it as distortion. One could define distortion of the second kind as occurring only when the reduction comes at the expense of other public program expenditures.)

On the other hand, a grant with a substantially higher federal share may allow the state to divert federal funds obtained in the categorical grant to other programs. An example of this is shown in Figure 6-1 by the budget line AGH. The diversion of categorical grant funds is indicated by the fact that, at the program level X_s (point G), the state is able to increase the level of other programs from Y_0 to Y_2. Finally, a categorical grant producing the budget constraint AEF, if it attains the standard program level X_s, produces no increase or decrease in other programs. Consequently, it produces no distortion of the second kind and does not result in federal funds being diverted to other uses than that for which they were designated.

Is this second kind of distortion undesirable? From the state or local point of view, one would have to say in theory that it is, because the grant has acted as economic coercion to induce the jurisdiction to forgo some other use for its resources. However, if the impact of the federal grant induces greater public spending and does not have a strong adverse effect on other public program expenditures, those in the jurisdiction who favor more public expenditures would perhaps view it as desirable.

---

[a] Advisory Council on Public Welfare, *"Having the Power, We Have the Duty,"* Report to the Secretary of Health, Education, and Welfare (Government Printing Office, June 1966), p. xii.

Figure 6-1.

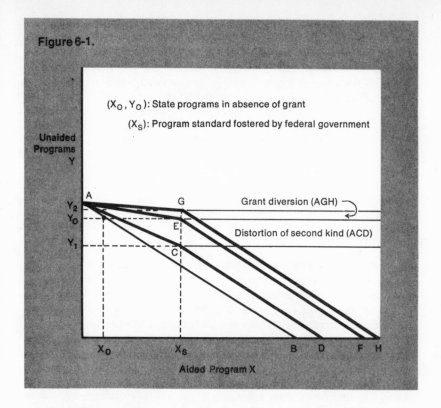

In considering the national stance in regard to the desirability of the second kind of budget distortion, we should rephrase the issue in other terms. What we have called budget distortion of the second kind is, from the federal government viewpoint, stimulation: i.e., as a result of the grant there has been an increase in state- and local-raised revenues devoted to the aided program. Conversely, grant diversion is equivalent to substitution: i.e., the grant has led to a reduction in state- and local-raised revenues for the aided program. For example, Figure 6-1 shows these two effects for a state's situation. The federal grant with the least generous matching can be described as stimulative in that it induces the state to spend more of its own resources (by an amount corresponding to Y_o-Y_1) for the aided program. On the other hand, the grant with the most generous federal matching allows substitution of some of the federal categorical funds to be used for other programs by an amount corresponding to Y_2-Y_0.

Since the national government has not articulated a clear position on general objectives for its grant-in-aid system, we cannot really say whether substitution (or stimulation) should be considered as a good or bad effect. However, if each federal grant program is viewed as an independent entity directed toward the achievement of a specific goal, then one might term stimulation of state- and local-raised revenues for the program as good and substitution as bad—that is, the less substitutive or the more stimulative the grant, the greater the effect per federal dollar expended for the program.

On the other hand, let us suppose that the grants-in-aid are viewed as a system, which (1) attempts to promote the achievement of specific objectives and (2) attempts to improve the private/public sector balance by making federally raised revenues available to the states and localities. In this case, in designing a grant formula for a specific program it is not at all clear whether we should be overly concerned about the possibility that substitution will occur. Even though it is true that, in this situation, one should attempt to design the system of grants to avoid substitution of federal funds for state or locally raised revenues in the aggregate, the fact that some of the categorical funds may be diverted to other public programs is not necessarily undesirable, provided that the program objectives for the categories are met reasonably well. Further, given the value structure of a state or locality, achieving a specific program goal may not be possible *without* making the matching incentive sufficiently high that substitution can and will occur. Finally, as Thurow has pointed out in relation to the multiple objectives that the national government might have, the promotion of two goals —a specific categorical goal and a broad objective, such as total level of expenditures in a jurisdiction—requires at least two intergovernmental fiscal tools. The categorical grant and the unconditional grant represent one feasible pair of such tools.[3]

REVIEW OF STUDIES OF STIMULATION AND SUBSTITUTION

We have talked thus far as if stimulation (i.e. distortion of the second kind) and substitution are observable phenomena. We now turn to a review of recent studies on this subject to discover, if possible, (1) whether these phenomena are actually observable in a meaningful sense and (2) what seems to have been the experience with existing grants-in-aid. The studies that we discuss below are mainly those that include some empirical work on the effects of federal grants (or federal and state grants) on state and local expenditures. There are, however, a number of other studies in this field that lend perspective to the matter; we therefore cite them, along with the studies specifically highlighted here, in a listing of references at the end of the chapter.

Let us first define what we consider the terms "stimulation" and "substitution" to mean. Figure 6-2 provides a schematic display of the concepts. The vertical axis Y is measured as the level of expenditure (public or private) for which the federal grant is *not* intended, while the horizontal axis X is measured as the level of the one (or more) activity for which the grant *is* intended to be used. Line AB is the budget constraint for the grantee prior to the grant. Point C is assumed to be the expenditure package the grantee would adopt in the absence of the grant. The shaded region is not considered; since it is assumed as a minimum, the grantee would not move to a point in that region when offered a grant intended to promote program X.

If, when offered the grant, the grantee were to move to any point on line CD, the grant would be said to be completely substitutive, since it would produce no increase in the level of program X. If the grantee were to adopt a program package anywhere in the region within the boundary represented by DCE, the grant would be considered as partially substitutive, since a portion of the added revenues would be diverted to programs other than those for which the grant is intended. Points on line CE would represent a situation in which the grant is neither substituted for other programs nor stimulative of increased expenditures from local sources for the supported program. For these combinations, each additional federal dollar increases the *total* expenditures for program X by one dollar, but does not draw any additional local funds with it. Finally, if the resultant program package were to fall within the region bounded by ECB and

---

[3] Lester C. Thurow, "The Theory of Grants-in-Aid," *National Tax Journal,* Vol. 19 (December 1966).

Figure 6-2.

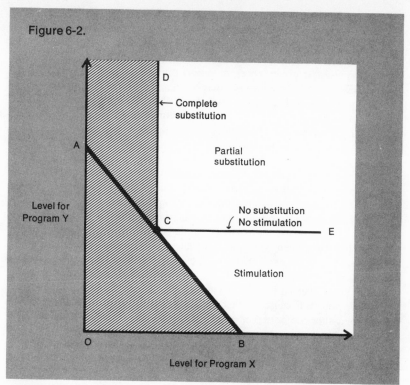

the X axis, the grant would be said to be stimulative of local expenditures for the supported program. In terms of regression analysis of determinants of expenditures, we have four correspondences, as follows: (1) line CD corresponds to a coefficient of zero for the grant variable, (2) the region bounded by DCE, to a coefficient greater than zero, but less than unity, (3) the line CE, to a coefficient of unity, and (4) the region bounded by ECB and the X axis, to a coefficient greater than unity.

One more explicit distinction must be made with respect to stimulation and substitution—their effect over time. A grant from the federal government to a state or local government may indeed, in the initiating periods, be stimulative because of the matching requirements. This, however, does not necessarily mean that the stimulation will persist over future periods of time. To determine to what extent it has persisted, "one must somehow predict what state or local governments would have spent in the absence of federal aid." [4] If, in the following periods, the actual amount of state and local outlay is less than what would have been spent in the absence of federal aid, we have a situation in which initial stimulation may have changed to substitution over the longer run. On the other hand, if the state and local government outlay is more than would have been spent in the absence of federal aid, there would be stimulation for future expenditures. By introducing matching requirements and other conditions, the grant designer in some cases can prevent initial substitution; over the longer run, however, this is much more difficult. It is to the longer-run impacts that the empirical studies we review here have been directed.

---

[4] O'Brien and Robinson, p. 5. (See listing of references at end of chapter; all citations by author from here on will be found in alphabetical order in that listing.)

Some of the studies are directed primarily toward measuring the response of expenditures by functional areas.[5] Others confine their attention to the response of the aggregate of public spending to grants-in-aid.[6] Henderson, for example, is concerned that it may be possible to allocate intergovernmental revenues indirectly to promote expenditures, by simply providing less for tax-financed expenditures than in the absence of intergovernmental revenues. Thus his analysis of expenditure and tax decisions is focused upon both "public" and "private" expenditures. He defines public expenditures as those made by the local government, and private expenditures as personal income less local taxes. Thus the latter includes taxes paid to state and federal governments, as well as personal savings.

Sacks and Harris (in their 1966 *National Tax Journal* article, p. 79) tried to resolve problems (raised in earlier determinant studies) by considering the issue of whether federal grants stimulate or replace state expenditures. Their view that federal grants should stimulate state expenditures is supported by several *a priori* statements: for example, "while not . . . from the taxpayer's point of view, federal aid can be regarded as outside money from the point of view of the state and local government and its availability should be expected to have a direct impact on raising state and local expenditures." They also state (p. 80): "In sum, it is expected that federal aid will increase expenditures of state and local governments because most federal aid is designed to do so." (In such statements the authors do not specify whether they mean "stimulation" when using the terms "direct impact" and "increased expenditures.") They say further (p. 85):

Since federal grants are usually for specific programs, we might expect a $1 to $1 correspondence between federal aid and expenditures when other variables are taken into account. On the other hand, one could argue that there needn't be this direct relationship, for if the federal aid represented merely a different way of financing a function which would be performed anyway by the state and local government, the impact might well be less than unity.

The empirical research in the Sacks and Harris paper suggests that educational, federal welfare, and highway grants to states have a significant stimulation impact on expenditures, i.e., the regression coefficients in their studies are significantly greater than 1 for these functions.

Osman concludes that, in general, federal aid has had the effect of stimulating those functions to which it was directed, and that the result has not been merely to substitute federal for state and local funds. In his model, the amount of stimulation can be calculated by the following method (p. 367):

If we could measure the magnitude of the state and local expenditure if federal aid to the particular function were zero, and then measure state and local expenditure from their own sources after including federal aid as a variable, we could measure the amount of stimulation.

In his empirical results, so long as the coefficient of the grant variable is positive, per capita expenditure will increase as a result of federal aid, but stimulation would result only if the coefficient exceeds unity.

Osman attempts to measure the stimulatory effect of federal aid to six functions (p. 366). For "Total General," he concluded that there was stimulation, i.e., each $1.00 increase in federal aid per capita was associated with a $1.94 increase in per capita state and local outlay. And since the regression coefficient of federal aid exceeds unity (1.94 > 1.00), stimulation is implied. "Each $1.00

---

[5] For example, Sacks & Harris (1966); Osman; O'Brien and Robinson.

[6] Henderson; Gramlich.

of federal aid was associated with a $0.94 increase in outlay from the state and local governments' *own* revenue sources." In the case of total educational expenditures per capita, a high degree of federal stimulation is implied. Each added dollar of federal aid was associated with a $5.11 increase in state-local expenditures, implying a $4.11 increase in outlay from the state and local governments' own revenue sources.

In "Local Schools" and "Higher Education," stimulation is again implied. The regression coefficient of federal aid for "Local Schools" was 2.71 and for "Higher Education" 2.59.[7] In the case of "Highways," we see that federal highway grants have stimulated state and local highway expenditures. The regression coefficient is 1.37 i.e., state and local highway expenditures increased $0.37 from own revenue source for each added $1.00 of federal aid to highways. In the case of "Public Welfare," the regression coefficient is 1.38. Again, stimulation is implied. Stimulation is also implied for "Health and Hospitals," the regression coefficient being 2.09. Thus Osman concludes that federal aid to state and local governments does stimulate state and local expenditures on a given function from their own revenues.

He points out that state and local expenditures on some functions may increase through federal aid to *other* functions. This would occur if the functions were complementary. For example, federal aid to "Total Education" may lead also to increased expenditures for such complementary functions as "Local Schools" or "Higher Education." It is very difficult to measure this second effect.

Henderson attempts to explain, on an aggregative basis, the behavior of local governmental leaders in metropolitan and nonmetropolitan counties and behavioral differences between the two groups of counties. And in his study, which included both federal and state aids, he found that "metropolitan counties show a much larger response than nonmetropolitan—$1.4231 of new local expenditures per marginal grant dollar contrasted with $1.0371 for the nonmetropolitan." The metropolitan response suggests an element of bandwagonism, in that the receipt of grants induces metropolitan counties to commit local funds beyond matching requirements to projects that would not otherwise have been undertaken. Thus, for nonmetropolitan counties there is little if any stimulation and for metropolitan counties there is strong stimulation. Henderson does not attempt to explain why the results were different.

Gramlich, in his 1968 article, compares the effects of several alternative federal policies which influence the total expenditures of states and localities. The policies of interest are matching grants-in-aid, unconditional bloc grants, and bloc grants conditioned with effort formulas. He theorizes that matching grants do stimulate some state spending in excess of the dollar amount of the grant. Thus, there would be an increase in state taxes to cover part of the expenditures.

Gramlich postulates that unconditional block grants will have less stimulatory impact on state expenditures than matching grants would. In fact, a dollar of unconditional grants will ambiguously stimulate less than a dollar of state expenditures. Thus the grants would increase, but not stimulate, expenditures and would reduce taxes. Later, he assumes that the suspected tax-reducing impact of unconditional grants could be avoided by conditioning block grants with various types of effort formulas. With an effective effort formula, the expenditure response would be one by definition, i.e., there would be no tax reduction and/or saving increases.

---

[7] It should be noted that total educational expenditures include scholarship support and manpower training programs that are not part of "Local Schools" and "Higher Education."

Using empirical estimates from a quarterly postwar econometric model, Gramlich measures the response of states and localities to a $1 billion increase in a policy variable. All of his estimates are aggregated, i.e., he does not attempt to measure the responses by individual functional areas. He found that matching grants do stimulate spending from states' own funds (each grant dollar induces a $1.120 increase in total expenditures), but the response is a good deal less than expected from his theoretical hypothesis. For block grants with an effort formula and for unconditional block grants, the estimated responses were .548 and .280, respectively. Thus, as he theorized, these grants substitute for, rather than stimulate, state spending. We see, therefore, that $1 billion of matching grants stimulate a little more than this amount of state and local expenditures. The other grants stimulated less than $1 billion. Unconditional grants increased expenditures by less than 30 percent of the grant; the remainder was used for tax reductions and saving increases. Block grants with effort formula increased expenditures by less than 55 percent; this means that 45 percent of the money was used for other purposes.

O'Brien and Robinson attempted to measure the stimulatory effect of federal highway grants. They note that, to determine whether federal grants stimulate or replace state spending, one must somehow predict what state and local governments would have spent in the absence of federal aid. Their study, which was the only analysis (of those we reviewed) not using multiple regression techniques, concludes that:

According to most reasonable assumptions about what state and local expenditures would have been in the absence of increased federal assistance, it is evident that federal funds —which were intended to stimulate increased highway construction—have acted as a substitution for state and local money.

Several assumptions are used in attempting to predict what state and local governments would have spent in the absence of federal aid. These figures are then compared to what was actually spent to determine whether federal highway grants stimulate or replace state and local expenditures. With all but one of the assumption made, the authors conclude that federal highway grants are a substitute for state and local spending:

Only if one assumes that no increase in state and local highway expenditures would have occurred is there any support for the argument that the federal aid program has stimulated state and local expenditures from their own funds.

And this assumption was the least likely of the several considered, given the status of the highways in 1956 and the power of the highway lobby.

*   *   *   *   *

From our review, it seems evident that studies on the problem of substitution are not conclusive. The processes by which grants-in-aid are translated into operation are complex. In most situations over a period of time, not even the persons using the grants seem to be able to ascertain whether (or how much) substitution has occurred, because the grant itself changes preferences and attitudes. We may well conclude that, except for the initial effects of new and large grants, the question of whether or not substitution has occurred may not be meaningful.

LIST OF REFERENCES ON SUBSTITUTIONS VS. STIMULATORY EFFECTS OF GRANTS-IN-AID

1. Roy W. Bahl, Jr., and Robert J. Saunders, "Determinants of Changes in State and Local Government Expenditures," *National Tax Journal,* Vol. 18 (March 1965).

   The article deals with the determination of factors that influence changes in the level of state and local governmental expenditures. It does not address itself to the problem of substitution or stimulation effects of grants-in-aid.

2. George A. Bishop, "Stimulative versus Substitutive Effects of State School Aid in New England." *National Tax Journal,* Vol. 17 (June 1964).

   This is a very useful article. The author defined stimulation and measured the effect of state school aid to local governments. He found that state aid was a substitute for local spending.

3. Solomon Fabricant, *The Trend of Government Activity in the United States Since 1900.* (National Bureau of Economic Research, Inc., 1952).

   Fabricant used multiple correlation analysis to study the local factors which are associated with variations in state and local government expenditures. The book does not deal with the problem of substitution or stimulation effects of grants-in-aid.

4. Glenn W. Fisher, "Determinants of State and Local Government Expenditures, A Preliminary Analysis," *National Tax Journal,* Vol. 14 (December 1961).

5. ————, "Interstate Variations in State and Local Expenditure," *National Tax Journal,* Vol. 17 (March 1964).

   This article attempted to identify the factors that determine state expenditures. It did not address itself to the problem of substitution or stimulation effects of grants-in-aid.

6. Roger A. Freeman, "State Aid and the Support of Our Public Schools," *State Government,* Vol. 26 (October 1953).

   An empirical study of state educational aid to local governments.

7. Edward Gramlich, "Alternative Federal Policies for Stimulating State and Local Expenditures: A Comparison of Their Effects," *National Tax Journal,* Vol. 21 (June 1968).

   This paper presents both a theoretical and an empirical explanation for the problem of stimulation. The empirical estimates deal with aggregates, and not with specific functions.

8. ————, "State and Local Governments and Their Budget Constraint" (to be published in a forthcoming issue of *International Economic Review*).

   The author undertook an empirical estimate of stimulation. The estimates deal with aggregates, and not with specific functions.

9. Mark A. Haskell, "Federal Grants and Budgetary Distortion," *Quarterly Review of Economics and Business,* Vol. 2 (May 1962).

   This article was directed to the study of measuring budget distortions. The author recognized, *a priori,* that stimulation may or may not occur when the federal government gives grants to state governments. In his empirical findings on the measurement of budget distortion, he concluded that stimulation of state and local expenditures on aided activities was not as prevalent as many economists would believe.

10. ————, "Federal Grants-in-Aid: Their Influence on State and Local Expenditures," *Canadian Journal of Economics and Political Science,* Vol. 30 (November 1964).

    While this article presented alternative definitions of stimulation, it was concerned with showing how the tools of microeconomics can be applied to the phenomenon of intergovernmental grants. It also indicated how the income effect and the substitution effect of modern price theory can be used to show whether federal grants have a stimulative or substitutive effect. The study is purely theoretical and applies to federal-state grants .

11. James M. Henderson, "Local Government: A Social Welfare Analysis," *Review of Economics and Statistics,* Vol. 50 (May 1968).

    The article helps to clarify some of the definitions of stimulation. Its empirical investigation was confined to explaining the differences in stimulation in metropolitan and nonmetropolitan counties.

12. I. M. Labovitz, *Stimulative Effect of Federal Grants-in-Aid: Some Illustrative Data* (Library of Congress, Legislative Reference Service, 1958).

13. Jerry Miner, *Social and Economic Factors in Spending for Public Education* (Syracuse University Press, 1963).

    An empirical study of state educational aid to local governments.

14. Wallace E. Oates, "Principle of Government Grants: A Report to the Office of Economic Opportunity" (Mimeographed; Princeton University, June 1966).

    The author presented, *a priori,* statements to support his view that federal (state) grants replace state (local) expenditures. His conclusions encompass state-local as well as federal-state relationships.

15. ————, "An Addendum to Principles of Government Grants: A Report to the Office of Economic Opportunity" (Mimeographed; September 1966).

    Same as above.

16. Thomas O'Brien and William H. Robinson, "Federal Highway Grants: A Theory of Stimulation, a Practice of Substitution" (unpublished study by the Fiscal Analysis Staff, U.S. Bureau of the Budget, February 1967).

    The authors undertook an empirical test to determine whether federal highway grants stimulated or replaced state spending. They found that the grants replaced state spending .

17. Jack W. Osman, "The Dual Impact of Federal Aid on State and Local Government Expenditure," *National Tax Journal,* Vol. 19 (December 1966).

    This article was very useful to us, especially in its two alternative definitions of stimulation. The author undertook an empirical investigation to support his conclusion; the findings are for federal-state relationship.

18. Edward F. Renshaw, "A Note on the Expenditure Effects of State Aid to Education," *Journal of Political Economy,* Vol. 48 (April 1960).

    An empirical study of state educational aid to local governments.

19. Seymour Sacks and Robert Harris, "The Determinants of State and Local Government Expenditure and Intergovernmental Flows of Funds," *National Tax Journal,* Vol. 17 (March 1964).

    The authors studied the factors that determine state and local government expenditures; they also introduced a rudimentary analysis of stimulation. Both state-local and federal-state relationships were described, and the analysis is both theoretical and empirical.

20. Seymour Sacks, Robert Harris, and John J. Carroll, "The State and Local Government: The Role of State Aid," *Comptroller's Studies in Local Finance, No. 3* (New York State Department of Audit and Control, 1963).

    The authors introduced two variables to try to explain some of the variation in state and local expenditure. They also made empirical estimates of the amount of substitution in state educational grants to local government.

21. A. D. Scott, "The Evaluation of Federal Grants," *Economica,* Vol. 19 (November 1952).

    This theoretical study concluded that federal grants may influence states to spend more than would be the case without their help, and will indeed sway state attitudes concerning proportions of total expenditure to be devoted to each revenue.

CHAPTER 7

Grant packaging:
A partial step toward a system
of grants-in-aid

PRESIDENT JOHNSON'S "Quality of American Government" Message to Congress, March 17, 1967, included a directive to the Bureau of the Budget to develop, in cooperation with relevant federal agencies and representatives of state and local governments, a workable plan for grant simplification, based on a review of existing grant-in-aid programs. The plan would be aimed at making it possible for related grants to be combined into a single financial package so that financial and administrative procedures under the many grant programs could be restructured.

The "Joint Funding Simplification Act," formulated as a consequence of the Bureau's study, was introduced in Congress in August 1967 (S. 2981 and H.R. 12631). Essentially, the bill provided federal agencies with a mandate from the Congress to: (1) bring together such federal aid programs as states and localities deem appropriate in pursuing their program policies in concert with national purposes, and (2) formulate packages of aids that would have a general applicability in a number of states and cities. The latter type of grant packaging was intended to serve as a trial for subsequent consolidation of grants. The bill's provisions did not affect such substantial requirements of existing federal assistance programs as eligibility, matching, and grant formulas.

PURPOSES AND AUTHORITY FOR UNIFORM RULES AND POOLING OF FUNDS

For the two general types of packaged grant programs, the legislative authorization would permit more effective use of federal funds in carrying out congressional intent, as well as state and community objectives. More specifically, it would reduce the delays and cost to states and communities in applying for and receiving federal funds.

The purposes of the bill are set forth as follows:

1. To enable states and local governments to use federal assistance more effectively and efficiently.
2. To adapt federal aids to the more particular needs of state and local governments by encouraging the wider use of projects that draw on federal resources from more than one agency, program, or appropriation.

3. To acquire experience which would lead to the development of legislative proposals on consolidation, simplification and coordination of federal grants.
4. To encourage federal-state arrangements to assist local governments (and other public or private agencies) in using the combined resources of those governments in support of projects of common interest and concern.

To carry out these purposes, federal agencies would be permitted, under regulations prescribed by the President, to identify programs that appear suitable for joint development and funding, to review and modify administrative regulations that impede the combining of grants in support of a project, and to work toward a joint or common application process for federal grants.

The bill seeks to eliminate difficulties that currently encumber states and communities in processing applications. It calls upon federal agencies to: (1) handle reviews of applications for funds expeditiously; (2) consider fully the state and local governments' timing problems, which affect the feasibility of the proposed project; (3) reduce to a minimum the number of federal officials that need be consulted; (4) inform the government applying for aid promptly of the federal decisions taken.

Authority would be given for establishing uniform technical or administrative requirements to remove presently inconsistent or conflicting regulations on (1) accounting, reporting, auditing, banking, (2) timing of federal payments, (3) merit personnel systems, (4) accountability for, or the disposition of, property or structures acquired or built with federal assistance. Federal agency heads are authorized to provide for review of proposals for projects by a single panel, board, or committee in lieu of review by separate groups. Furthermore, on the request of the head of a state, city, or county, requirements for a single or specified city or state agency may be waived, if it is determined that administration by another public agency is in accord with state or local law and with the objectives of the federal assistance program. (The Intergovernmental Cooperation Act, P.L. 90-577, which was approved in October 1968, takes the further step of permitting federal agencies to waive, at the request of a state's governor, single state agency or multimember board or commission provisions that prevent effective organizational arrangements within the states.)

Federal agencies would be authorized to delegate to other federal agencies such powers as would promote the purposes of the proposed Act. It is contemplated that "a lead" federal agency would be designated to assume responsibility for processing applications and managing the aided project. Importantly, the bill also provides that joint management funds be established for joint projects. The accounting for funds would be approved through this joint management fund, to which would be advanced a proportional share of amounts from each affected appropriation as needed to make payments. The agreements worked out by the federal agencies would have to assure to each agency such information as it requires. The agency administering the joint management fund would be responsible and accountable for the total amount provided for each project; any repayments would be made to federal agencies in accord with a mutually agreeable formula. For any project a single matching requirement could be established, according to the federal share ratios applicable to the several federal aid programs involved and the proportion of funds transferred to the project account from each of those programs.

PRECEDENTS

Joint project or plan submissions are not altogether new. Single state plans for child health and public health programs were developed many years ago. Procedures for single reviewing of compliance with merit personnel systems through a single state civil service agency were pioneered much earlier. Procedures for single audits were also established for some closely related grant programs administered by the same state agency. A Budget Bureau circular issued in 1965 encouraged federal agencies to make use of audits conducted by the states or other federal agencies to the maximum extent feasible, further reducing the separate auditing requirements placed on the states. The proposed Act is an extension of these earlier steps toward more order in federal aids.

In 1967 the Economic Opportunity Act was amended to provide, pursuant to regulations prescribed by the President, that where funds are advanced for a single project by more than one federal agency to any agency assisted out of economic opportunity funds, any one federal agency may be designated to act for all in administering the funds advanced.[1] The amendment also provided for a single matching share and for waiving technical grant or contract grant requirements that lead to inconsistent rules.

In the 1964 Economic Opportunity Act, an Economic Opportunity Council was directed to promote better coordination among programs so as to reach and better serve the poor. The Council was also charged with assisting state and local agencies to (1) adapt diverse federal programs to varied local conditions and (2) stimulate new and more imaginative ways of combining complementary federal resources in the solution of specific problems.

REACTION FROM THE STATES

In October 1967 the 59th Annual National Governors' Conference passed a resolution that urged enactment "without delay of the Joint Funding Simplication Act." To give greater specificity to the resolution, the Conference's Committee on Revenue and Taxation, with Governor Philip Hoff of Vermont as chairman, employed a survey questionnaire to solicit the governors' experience in putting together federal grants to achieve state objectives. The responses indicated that the governors considered it urgent to take action toward more uniformity in the procedures for grant application, condition-meeting, and accounting. Also clearly manifested was the states' desire for more federal initiative in, for example: formulating packages of federal grants; providing more specific information on what is available to carry out state and city objectives; serving as grant-in-aid coordinators on program or project plans developed by state or city to serve national as well as local purposes; reducing time, personnel, and other costs involved in applying for federal project aids; placing primary emphasis on the general program purposes sought by the U.S. Congress rather than on controls and safeguards.

The inquiry sent to each of the governors was as follows:

(1) Has any single agency (or combination of agencies) in your state been successful in packaging two or more federal grants to achieve a specific state objective under existing federal legislative authority?

If so, list the federal grants that were combined as follows:

State Objective	Title of Grant Programs	Federal Agencies	State Agencies

(2) Please cite examples where a state agency (or combination of state agen-

---

[1] An identical provision is included in the Juvenile Delinquency Act (P.L. 90–445).

cies) has been unsuccessful in their attempt to package federal grants, or discouraged from such attempts by presumed lack of federal authority.

Provide the same details about the programs and agencies as in question (1).

State Objective   *Title of Grant Programs*   *Federal Agencies*   *State Agencies*

_____

_____

(3) Do you have pending one or more proposals for federal funding that involves an attempt to package federal grants? Please give the same details about programs and agencies as in questions (1) and (2).

State Objective   *Title of Grant Programs*   *Federal Agencies*   *State Agencies*

_____

_____

(4) Do these steps toward simplification appear adequate in the light of your policies? Should additional steps be taken?

(5) What additional steps might be taken by the federal agencies to give support to public programs in your state?

SUMMARY OF RESPONSES [2]

To help assure that the questions would be referred to other appropriate state officials, a copy of the inquiry was also sent to the federal grant-in-aid coordinator in each state.

The responses varied materially in their detail and perspective. Many threw considerable light on the potential of the Joint Funding Simplification Act to create "order out of confusion" in grantsmanship.[3]

Combining federal grants-in-aid to carry out state projects and programs was reported by a number of states. Involved in various of the combinations were programs to improve reading skills of children, manpower development and training, mental health facilities and services, job training and neighborhood youth corps activities, day care services, professional training of Department of Education personnel, better transportation in localities, and so forth. As this partial listing suggests, the public objectives of the states calling for combinations of existing federal aid programs were varied. In some instances the purpose was coordination of planning activities. In others, improved sewer and water system services were being sought. In still others, the search for more adequate health care for lower-income groups or for specific classes of public beneficiaries—such as migrant workers and Indians—led to the combinations as helps in financing required programs. Additional packaging reported included rehabilitation of both disabled and nondisabled workers, construction of hospital and health facilities, and development of recreational programs. In

---

[2] The summary presented here is necessarily brief. It was gleaned from a full summary of the replies received from each of the responding states, plus comments added by some of the states. This full summary also furnished the basis of part of Governor Hoff's testimony in hearings on H.R.12631 before the Subcommittee on Executive and Legislative Reorganization, the House Committee on Governmental Operations, June 10-11, 1968.

[3] Although not all states replied in full, we considered that the number and quality of replies were adequate to provide a representative picture.

one state, approval had been granted for packaging of funds for a state data bank; in another, a coordinated plan of health care, including smoking control, was successfully packaged.

The states also reported on their unsuccessful packaging attempts. One state told of failure to gain federal approval of funding for an Opportunity Center that would include job assistance training and career development. Another was not able to achieve a desired combination of grants to assist in financing a Training Center for School-Disoriented Youth, and a project for job production activities failed to be federally funded in still another. The range of program purposes and program content for which packaging was unsuccessfully attempted was wide—including programs directed toward water pollution control, highway safety measures, park and recreation land acquisitions, provision of state leadership and technical assistance for local education agencies, child health programs, and industrial development.

A number of states reported packaging proposals that were pending. These also covered a wide range of activities: for example, a proposal for training community development personnel; a program for highway and airport expansion; and a program for urban beautification and open space. Additional pending proposals included an umbrella program to administer federal education programs; a pilot neighborhood center; a comprehensive state planning program; construction of college facilities; community development; airport development; and a PRIDE project. One state had proposed a program to strengthen local governments and another, a program to reduce red tape and simplify reporting and accounting.

Attempts to reduce delay and frustration. Several states reported on the difficulties of timing, when trying to coordinate and package grants. The President's "Quality of American Government" message and the subsequent move toward joint funding encouraged the State of Vermont, for example, to develop a packaging of Section 701 Urban Planning Assistance grant under the Housing Act of 1964 and Section 301(b) of Title III of the Public Works and Economic Development Act of 1965.

In seeking such a package of aid, Vermont's objective was development of an integrated Planning, Programming, Budgeting system for the state, together with a supporting state-wide information system. Both purposes had been urged by national agencies to obtain better coordination and more effective and efficient use of federal dollars, as well as of state revenues. The federal agencies involved, despite a high order of cooperation, deemed it not possible to work out a joint interagency project that could be jointly funded. Rather, an "in tandem" approach was adopted. Subsequently, Vermont reported that the grant "was achieved after considerable time spent in recurrent and at times repetitive discussion and negotiation . . . the procedural problems at the Federal level usually cooled our enthusiasm before serious efforts were made."

From Michigan came a formulation of the timing problem in terms of the uncertainties created by partial approval of grant support under one grant authorization and delay in approval of other grant support for a single project. The project—an adult work-training program based in a school in Kalamazoo—was finally carried out; however, the six-week delay from the time one part of the project was approved and funded caused considerable turmoil for the school: e.g., was it wise to staff for the entire project, to commit facilities, and to announce a starting date before funding was complete? If single projects are to be funded from more than one source, closer cooperation among federal agencies is urgent.

Even more uncertainty and delay is likely if each federal agency conditions its approval on favorable action of other federal agencies. Rhode Island reported that "the problem of joint or multipurpose projects is usually one of timing: one of the agencies concerned is ready to act (or must act), while the other needs an additional year or two." The problem was noted in New Jersey as well: "The inability of one federal agency to make a decision can delay or condemn the entire proposal."

ACHIEVING GREATER UNIFORMITY IN GRANT-IN-AID RULES

Although a number of federal planning and project grants are closely interrelated, their requirements for administration sometimes differ widely. Accounting and reporting requirements vary; there are different requirements for the "grant" and the "contract" that relate to the time period for which the funds are available; personnel system requirements differ; overhead allowances are markedly variant; equipment and property controls are disparate. Some federal grants allow advance payments; some allow payment on a quarterly basis; others allow payments only as a reimbursement of documented expenditures. As noted earlier, the questionnaire responses showed much awareness of the need for greater uniformity in the grant rules.

A state or city that undertakes to bring together federal grants-in-aid and other assistance faces a large task of coordination. Assuming that information on the sources of federal assistance is at hand, together with a reasonably up-to-date list of names and addresses required to follow through to an application or required plan submission, the state or local government is still confronted with a range of conflicting but detailed requirements.

In recognition of these conflicts, the Joint Funding Simplification Act would call for a review of the rules under each grant and for answers to such questions as: Are these rules essential? What changes in regulation would help gain greater uniformity? From one state agency came a plea for the speedy enactment of at least the part of the bill that calls for establishment of common technical and administrative rules among related programs. Even if joint funding were not authorized, the steps toward simplification "would be an aid in eliminating a coordination effort that causes significant workload under the present system." Another state urgently requested enactment of the bill's proposal of delegation of authority for approval and supervision, so that joint management funds could be realized.

DESIGNING GRANT PACKAGES TO MEET STATE AND LOCAL POLICIES

Implementation of public purposes often requires a coordinate funding and carrying out of a number of different activities or programs. Economic development objectives in the backward areas of a state are set forth by the states as clear examples of the need for such activity or program coordination. A wide variety of federal aids can be applied to facilitate the implementation of such an objective. The separate activities or projects involved, in turn, may look to many different federal aid programs. The combination of projects, activities, and programs best suited to achieve the general purpose can be best designed by a specific state to meet its specific needs. The combinations may involve airport construction, runway extension and lighting, access roads, new terminals, community colleges and area vocational centers, outdoor recreational facilities and services, sewage treatment facilities, and so forth. The formulation of the policies, plans, and activities by the state under present procedures would then call for a search of federal funding sources among the many possible grants.

It should be possible, under the Joint Funding Simplification Act, for a state or local government to formulate its specific project or program proposals and to call upon an appropriate federal agency (with substantial granting authority) to seek out a coordinated grant approval plan and to work with other appropriate federal grant and assistance sources to develop it.

The possible combinations of two, three, or more grants within an aggregate of well over 200 to 300 demonstration and physical facility project funds are too numerous to look toward standard federal packaging. Nevertheless, some "standard combinations" that would be applicable to common problems in a number of states are possible. Such packages need identification, both because their use should be encouraged and because subsequent consolidation legislation seems likely.

Under present practices, a state seeking federal aid for a project that requires funding from more than one grant authorization must first engage in a discovery procedure on what is available. It then submits separate applications for each aid. Each application form may have its own unique requirements, and each is processed separately and independently, according to the practices for that particular program. For each grant the special requirements must be administered by the state to accord with the federal practices on reporting, accounting, payments, auditing, and so forth.

No detailed accounting has ever been made of the total costs of applying for and receiving federal assistance. However, the costs are many and usually include:

1. The cost of information, e.g., on the availability of federal assistance, and on the requirements for federal assistance.
2. The cost of processing project submissions, e.g., formulating projects, preparing applications, obtaining any state or local legislative approval required, reviewing and following through on stages of review, amending project applications, accepting and fitting the aids into own governmental budetary and other procedures.
3. The cost of administration, e.g., preparing and submitting audit reports, preparing and submitting data required, accounting for procurement financed with federal aids, reporting on progress, responding to site visit requests, and so forth.

NECESSITY OF INTERAGENCY COOPERATION

In response to the President's directive, some steps have been taken by agencies and departments to improve the granting procedures under current legislative authority. Several states in their survey responses reported on these steps toward packaging. The Federal Concentrated Employment Program, for example, represents an attempt within the U.S. Department of Labor to package the manpower aid programs the Department administers. Allocations of Department funds are made to a single agency or committee in target cities on the submission of a *single* work program and are reviewed *en bloc* by a single federal committee. Application procedures are thus simplified. Nevertheless, without joint fund management authority, program components still must be identified by funding source, and spending by the target city must be allocated for activities precisely in accord with the earmarking of that source. Importantly too, other federal aids administered by other federal departments and agencies for job creation, training, manpower development, and related activities are not included in the Department of Labor manpower package program.

The State of New Jersey commented on such packaging efforts:

. . . The Federal government is at least aware of the problem and is groping toward some form of solution, but the apparent competitiveness and frequent insularity of the various federal bureaus and offices do not raise hopes for significant, substantive federally guided steps toward program integration at the operational level.

ADMINISTRATIVE ACTION

Legislation is being sought to simplify grant machinery and is complemented by administrative action. Several steps have been taken toward coordination and administrative simplification.

On May 11, 1967, President Johnson instructed the Secretaries of Housing and Urban Development, of Labor, and of Health, Education, and Welfare and the Director of the Office of Economic Opportunity to review their procedures for the development and processing of grant-in-aid applications and to recommend steps for reducing the time involved by 50 percent. The Interagency Administrative Task Force, under HUD's direction, was created to implement the instruction. A final report, "Reducing Federal Grant-in-Aid Processing Time," was submitted by the Task Force in September 1967. Reductions in processing time put into effect or planned are intended to reduce the costs of delay to states and cities.

A follow-up activity of the Task Force was requested by the President to effect other administrative improvements in aid programs of the four participating agencies. Moreover, all departments and agencies with grant-in-aid programs were directed to analyze their programs and report to the Bureau of the Budget by March 31, 1968, on steps taken to reduce processing time. As a consequence of this directive, eleven additional departments and agencies identified and analyzed a total of forty-six assistance programs or program components in "An Interagency Report to the President on Improved Grant-in-Aid Processing."

This report made the following prominent and recurring recommendations for:

1. Increased delegation from Washington to field level, and in a few instances to state level.
2. Increased pre-application assistance to state and local governments.
3. Improved processing control and work scheduling.
4. Increased use of parallel and concurrent processing.
5. Simplified application and review procedures and forms.
6. Increased interagency consultation on problem areas.
7. Differentiation of processing detail, according to project complexity and size.
8. More precise delineation of program criteria.
9. Improved quality of technical assistance to state and local governments.
10. Improved intra-agency communication, through such devices as periodic headquarters-field conferences.
11. Increased use of mechanized automatic processing techniques.
12. Increased emphasis on federal training and personnel development.

The detailed reviews by each of the departments and agencies led to reduction in the time lag of processing and payment and to some delegation of authority to state agencies, with elimination of a few stages of review and of certain rules, and so on. Such simplifying improvements in grant administration are being effected in part through interdepartmental task forces, and in part through direct action of individual departments and agencies. The Department of Labor, for example, has sought to achieve the packaging of manpower programs, as indicated earlier. Over fifteen major federal manpower programs support state and community policies on training.

The Department of Health, Education, and Welfare has made several administrative changes. It has developed a standard departmental application form for assistance; multiple copies are provided to applicants for distribution to the reviewing agencies. A coordinated review is carried out by the agencies within the Department, and a "lead agency" is designated for purposes of federal administration of projects approved for joint funding.

The recent endorsement by the U.S. Office of Education of a combined packaging of educational aids proposed by the State of Texas has provided a design for comprehensive packaging and planning of federally assisted educational programs.[4] State plans for the Elementary and Secondary Education Act (Titles I, II, III, V, and VI), the National Defense Educational Act (Titles III and V), the Vocational Education Act of 1963, and the Educational Professions Development Act of 1967 would be modified to permit the packaging of federal funds for these programs and the use of the funds in accord with the developed state policy. In harmony with this policy, local school districts may generally submit single plans for federal aid, and single reports.

Administrative action has helped to achieve interagency funding arrangements for neighborhood centers. The Neighborhood Centers Pilot Program is attempting on a trial basis to simplify application procedures for federal grants, with fourteen cities and four federal agencies participating. Reporting requirements have been streamlined so that each city may submit general data bearing on the proposed neighborhood program in a single information package. Similarly, five federal agencies are participating in a coordination effort under which thirty-six local parent and child centers are aided. And attempts are also being made to link neighborhood centers with target areas of Model City projects and with the Labor Department's Concentrated Employment Programs and Comprehensive Area Manpower Planning (CAMP) program. Neighborhood health centers are being funded through combinations of OEO and Partnership in Health grants. Steps are in process to develop joint funding for day care services using HEW, OEO, and Labor Department grant authorizations and funds.

SUMMARY OF PRESENT STATUS

As of July 1968 some administrative action has been taken to simplify procedures largely by reducing processing time, providing for single or common project applications, and providing for single or common reviews.

Legislative authority to jointly fund and establish a single weighted average of state and local matching shares is fostering simplified application and funding procedures for certain federal aids in a way that can be adapted to local requirements and project design. Hearings have been held on the new legislative authority sought through the Joint Funding Simplification Act. Congressional cautions on the legislation suggest the need for concern about the forces that have been put into play, along with the flexible adaptation of the grant-in-aid tool as an instrument for intergovernmental relations.

CAUTIONS AND COMMENTS

The packaging of federal assistance as a step toward achieving more system in the present patchwork of grants does not essentially apply to the large support grants that account for the majority of federal dollars going to states and localities. Although included in the provisions of the Joint Funding Simplifica-

---

4 In connection with S. 3770, the Vocational Education Bill, action along this line is being considered by Congress, with a possibility of a prohibition of such packaging.

tion Act, this class of aids does not originate most of the problems that the packaging proposals are designed to meet. Rather, it is the large number of demonstration, innovation, and experimental aids—as encouragement to new public products and new methods of producing and delivering them—together with aids for physical facility, equipment, construction, and so forth, that create the frustrations. They involve sorting out of what is available and a host of other information difficulties, as well as separate applications, separate reviews, separate accounting systems, and separate funding.

As indicated elsewhere, such demonstration aids are not all of a kind. They may, for example, be an assortment of initial federal responses to a recently identified large problem; they may be demonstrations for intercommunity transfers of social program techniques; and they may also be truly experimental. In any case, their basic purposes are best carried out by allowing the states and localities wide latitude in designing projects adapted to their own needs and arranged to buttress their own policy directions and own funding. Communities may serve as laboratories for trying out new public service combinations to meet public objectives. (Clearly, if intercommunity results are to be compared in yielding experimental findings, some experiments require controls that point to considerable federal assistance in design of the program.)

The proposed Act and the present administrative measures that are being taken under existing authority deal with a broader range of grants and other federal assistance programs than those that raise the major problems of multiplicity. At the same time, these proposals—both legislative and administrative —fail to come to grips with the problems and cost of information about the availability of federal assistance. There is no clear shifting to the federal government of the cost of "grantsmanship" on such small aid programs. As a consequence, a costly structure is continued, and the expenses of expertise that can seek out relevant (or even barely relevant) grant support and process applications for the support still fall on the states and localities. This structure includes the expert private consultant on federal grants, the federal grant coordinator at state and community governmental levels, and the state and local offices maintained in Washington, D.C. The price for lack of expertise may be high in reduced federal aid.

Even in this beginning of a system through packaging and joint funding—a beginning that is not intended to affect such substantive requirements as eligibility and matching of existing federal assistance programs—the traditional concern of individual members of Congress to be responsive to their constituencies on specific public projects has become a barrier to favorable and speedy congressional action.

Moreover, confusion appears to exist about the structuring of the building blocks represented by federal aid programs. States and communities with considerable information and expertise can bring grants together in a package to meet their own purposes through carefully formulated projects. The projects and the grant combinations necessarily will differ from one place to another, because the problems and the public purposes served are not always the same. One community may place high priority on providing a range of services that will result in independent, satisfying living levels for the physically handicapped. A vocational rehabilitation center may serve trainable adults by using vocational rehabilitation grant funds; it may also serve as a training center for teachers by using Office of Education aids, and as a sheltered work shop for a group of disabled, and so forth. Another community may wish to give priority to a combined medical-social service-education center for the children in a depressed neighborhood. The possible combinations of the building blocks as suggested earlier are too numerous to make into standard uniform packages that can (or should) be applied everywhere. Consolidation of grants to broad functional areas will not serve the purposes of projects that call for combinations across functional areas. At the same time, unless the vital purposes of transfer of techniques and experimentation are preserved by earmarked federal dollars, incentives for such transfers and experiments will be lost.

Repeatedly, in the testimony on the Joint Funding Simplification Act, consolidation of grants was offered as a substitute for joint funding. For example, the Deputy Director of the Civil Division of the General Accounting Office in his testimony before the House Committee on Government Operations stated:

We believe that the real key to significantly improved administration lies in the legislative consolidation of programs into broad categories of assistance, and the placement of like programs in a single agency, rather than establishing an administrative apparatus to deal with a continuing proliferation of single narrow purpose programs.

Under the proposed Act, experience with standard packages, where appropriate, would yield guidelines for future recommendations or consolidations.

The governors at their 59th Annual Conference recommended action that would reduce the costs of information about the more than 200 federal demonstration aids. More specifically, the Conference Committee recommended that these demonstration or innovational grants be consolidated into a single demonstration grant authority for each federal department and independent agency that had substantial intergovernmental programs.

The authorization for innovation grants to state and communities for demonstration and experimentation regarding new public services should not be fragmented; rather, it should be broadly designed to encompass the wide range of each department's program responsibilities. For example, the Department of Health, Education, and Welfare would have a single authority to support demonstrations of new services or of more efficient methods of delivering services in the health, education, and welfare areas. This new broad authority would take the place of specific demonstration grants. As a consequence, state and local governments would no longer need to spend their resources to determine whether the federal government is authorized to support a particular demonstration or innovation of concern to them.

Concomitant provisions of two types are needed:

1. Substantive committees of Congress are concerned necessarily with the types and directions of innovation and demonstration in public services. These committees might designate each year, as a directive to the federal departments, the type of programs in which, in their judgment, innovation should be encouraged. Departments might be required to report back each year to the committees the steps they have taken to carry out the congressional directives.
2. The federal agencies that encourage demonstration and innovation in states and communities require strong professional staffing capable of giving guidance on technical problems to states and communities.

CHAPTER 8

Consolidated and target grants

THE COMPLEX OF LEGISLATIVE AUTHORITY FOR GRANTS, variations in appropriation provisions, multiplicity of granting agencies, and differences in regulations point to changes in the existing grant-in-aid structure. The proposed Joint Funding Simplification Act discussed in the preceding chapter in general leaves the complexities, the insularity, the multiplicity, and the statutory variations unaltered. It does, however, seek to obtain more orderly procedures by calling for submission of program package proposals by states and communities and for a combining of grant authority and funds to help carry them out. The measure is also viewed as a step toward grant consolidation, where combinations of grants would achieve program policies more effectively in a number of states.

Consolidated or "block grants" are increasingly offered as the preferred solution to the present overly complex structure of federal financial assistance. The "purest" concept of a block grant is assistance to a state for a broad functional area—such as health—in which the state would be free to use the funds as it sees fit. In this chapter we discuss a more general notion of consolidation, which includes any steps (except the totally unrestricted fiscal grant) to reduce the constraints on the use of federally raised revenues. The chapter undertakes to (1) review the origin of proposals for block grants; (2) describe the present status of consolidation of grants; (3) assess the national purposes as they relate to grant consolidation; and (4) suggest some new directions in achieving the purposes for which consolidation is sought.

ORIGINS AND CURRENT PRESSURES

A proposal for consolidated or block grants emerged from the 1949 review of federal grants-in-aid by the Commission on Organization of the Executive Branch of the Government (the first Hoover Commission). The term "block grant" was applied, not as earlier to an unconditional fiscal grant, but to a grant restricted to a broad program purpose. The Commission urged that "a system of grants be established based upon broad categories—such as highways, education, public assistance and public health—as contrasted with the present system of extensive fragmentation." [1]

A number of legislative proposals for block grants, particularly concerning health and public welfare, followed from this recommendation. In the 80th Congress, for example, and again in the 81st an omnibus health bill sponsored by the Administration provided for a single grant for public health services and called for a single allotment of funds to the states and a single matching requirement. Even before the Commission report was issued, a bill introduced in the 79th Congress authorized the states to determine whether they would continue categorical programs for public assistance or would combine their programs into a general public welfare program. Later bills introduced at the request of President Truman also followed this same pattern.

During the mid-1950's, the Eisenhower Administration concerned itself in a major way with intergovernmental fiscal relations. The first Secretary of the then new Department of Health, Education, and Welfare, for example, urged a concerted effort to simplify the structure of grants-in-aid. However, of the legislation introduced as a consequence of the Department's reassessment of grants-in-aid and the use of block grants for health, child health and welfare services, and vocational rehabilitation, the only actual enactment prior to 1960 was for vocational rehabilitation. This early experience of HEW has been summarized as follows:

> The repeated rejection of block grants leads us to the conclusion that the assumptions on which the block grant proposal rests are not valid in all instances, or, at least run counter often to other objectives which are more compelling.[2]

Despite these early frustrations, the concept of a grant for broad functional areas was not abandoned. In 1967 and 1968, the Johnson Administration, the Advisory Commission on Intergovernmental Relations, and the National Governors' Conference were all urging grant consolidation.[3] And the Congress, by combining a number of grants, had taken steps toward consolidating federal aids.

Why the change in receptiveness of the Congress and the public to grant consolidation?

Perhaps the most important of the many factors which contributed to the change was the sheer number of categorical grants. Between 1955 and 1967 the number of new grant enactments had multiplied many times, and this large increase was seen to be markedly altering the quality of intergovernmental relations. In 1967, Charles Schultze, then Director of the Bureau of the Budget, in testifying before the Senate Subcommittee on Intergovernmental Relations explained the choices that were faced in responding to demands for national action:

> We could have sat on our hands and played it safe. There would certainly be fewer complaints. There would, also, however, be an even worse gap—that between mounting social

---

[1] Commission on Organization of the Executive Branch of the Government, *Overseas Administration, Federal-State Relations, Federal Research, Report to Congress* (March 1949), pp. 31-32.

[2] Selma J. Mushkin, "Barriers to a System of Federal Grants-in-Aid," *National Tax Journal,* Vol. 13 (September 1960), p. 198.

[3] Remarks by Charles J. Zwick, Director, U.S. Bureau of the Budget, at the Annual Conference of the National Association of State Budget Officers, San Antonio, Texas, Aug. 12, 1968; *Fiscal Balance in the American Federal System,* Advisory Commission on Intergovernmental Relations (1967); *Resolution 12* adopted by the National Governors' Conference, Cincinnati, Ohio, July 21-24, 1968.

costs and responsible policy initiatives. In closing one gap, we opened another, but it is the one we prefer. I dislike to see evidence of faulty coordination, spinning wheels, frustrating delays, failures of communication, and all the other dross that comprises the symptoms of uneven administration and program execution. At the same time, it would be surprising if everything clicked smoothly in the wake of such an immensely productive period of legislations.[4]

A second factor was the marked change in the underlying motivation for consolidation. The block grant proposal of the 1950's was an "economy" measure, i.e., a way to reduce federal aid and to divert the pressures for political action on specific programs from the Congress to the states and localities. But the combining of grants in the 1960's was accompanied by larger federal appropriations, so that between fiscal 1964 and 1969 federal funds for grants-in-aid doubled. The basic rule—"improvement through enlargement"—was followed, thus offering the immediate prospect of higher, rather than reduced, allotments to governments eligible for assistance.

Furthermore, Congress has recently safeguarded its specific program interests by special statutory requirements. (The need for "safeguards" for special programs was a lesson drawn from the congressional debates of the 1950's.) For example, the "Partnership for Health Act" of 1966 earmarked at least 15 percent of a state allotment for the state mental health authority and further provided that no state's allotment under the new Act "shall be less for any year than the total amounts allotted . . . for cancer control, plus other prior allotments under this section," for the fiscal year prior to enactment of the new legislation.

Additionally, a stronger emphasis was placed on federal aid to help assure a minimum standard of performance of state governments. If effectuated, these complementary measures open the way to improved state program decisions and operations that underpin greater flexibility in federal grant use.

Such emphasis on trying to assure standards of state performance had its beginnings in the Social Security Act Amendments of 1939, which conditioned federal assistance on state merit systems for personnel employed in carrying out federally aided programs. Experience under that Act and the clear dependence of quality of program administration upon the caliber of state and local employees led to conditioning of other grant programs and to aid given for personnel training. Nevertheless, personnel practices in many states have fallen short of what is required for effective administration.

The Intergovernmental Personnel Act of 1967, still (as of August 1968) awaiting congressional decision, would broaden the existing merit system aids to states and localities for training to upgrade and refresh the skills of their employees. Senator Edmund S. Muskie, who introduced the measure, stated:

But where the Federal Government is so concerned with the effective implementation of its grant-in-aid programs, it should be equally concerned with providing incentives for the modernization of personnel systems and training for those who administer these joint-action programs.[5]

At the same time, federal encouragement of state and local planning and state program development has been gaining acceptance. An increasing number of federal grants are conditioned upon adequate state or local planning or are supplemented by federal assistance for such planning activities.

---

[4] *Creative Federalism,* Hearings Before the Senate Subcommittee on Intergovernmental Relations (Government Printing Office, 1967), Part I, p. 389.

[5] Congressional Record, Vol. 113, No. 11, Jan. 26, 1967, p. S965.

PRESENT STATUS OF GRANT CONSOLIDATION

In this climate of grant revision Congress has enacted legislation combining federal grants-in-aid for public assistance, public health, and child health.

Combining formula grants. The Public Welfare Amendments of 1962 provided for a single state plan, instead of separate plans for aid to the aged, the blind, and the permanently and totally disabled. At the option of each state, such combining may be done and medical assistance may also be included. In addition, with the enactment of the Social Security Amendments of 1965, each state with an approved medical assistance plan was given the option to choose the basis for federal financial participation—that is, the matching ratio for cash payments, or for medical assistance. This change in general achieves flexibility in expenditures among categories under a single and higher overall federal matching share. The combining of plans and the single matching ratio all somewhat short of the initial proposal for block grants for public assistance, especially in the continued exclusion of general assistance, but the single matching ratio does move substantially to effect the combining proposed.

The Partnership for Health Act of 1966 (P.L. 89-749), which is now being urged as a model for block grants, combined almost a dozen specific categorical grants into a grant for comprehensive public health services. A brief review of the purposes of the consolidated grant legislation and its provision may help to put in context the model that is being urged. Section 2(a) of the Act states:

> The Congress declares that fulfillment of our national purpose depends on promoting and assuring the highest level of health attainable for every person, in an environment which contributes positively to healthful individual and family living; that attainment of this goal depends on an effective partnership, involving close intergovernmental collaboration, official and voluntary efforts, and participation of individuals and organizations; that Federal financial assistance must be directed to support the marshaling of all health resources—national, State, and local—to assure comprehensive health services of high quality for every person.

Under the new legislation a series of grant programs takes the place of the categorical disease programs. The series includes (1) grants to states on a formula basis for comprehensive state health planning; (2) project grants for areawide health planning on a comprehensive regional metropolitan basis; (3) project grants to public or nonprofit private agencies for training, studies, and demonstrations, looking toward the development of improved or more comprehensive health planning throughout the nation; (4) grants to states on a formula basis for comprehensive public health services; and (5) project grants to public or nonprofit private agencies for actual development of health services.

A 1967 amendment to the Act brought three other kinds of project assistance within the scope of the comprehensive legislation: assistance for (1) construction of experimental facilities, (2) development of experimental equipment, and (3) demonstrations in new careers in health manpower and new ways of using and training health personnel. Moreover, instead of a separate categorical grant for purposes of rat control, Congress raised the appropriation authorization for comprehensive health services. While the higher appropriation was specifically linked to rat control, the funds were not earmarked by statute. The clear legislative intent, however, calls for a *de facto* earmarking at this time.

Appropriation authorizations for each of the separate grants within the Partnership for Health program are set as follows:

1. Comprehensive state health planning: $10 million for fiscal year 1969 and $15 million for fiscal 1970.
2. Areawide health planning: $10 million for fiscal year 1969 and $15 million for fiscal 1970.

3. Project grants for training, studies, and demonstrations in planning: $5 million for fiscal year 1969 and $7.5 million for fiscal 1970.
4. Grants for comprehensive health services: $70 million for fiscal year 1969 and $100 million for fiscal 1970.
5. Project grants for health services development: $95 million for fiscal year 1969 and $80 million for fiscal 1970.
6. Project grants or contracts for research and demonstrations relating to health facilities and services: $40 million for fiscal year 1969 and $60 million for fiscal 1970.

As indicated earlier, the Partnership for Health legislation sought to overcome earlier barriers to congressional approval of consolidation of categorical grants by earmarking a part of the grant for comprehensive health services for mental illness, and by preserving a distinct role for mental health commissions in the states.

Among the special circumstances that led to enactment of the Partnership for Health amendments was the awareness of resources being frittered away on small individual grants under the separate categorical programs. In 1963 the federal funds for categorical disease control programs averaged $46,000 for cancer control; $64,000 for heart disease control; $48,000 for tuberculosis control; $2,000 for diabetes control; $118,000 for mental health work; and $72,000 for venereal disease control.[6] But averages do not tell the whole story. For example, in the smaller states, a number of grants for specific disease control programs fell below $6,000. All but venereal disease control program grants were distributed among states by formula; the small amount of funds for venereal disease some years earlier led to a focusing of the federal funds on identified projects through project grant support.

Of far greater importance in moving to grant consolidation was the altered perspective on public health work that emphasized health services for *people,* rather than services according to the earlier categorical programs. The content and role of public health services have been in process of change over many decades. In earlier periods, disease control meant, essentially, control of the infectious and communicable diseases through provision of safe water, milk, and food supplies, and by isolation of the individual. In recent years, new vaccines and therapeutic products have provided methods for eliminating many of the infectious and communicable diseases and for specific treatment of a range of others that less than three decades ago were important causes of death in the United States.

The great increase in knowledge about treatment and prevention of disease and about rehabilitation pointed to personal health care rather than traditional public health work. Pressures developed for a broadened public responsibility, to be evidenced in programs that would provide, or finance, greater equality of access to medical care. Adoption of the medicare and medicaid programs broadened this protection and gave new impetus through federal-state contracts, as well as grants, for advancement of personal health work in the states. Moreover, the increasing concentration of population in urban centers along with new industrial technologies were generating new threats to health (for example, air and water pollution from community and industrial wastes and by-products; the not fully understood hazards of radiation levels; and the difficult to measure stresses of urban living and congestion) which called for a very different emphasis from that of traditional public health work.

---

[6] Selma J. Mushkin, *Health and Hospital Expenditures of State and Local Governments: 1970 Projections* (Chicago, Council of State Governments, May 1966), p. 53.

The above brief review suggests the following characteristics of the Partnership for Health model:

1. Planning is federally aided as is training of personnel to help assure effective use of federal grant funds that are not tied to specific narrow categories.
2. Demonstration and experimental purposes are preserved through special project grant provisions.
3. General health support grants are distributed by formula to states.
4. Communities as well as states, and nonprofit agencies as well as public, are eligible for project grant assistance.

We see that the constraints imposed by the disease control grants have been eliminated, but a significant number of controls are retained by the federal government. Thus, this consolidation falls far short of the pure concept of a block grant.

Combining project aids. A different model for combining grants is suggested by the approach to child health services in the Social Security Act Amendments of 1967. This "consolidation" permits greater state control over the selection of projects. Certain project grants for maternal and child health, for health of school and preschool children, and for dental health of children are to be combined after 1972 with the basic formula grants for maternal and child health and for services to crippled children. Also, after 1972 (as well as in the years before), a portion of the funds is to be earmarked for family planning.

The child health model for the period after 1972 is that of federal allotments to states under statutory criteria. It would shift to the states responsibility for case-by-case project selection, with, however, standards or conditions for the development of a state program. This program would be carried out directly or through grants or contracts to meet the purposes of the earlier federal project grant assistance. Approval of the state program plan by the relevant federal agency is a condition for assistance. Separate categorical grants, however, are continued for child and maternal health and for services for crippled children. Within these grants, legislative provision is made for even more specific categorical programs such as prevention of mental retardation and dental health of young persons in low-income families. As indicated earlier, funds also are specifically set aside for family planning activities.

The characteristics of this model may be summarized briefly:

1. Specific national program purposes are not relaxed, nor is more flexibility of fund use given to states. In contrast, the Partnership for Health model widens the latitude of state program decision.
2. State program development is encouraged by converting federal project grant authority (beginning 1973) to federal formula grants that give the state decision on projects to be supported (subject to federal legislative standards and federal controls). The Partnership for Health model not only retains direct federal project grants but also enlarges these project supports relative to formula grants for public health services.
3. Funds are set aside for training of personnel and for research projects by project grant support much as in the Partnership for Health Act.
4. No specific grant is made to support state program planning. However, the grants for Comprehensive Health Planning should, if comprehensive in scope, include child health services as well as other health care.

Target grants. Still another fairly broad grant-in-aid pattern has emerged in the push for intergovernmental attack on social and economic problems. This involves a grant that governments eligible for financial assistance may use for a broad range of programs within the general purposes of the national grant. We term it a "target grant" because it permits use of funds for possibly wide-rang-

117

ing public services that are all to be focused upon a complex problem existing in a specific target population or geographical area. Wide latitude is given to the grant recipients on the program design and services and facilities to be provided, but the standards of the proposed programs are subject to review. Controls and standards are fairly specific and numerous.

The prime example of such target aid is the Model Cities program. Under this program, project grants are made to help cities plan, develop, and carry out demonstrations of methods to remove or arrest blight and decay in entire sections of neighborhoods and to reduce social and educational disadvantage, ill health, underemployment, and enforced idleness. Grants are authorized to cover up to 80 percent of the cost of the city demonstration program and also, under specified conditions, up to 80 percent of the nonfederal matching share required of new grants under other federal aid legislation that can contribute to reducing disadvantage and blight. Grants for planning are provided, and cooperation among functional agencies is sought. To obtain project grant support, compliance is required with the standards and controls set forth in the Demonstration Cities and Metropolitan Development Act of 1966. Project proposals are made by cities to the administering federal agency, and review is carried out by that agency prior to grant approval and funding. Priorities for projects are established as required to limit the amount granted in the aggregate to the appropriation level.

In effect, this model of a target grant without restriction on function for which the grant may be given is a form of general support aid, *but* with many strings or conditions attached. Programs are reviewed in detail to assure the carrying out of the pinpointed objective—advance from blight and poverty in a specified location.

Pressures for grant blocking. In the 1967 congressional debates on federal aid for education, as well as on the Crime Control and the Juvenile Delinquency Prevention and Control Acts of 1968, much of the discussion centered on the role of the states with federal grants exclusively to states. The concept of block grants "to the states to be distributed by the states under a master plan as a substitute for existing federal grants to local governments for specific projects" was the main thrust of the 1967 congressional review of federal assistance for education.

Following the debate on the Crime Control Act, the legislation adopted provided assistance for planning and law enforcement purposes exclusively to state governments. In commenting on an earlier version of the bill that would have provided grants to cities with populations of 50,000 and over as well as the states, the minority committee wrote:

The days are long overdue when the unmanageable and unworkable proportion of 495 separate authorizations for federal aid programs should be revamped, repackaged, and consolidated where feasible in the form of block grants to the states in broad program categories. . . . The federal government should concern itself with the coordination of 50 state programs rather than trying to evaluate, judge, and fund the projects of thousands of local governments. The states are ready to assume their responsibilities for action." [7]

Senator Hugh Scott, in his remarks on that earlier version of the bill, quoted from the President's Commission on Law Enforcement and Administration of Justice: "One of the major problems of effective law enforcement is the fragmentation of police efforts," and added his own comment that intra-state and

---

[7] Senators Dirksen, Hruska, Scott, and Thurmond, *Report No. 1097,* Report of the Senate Judiciary Committee on the Omnibus Crime Control and Safe Streets Act of 1967, pp. 228, 229.

interstate cooperation must be stimulated through a block grant approach.[8]

In the Juvenile Delinquency Prevention and Control Act, as reported by the Conference Committee, the approach taken was that of project grants to local agencies rather than to states.

In each case compromises were in effect worked out. In the crime control legislation, funds are provided to states for planning and for law enforcement purposes, but additional standards and requirements are included to help assure local government participation. Forty percent of the planning grants and 75 percent of the federal grants for law enforcement purposes are required to be set aside for units of general local government or combination of such units. Federal grants directly to local units are authorized if any state fails to act. The Juvenile Delinquency Prevention and Control Act authorizes direct federal grants to city and counties for both planning and program purposes, but limits the direct local grants for rehabilitation and prevention until such time as a state has an approved comprehensive juvenile delinquency plan. To be approved, the plan must provide for participation by local and areawide public groups and give assurance that the state will furnish at least one-half of the matching funds. The compromises required more, rather than fewer, statutory conditions and standards along with the granting to states. In the case of aid for elementary and secondary education, while federal assistance to gain payments to school districts was retained, a boost was given to state planning for education.

The smaller block. The consolidations and combinations of grants and the packaging of public services and facilities that can be funded to carry out a specific national purpose follow the general direction of the 1949 block grant proposals. The steps that have been taken, however, fall far short of the concepts of (1) federal financial assistance for the major broad functional areas, and (2) removal of federal restrictions on state or local program decision.

Congress gives no indication of relinquishing its access to a tool of specific categorical assistance in responding to public demands for services. Nor do the actions taken suggest fewer (or loosened) grant strings to any appreciable extent.

In this context it should be noted that, when a dozen or so categorical disease grants were combined by the Partnership for Health program, there were also some ninety-five or so separate authorizations for federal technical and financial assistance for health purposes.[9] As new needs are identified and program approaches develop, additional categorical aids or earmarked portions of existing aids may be anticipated.

Federal financial incentives have evidenced their effectiveness as a tool to encourage states and localities to provide the quantity and quality of specific public services deemed, in terms of national values, an essential right of citizenship. Such incentives can serve especially to weight the balance in favor of state and community action on behalf of disadvantaged groups in the population. The lowered tax price of such services reduces resistance to paying local taxes for the benefit of others less advantaged.

Similar incentives are required to meet the costs of marketing new public

[8] Senator Scott, *Ibid.,* p. 218.

[9] See William H. Robinson, "Recent Trends in Federal-State-Local Fiscal Relations," in *Revenue Sharing and Its Alternatives: What Future for Fiscal Federalism?*, Vol. I, Prepared for the Subcommittee on Fiscal Policy of the Joint Economic Committee (Government Printing Office, 1967), p. 69.

products or new delivery systems for such public products. And the conditions attached to the grants are essentially the only way short of a direct federal administrative undertaking for specifying the public product that is sought.

GRANT CONSOLIDATION AND NATIONAL OBJECTIVES

Two considerations are central to the enthusiasm for consolidation of categorical grants-in-aid: (1) a reduction in the number of specific grants would ease the administrative burden; (2) the freeing of monies from narrow categories would give the states and localities greater flexibility in using the monies made available to them.

We must agree that progress in these two consideration, per se, is a laudable objective. We must ask, however, how far this objective could be pursued without sacrificing the national objectives which gave rise to the grant-in-aid system in the first place. It must be recognized that the most desirable grant-in-aid system based on the criteria of simplification and flexibility would be an unrestricted fiscal grant designed to provide funds to states (and localities) on an automatic basis—in other words, a system that would routinely earmark a specific portion of federal revenues for use by the states and cities. There are, however, objections to such an approach—as is demonstrated by the absence of any strong political force now pushing toward the goal of totally unrestricted federal grants to the states and cities. In fact, our earlier discussion of the Partnership for Health grants indicated that there seems to be considerable reluctance to move toward a complete freeing of monies even within functional categories.

The framework for a system of grants presented in Chapters 2 and 3 of this report contained, as the basic rationale for categorical grants, the concept of national promotion of acceptable or at least minimum levels of public services in programs of national concern. The argument presented there put forward two roles or uses for national or regional categorical aids: (1) as a corrective device for program externalities (benefit spillovers); (2) as a means of assuring the birthright of the citizenry. Related to these was the possible use of controls in grant expenditures to ensure effectiveness of approach in the attack on public problems.

These broad objectives provide a general rationale for some kind of federal action. However, they are not adequate to define criteria for specific grants-in-aid design decisions. We must ask, more specifically, on what basis the degree of federal funds to be earmarked to limited categories should be decided.

In large part, the historical development of the categorical grant-in-aid complex can be traced as the reaction of the national government to public problems or to disparities between what are considered to be acceptable standards and the existing levels of services in state and local programs. The approach has been pragmatic—which is one reason for the proliferation of the grant-in-aid today.

In this pragmatic approach, an obvious concern of the national government is the efficiency with which it can induce the achievement of the objectives set in regard to the problems identified. In the national view, federally provided revenues intended for specific problems can be dissipated in two ways: (1) the funds may be diverted to other uses; (2) the funds directed at the specific problem may be used ineffectively. These dangers are discussed in the two following subsections—"scope of the problem" and "ensuring program effectiveness."

Scope of the problem. As a specific example, let us suppose that a national study has revealed the existence of disproportionately high rates of infant mortality and birth defects for certain identifiable population target groups in the nation. This problem can be viewed both as one of externalities, on the basis of the future burden that defective children will place on other communities, and as one of concern for the right of these children to a normal life.

In a unitary government the response would be straightforward, that is, the government that perceives the problem would be the same government that is responsible for taking direct action to deal with it. However, in a federal system, with certain traditional spheres of action and some degree of independence on the part of state and local governments, the response is more complicated.

In the case of a federal system, the first question to be asked is: Should the national government have a concern for a health problem at the level of specificity described? Or, stated another way, is there any objective basis for deciding what the scope of problems appropriate for the national concern should be? The answer cannot be stated *a priori*. If a problem once known to exist should persist and not be dealt with, the national government cannot be denied the right to bring to bear the necessary measures for action. This would be the case for any problem affecting a portion of the population sufficiently large to be brought to congressional attention, whether the problem is related to health care, educational opportunity, pollution, or unemployment. As a consequence of our national entity *within* a federal system, there is always some degree of national conscience that will react to inequities or unmet problems.

The acceptance of the reality of national concern for specific problems, however, does not necessarily imply that a specific categorical grant-in-aid should be designed for any given problem area of specific scope. For example, there is a wide range of options for the extent of earmarking federal funds intended to help solve the infant mortality and defect problem. At one extreme, the funds could be totally unrestricted. Or, moving to only slightly more limitation, they could be directed for use in the broad functional area of health. They could be further limited to use in maternal and child health programs—or more specifically, for maternal and infant care programs within identified population groups. Finally, they could be very highly controlled, through specifying the means to be used in attacking the problem. However, we will reserve this last approach for discussion later (in the section on ensuring effectiveness of approach).

For further guidance, we need to know why the specific problem has not in the past been dealt with by some level of government. Is it because the problem was not recognized? Or were its causes so insufficiently understood that there was no clear notion of how to attack it? Were the available resources inadequate? Or, in a particular jurisdiction, was the target population without sufficient political "strength" to overcome the existing objections to expenditures? Or is the value perception of a given jurisdiction such that the problem was not even viewed as a *public* problem and/or responsibility? Depending on the answers to questions like these for each problem, the national action required to assure a reasonable attack on it could vary substantially.

If the reasons for past inaction were unawareness or lack of sufficient knowledge to proceed, the national action would depend on the national attitude regarding rapidity and evenness of state response. When the national government is not concerned about the rapidity and evenness of response, there would be little need to earmark grants for the specific purpose. On the other hand, if these factors are seen as critical, categorization of funds to the problem would be called for.

In some cases, limited availability of resources may be a prime factor contributing to the absence of adequate programs. Stated in another way, in our hypothetical case, the jurisdictions involved have demonstrated by past actions that (with the current availability of resources) the problem of infant mortality and birth defects has had lower priority than those other problems to which current programs are directed. If resources just adequate to provide an effective program for dealing with the infant mortality and defect problem were supplied to the jurisdictions—but with no strings attached—there is no particular reason to believe that the monies would actually be devoted to that problem. Stated more strongly, if the jurisdictions act in accord with their own previously demonstrated priorities, injections of funds that are not only rather limited in amount but also not earmarked will very likely be diverted mostly to other program areas.

On the other hand, the case could be somewhat different when "large" additional injections of funds are planned. (We use the term "large" somewhat loosely here to mean an amount of revenues of sufficient magnitude to both relieve the pressure of funding ongoing programs and provide a significant amount of funds for new programs.) Whether or not a given injection of federal funds is large is then relative to the scope of programs for which it can be used—the narrower the scope, the "larger" is a given amount of funds.

Thus, if large additional revenues are contemplated, say in the form of unrestricted grants or grants restricted to the broad functional area of health, and if the consensus values of the recipient jurisdictions are not believed to deviate substantially from those of the national consensus, there would be reason to hope that the specific problem would be dealt with by the states and localities.[10] The likelihood of an attack on the problem might possibly be increased if a state plan of action for the program area were required for federal review. This idea is discussed later in the chapter.

Finally, when the reasons for the continued existence of the problem include, to a substantial degree, a lack of concern by those who influence decision in the individual jurisdiction, the need for tight earmarking of the federal funds—possibly to the extent of requiring the funds to be spent by a specific local government or organization—is paramount. For example, it can be argued that the directing of funds to maternal and infant care programs for Negroes in some of the southern states can be assured only if the categorical grant has very strong strings attached to it.

A continuing commitment by the national government to allocate its resources on a *problem-oriented* basis requires that each problem of national concern be addressed in turn to ascertain the appropriate grant mechanism needed to assure that funds will be applied to the problem and not diverted to other uses. Concomitant with that is the responsibility to review existing grants that were categorically directed to earlier public problems and then to ask: do those problems in fact still warrant specific program attention? For example, at some point in time (perhaps already passed) such a question must be raised about the specific grants that were aimed in the late 1950's at upgrading the teaching of science and other critical subjects. Obsolete categorical aids can in themselves create undesirable distortions in the priorities of states and localities. The Intergovernmental Cooperation Act of 1968 provides for periodic congressional review of grants.

The concept of categorization is not, and should not be, limited to the factor of function. In some cases, categorization re a target population—whether on

---

[10] It should be noted, however, in the strict logic of benefit spillover correction that the federal grants must be earmarked as narrowly as the scope of the spillovers. Otherwise, the matching grant would not act to offset the "distortion" produced by the spillover effect.

the basis of geographical location, income, or some other population characteristic—may be much more important than functional categorization and may present an acceptable tradeoff in the push to keep constraints within reason. This is particularly true when the various public problems being addressed are highly interrelated, as in the core cities.

Another "nonfunctional" categorization that must be retained is the promotion of experiment and demonstration across a wide range of functional areas. As pointed out in Chapter 3, projects serving this broad objective should be funded specifically and in a major share by the national government to assure the adequate development of new concepts and understanding.

Not all federal grants-in-aid need to be oriented to a specific problem. (In Chapter 2, other objectives were offered for a system of grants-in-aid). To the extent that objectives of general support and an increased share of federally raised revenues are also envisioned for aids, other formulations are called for. There is little apparent justification for earmarking federal funds even into broad functional categories if their function is a support role. If we are not addressing very specific problems, who in the federal government is to say what the balance should be among broad functional categories in the states and localities? Further, the act of constraining a state to apply a grant only to health, for example, is much too blunt a device to ensure that the money will be spent effectively or equitably. Finally, incremental funds for broad program areas are highly fungible, unless the matching funds required to obtain the incremental federal revenues are of the same order of magnitude as the growth in spending for that program that normally would occur in the state and localities. Broad functional aids, unless accompanied by fairly intricate strings (which might be described as hidden categorization), give only the illusion of federal control and direction of purpose. The illusion may, however, be of importance politically.

Earlier we made the point that problem-oriented grants ought to be reviewed periodically and eliminated when obsolete. This is easier to say than do, since, for most recipient jurisdictions, funds narrowly controlled are still better than no funds at all. The notion of consolidation of grants may be a particularly appropriate way to allow old and obsolete problem-oriented grants to die.

An explicit mechanism might be built into new problem-oriented grants so that after a specified period of time (open to review) the grant would be merged with a broader support grant. At the time of merging, conditions could be set so that each state would receive an increment to its support grant equal to the average of the amounts of the categorical grant utilized over some specified time period. This would be similar to the procedure used in consolidating the narrow disease control grants into the Comprehensive Health Services grants.

While it is true that these increments to the support grant might in the long run be illusory, in the short run the technique would assure the states that the money is not being withdrawn and might ease considerably the political problems of eliminating obsolete categories.

A similar approach might also be advocated for problem-oriented grants which have in effect already become narrowly defined support grants for established state and local programs. The option of merging discrete public assistance grants into a single matching grant is consistent with this concept. Of course, if the notion of broadening the eligibility for federally aided public assistance is promoted, it might be necessary to earmark funds for new eligible groups, depending on the circumstances at the time.

In summary, we can make the following points:

1. In the foreseeable future the national government will most certainly continue to have concern for the resolution and alleviation of rather specific public problems of various types.

2. There must be assurance that federal revenues appropriated to deal with specific problems of national concern are in fact directed toward solution of those problems. Depending on the conditions, this may call for the earmarking of federal funds into narrow categorical grants sometimes by function, sometimes by target population, sometimes by both.

3. When the problems for which narrow categorical grants have been designed are alleviated, those grants should be eliminated. Consolidation into broader support grants may be an appropriate means for accomplishing this.

4. If narrow problem-oriented categorical grants have become narrow support grants for established programs, consolidation into or with broader support grants would be appropriate.

The primary reason for categorization of grants-in-aid by the scope of the problem is to increase the likelihood that resources will be directed to problems of national concern when there is reason to doubt that states and localities will act without federal encouragement. In most cases this calls for tight categorization of new programs, which can be relaxed over time as the programs become established or as the problems are seen to be alleviated. The relaxation is not easily achieved, owing to the institutional patterns developed in the states in response to the federal aid categories. The purposes of the national government, however, call for a mixed and dynamic system which ensures that problems will be addressed and at the same time avoids strangulation by red tape.

Ensuring program effectiveness. Turning again to our problem example of infant mortality and birth defects in an identifiable target population, let us suppose that a grant has been designed to earmark specific federal funds to the problem. Are additional or alternative conditions needed to ensure effective use of the federal funds?

In the logic of resource allocation, the amount of resources to be devoted to attacking an identifiable problem depends on how much can be accomplished in alleviating the problem. When resources are scarce, one attempts to allocate them to achieve the greatest progress possible. Thus, even when a problem is critical, resources that do not contribute significantly to its resolution should not be spent. (Psychological and political factors arising from certain crisis problems may, of course, dictate that some resources would be wasted in any event). Further, the very process of defining minimum or acceptable output standards for public services cannot be separated from the cost of the standards —and the cost in turn is directly related to how effectively the resources will be used.

In Chapter 3, we briefly sketched the wide variety of program options that could contribute to a reduction of infant mortality rates. Each of the options had a potential effectiveness and a price tag that differs from the others. Analysis would probably show that certain combinations of programs are preferable to others. For example, it might be concluded that the most effective progress toward the objectives could be made if a major portion of the resources should go, not to direct health care for expectant mothers, but rather to family planning. In such a case we must ask whether the federal government should try to control *how* the grants are used, as well as for *what* problem areas.

Here we come face to face with a major part of the straitjacket of federal grants-in-aid. If categorical aids are to be allocated primarily on an objective formula basis, the extent of earmarking to ensure that the funds are directed to specific problems *and* that preferred program approaches are used would be great. The complexity of the grants could rapidly become overwhelming. Even worse, the balance of activities that is appropriate from the aggregated view of the national government will frequently not be appropriate for the particular manifestation of the problem at the local level. Local administrators would have very little freedom to tailor the federal funds to their own needs. This straitjacket problem becomes even more critical when there are many functional categories that can deal with the same complex problem, as in the case of blight and poverty in core cities.

The project grant route avoids some of these problems. A given jurisdiction applies for specific project grants to implement family planning centers, to build neighborhood clinics for prenatal care, to install intensive care units for high-risk births in specific hospitals, and so on. This approach has already been followed in many program areas, not only because certain approaches to public problems are thereby fostered, but also because limited funding has prevented an across-the-board program applicable to all (so-called "programs-on-the-cheap" labeled as demonstrations). However, (as we indicated in Chapter 7), it is the project grant phenomenon that has led to much of the dissatisfaction with the present grant-in-aid scene.

From an overall consideration of effectiveness, some freeing up of funds appears to be essential. However, there are at least three directions in which strings could be relaxed to allow flexibility: (1) functional categorization could be broadened; (2) targeting of funds to identifiable population groups could be eased; (3) earmarking by standards on specific program approaches could be relaxed. Of these options, the third represents the most feasible direction for reducing grant complexity without sacrificing the important objectives of categorical aids.

It has been convincingly demonstrated that grants intended to foster a new attack on specific problems not hitherto dealt with by states and localities must be targeted precisely; otherwise they become nothing more than general support aids. If the problem is one that falls into a narrow functional category, the funds must be categorized that way; if it is confined to an identifiable population group, the funds must be targeted to that group. And in some cases, both functional and target earmarking will be required.

The difficulties in channeling monies to a problem through formulas are illustrated by the short experience with Title I of the Elementary and Secondary Education Act. As reported by Ronald Kessler in the *Wall Street Journal,* January 10, 1968:

Officially, the U.S. Office of Education, which administers Title I, says the distribution formula "is based on the premise that the children of poverty, wherever they may live, need an enriched educational program if they are to overcome the learning handicaps they bring to school with them. Funds are therefore to be concentrated in school attendance areas having high concentrations of such children, regardless of the fiscal capacity of the district or county as a whole."

This leads to the following situation:

Any child in a school approved for Title I funds can benefit from the money—even if he is wealthy. In the Larchmont-Mamaroneck School District . . . [it is conceded] that many of the children enrolled in the Title I guidance counseling program come from wealthy backgrounds. . . .
With median incomes in the 1960 census of $11,915 and $7,642, Larchmont and Mamaroneck (N.Y.) have been able to afford to spend an average of $1,100 per child for education, exclusive of capital expenditures and debt service. . . .
Larchmont-Mamaroneck gets for its high per-pupil expenditure a superior teaching staff and a full staff of psychologists, psychiatrists, social workers, and remedial reading teachers. The 6,100-pupil school system has a television studio, 200 television sets, 195 projectors,

and 47 tape recorders. With its $88,000 Title I grant, Larchmont-Mamaroneck has bought more audio-visual aids and hired additional special personnel.

At the same time,

> Title I has increased Newark's per-pupil expenditure to $856—still well below the suburbs—for about one-third of its pupils. Although the remainder have far greater problems than students in Larchmont-Mamaroneck, about half as much is spent to educate them.

One approach to dealing with these difficulties is to add conditions to the formula so that the funds are better targeted:

> Senator Brooke has proposed an amendment to cut off Title I funds to school systems with less than 10% of their students from poor families. Others have suggested that schools with high per-pupil expenditures be denied poverty money.

Another approach is to increase the number of aids to obtain better targeting:

> Senator Kennedy says he plans to file legislation that would permit the current system of allocating Title I funds to continue while at the same time authorizing additional grants to genuinely needy school systems.

Kessler's comments highlight the difficulty of targeting funds to an identified problem. If anything, not fewer but more constraints are required to ensure that funds are used to deal with the problem as perceived on the national level. Considering this essential complexity for targeting, the notion that further constraints are warranted to control the specific means by which the problem is attacked seems unreasonable.

A REASSESSMENT OF DIRECTION

The clearing out of underbrush from what has been called the federal grant-in-aid jungle requires, not just a single prescription, but a series of remedies, each one tailored to the specific purposes being sought and to the special characteristics of each type of public product. Among the approaches to simplification which show some promise in the foreseeable future, we include: (1) joint funding; (2) consolidation of categorical formula grants; (3) consolidation of project grants; and (4) conversion of project grants to formula grants. These options are discussed below.

Joint funding. The combining of federal grants through legislation such as the Joint Funding Simplification Act represents one approach. A review of the disparities in regulations and requirements could eliminate unnecessary or outdated strings and is clearly called for, whether or not joint funding is authorized by the Congress. (This approach was discussed at some length in Chapter 7.)

Consolidation of categorical formula grants. Consolidation of categorical aids along the model of the Partnership for Health Act offers a means to simplification in still other cases. Even a summary review suggests that a number of public services, other than the categorical disease programs, have undergone a substantial change over time. A combining of existing formula grants for such altered public services would facilitate a broad approach and the flexibility to alter the product as needed to meet the changed circumstances. Grants for vocational education are an example. The "Partnership for Learning and Earning" legislation before the Congress in 1968 would combine federal vocational education grants including the George-Barden Act of 1946 and the Smith-Hughes Act of 1917 into a single and more flexible statute, and also encourage links between school and work by earlier training in occupational opportunities. Updating and revision of vocational education has been urged for some years.

But the pace of technological change has been accelerating, with its concomitant transformation of the job market and occupational training required for satisfactory employment opportunities in that fluid market. Unless vocational education is continuously adapted to meet the job market requirements of the period ahead, the national purposes cannot be achieved.

The problem that is posed for both the Partnership for Health program and the proposed new Partnership for Learning and Earning is whether a greater latitude for state discretion will produce the program modifications that are required. We know that consolidation (as in the Partnership for Health) is a politically feasible means for eliminating federal support for outmoded categories, but we do not know whether this new freedom will encourage a better response to the new complex of problems. The period of operation of the Partnership for Health is still too brief to provide an answer drawn from actual experience. The fragmentary experience thus far accumulated suggests little alteration of state health programs. More, rather than fewer, federal requirements for state in-depth analyses of health programs and evaluation of effectiveness of the ongoing program, coupled with federal technical assistance and state personnel training, would help attain the necessary reassessments. Federal sanctions in the form of withdrawal of federal support would need to be strengthened if the time period for health program revision were shortened to any great extent. Exercise of such sanctions, however, would cause tension between national government and the states. And, given the small share of federal funding of public health work in many states, such sanctions might prove an ineffective means of affecting state health program decision.

The outlook on consolidation of specific categorical grants may be summarized somewhat as follows:

1. Consolidation is more likely to be acceptable to the varied interest groups in those functional areas in which (1) the national purposes in stimulating program have become outdated by technological, economic, or social conditions, (2) the federal grants-in-aid in the aggregate represent a relatively small share of ongoing public expenditures, and (3) there are many alternative uses of the relatively small federal funds that would serve the altered national purposes equally as well, or nearly so.

2. Congressional encouragement of new public services of a more innovative type may be expected to take the form of specially designed categorical grants of a formula or project type, or of earmarking of some fraction of a consolidated grant that in effect is at least a short-term categorical grant within the broader grant program.

3. Consolidation of all federal grants into a fairly limited number of broad functional grants—such as "education," "health," "transportation," "welfare," "public safety"—with wide latitude to states in programming as a complete substitute for categorical grants has been suggested. This is neither a feasible prescription for the Congress, nor one that can serve the national purposes of (1) achieving nationwide standards of specific public services, (2) reducing state and local tax deterrents to the provision of compensatory services for low-income groups, (3) leading state and local governments in their provision for more efficient and effective public services, and (4) responding to the citizen and the groups with which he aligns for public action.

What are the considerations that underlie these conclusions? A major consideration is the fabric of our functional federalism, which allows national, state, and local governments to harmonize their policies through intergovernmental exchanges and cooperation. Division of responsibility among governments has long ago been abandoned as unfeasible in the case of taxation. A cooperative partnership of government in tax administration, together with interjurisdictional tax deduction provisions, has evolved as a substitute for a clear separation of tax sources between governments. Harmonization of expenditure policies also is following the route of intergovernmental communication and exchanges on a more or less institutionalized basis, with provisions for (1) review prior to issuance of federal regulations on grants-in-aid, (2) information exchanges on grants-in-aid and other intergovernmental issues, and (3) intergovernmental partnership in planning and public personnel training[11]. The notion of a rigid separation among governments in program responsibilities has been abandoned, just as the notion of separation of tax sources was earlier. The major exception is the assignment of primary responsibility for economic stabilization, income redistribution, and defense policies to the national government. The monetary and fiscal powers of the national government in controlling economic activity have no state or local counterparts, and the superior access of the national government to social insurance and income-taxation tools for redistributive purposes also has no essentially similar state or local counterpart.

As we noted in Chapter 1, the voters' view of "government" in a federal structure necessitates an intergovernmental harmonization of policies. Clearly, the voters turn, not exclusively to one level of government, but to the national government, states, and their own communities to provide the public services they seek, with the "mix" of intergovernmental action depending on the responsiveness of each of the governments to the demands for public action. Congressional responsiveness to the voters generally leads to categorical aid, earmarking of funds within a broader consolidated grant, and statutory formulation of standards and requirements for receipt of federal funds. (Direct national programs are always an option, but one that does not yield the local administration that appears to be preferred by most voters.)

Project grant consolidation. That the greatest problems of proliferation and complexity in the grant-in-aid system are related to the project grants is abundantly clear. The federal government has allowed this proliferation for several reasons, including (1) a desire to foster experimentation in new programs; (2) a concern that existing formula grants are not adequate to assure that resources reach the problems; and (3) a concern that greater influence on the part of the national government is required in the specifications of how the federal aids are applied to the problems. The concerns have been legitimate, but we have reached a point at which other methods are essential to meet them, lest we become hopelessly bogged down in complexity.

Two measures for reducing the number of project grants are suggested below. These are followed by proposals for converting project grants to formula grants.

1. As a first alternative we consider the consolidation of experimental project grants. The objective of fostering experiment in new program development is a legitimate national concern. In the theory of grants-in-aid, there are strong arguments for categorization of support for projects of this type (see Chapter 3). While the reasons for tight categorization and federal control of monies to be used for experimentation are compelling, measures which can simplify the administration of these grants are available. Strong consideration should be given to the proposal that project grants which have as their purpose experi-

---

[11] The Office of Emergency Planning, as the Presidential liaison with the states, has carried out an extensive program of state visits and consultation with officials of those governments; the Vice President's office as liaison with local governments has, in addition to many consultations, prepared a *Handbook for Local Officials;* and the U.S. Bureau of the Budget has strengthened its communication channels with state governments.

mentation with new or improved public products should be consolidated into a single authority for each major federal department. (The concomitant provisions to assure congressional direction were set forth in Chapter 7). These measures would not only reduce the burden to states and localities of finding and applying for project aids but also retain federal direction of the experimentation.

2. The second option for reducing the number of grants is related to those other project grants that are not primarily experimental in nature. Their consolidation would involve broadening the concept of the interfunctional target grant. A beginning has been made in this direction through the Model Cities program, which remains a project grant but permits bringing together a multitude of federal aids into a single package, subject to federal guidelines. This approach is particularly appropriate for the range of project grants dealing with various facets of a broader problem endemic to a particular geographic location or target population. For example, broadening the concept of the Model City approach would enable a city to both plan and request approval for a total package of programs, instead of seeking funds for an employment program from one federal agency, for a neighborhood health center from another, and so on.

Conversion of project grants to formula grants. The steps outlined above would make some progress toward reducing the number of grants and the procedural complexity of obtaining them. However, the measures still retain all of the encumbrances of preauditing the proposed projects at the federal level. Other options are available for decentralizing the preaudit procedure or in large part eliminating it. We present two such options here, both of which would in effect mold project grants into formula grants.

1. One alternative approach to project aid is to give the states control over project selection and approval, thus removing the discretionary authority from the federal agencies to state agencies and converting the limited federal sums from project support to formula distributions among states. This is essentially the route that is projected, beginning in 1973, for the child health grants. The pattern of change, however, cannot in many cases serve purposes that require truly experimental program designs, especially when interproject comparisons are looked to for scientific findings on program effectiveness or for quantifying the relation between program inputs and outputs. Nor is there much purpose served by moving the selection of projects to a state level, when only small sums are made available to meet large public problems. Control by the state is substituted for control by the Congress and the federal administrative agencies, without necessarily augmenting the available resources and with no assurance of enhanced effectiveness in their allocation. The child health grant meets these problems by imposing additional federal regulations on the states, e.g., (1) requiring state financial participation, (2) defining the general content of the projects to be funded, and (3) calling for progressive steps by the state toward the development of a state-wide child health program. Federal direction thus is broadened without substantial additional federal commitment to facilitate the financing of the broadened program.

2. The second approach involves what may be termed *differential* grants. In general, the national government has provided financial assistance to state governments under uniform statutory rules, uniformly applied throughout the nation. The well-known need for differentiation in treatment of state and local governments in disparate economic, social, and political circumstances has contributed to the case-by-case grants. The wide differences that exist among

states and communities in public service requirements, in population concentration and characteristics, in governmental organization, and in responsiveness of legislative bodies to public demands on expenditure, taxing, and borrowing policies are sharpening rather than narrowing. As the differences continue to sharpen, the desirability of a change in federal grants-in-aid will become more apparent. Even now, state government officials are questioning the uniformity of federal grant rules in the face of intergovernmental differences.

An alternative to the use of more and more project grants to compensate for these intergovernmental differences is to develop new and more sophisticated formulas for grants. Such new formulas would incorporate both the project grants and the existing problem-oriented formula grants into one system. Such formulas would need (1) to take into account the differences among state and local governments and the effect of the differences on the need and cost of providing a particular public service, and (2) to direct federal funds to those governmental units which are responsible for the production of that service. Requirements and standards must also be altered to reflect the relevant differences in public programs from place to place.

This conversion of project aids and the existing formula aids to a more adequate system of formula grants would call for the following:

1. A clear identification of the national purposes of the intergovernmental program that is sought through the stimulus of federal assistance.
2. An identification of the general governmental units that appropriately could be called upon to provide the services to the beneficiaries taking account of (1) economies of scale, (2) political responsiveness, and (3) ongoing responsibility of the government.
3. An estimate of a reasonable minimum public expenditure that is required to give effect to the purposes that are sought.
4. An identification of the components that reasonably measure "target" area product requirements.

Given these findings, it would be possible to develop federal aid programs in which federal funds are distributed to state and local governments in amounts reasonably related to purposes which are intended, allocated by formula, and paid to those governments best able to carry out the national objectives in a manner that is responsive to national purposes and local citizen concerns and interest. These programs could be defined in terms of narrow functions or as broader interfunctional target grants as the nature of the public problem dictates.

Modern computer technology offers the means to deal with the complexity of multifunctional approaches without placing on federal administrative officials the difficult task of case-by-case project proposal review. While existing data that can be fed into computers are far from precise, they do provide objective measures for use in converting project grants to formula grant offerings. Grants can be tailored to the size of the relative need of even small geographic areas, without requiring local outlays of funds to define program "need." Existing data sources permit, for example, a determination of neighborhoods with high ratios of substandard dwellings and high infant death rates. With some additional data collection along the lines of information that have already been tested, data can become available on unemployment and subemployment rates, numbers of families below poverty levels, and so forth.

The pattern suggested here is similar to that of Title I of the Elementary and Secondary Education Act. Grants under Title I may be construed as target grants. They are provided to school districts, and funds may be spent for a range of public services that includes school meals and health services as well as services to enhance education. This type of grant was adopted "in recognition of the special educational needs of children of low-income families and the impact that concentrations of low-income families have on the ability of local educational agencies to support educational programs." [12] (The difficulties created by data inadequacies in differentiating communities by product requirements of target groups were discussed earlier in this chapter.)

Funds are provided by formula to state educational agencies for grants to local educational agencies. The amounts going to each state and county are determined by the relative number of children in low-income families (with some additions such as numbers of children receiving public assistance) multiplied by one-half of the average educational expenditures in the state or the nation, whichever is higher. From these allotments, payments are made by the state to local educational agencies, on the basis of the number of children from low-income families and the average expenditure. Local educational agencies have fairly wide latitude in the design of their projects but must carry out effective procedures for measuring educational achievement. States are restricted in their disapproval of local project plans by a federal requirement for a fair hearing.

As techniques for assessing program effectiveness improve, prior project approval as a condition for federal assistance might be abandoned in favor of postauditing the effectiveness of the programs. Such measurements would require, however, federal technical assistance, such as training of personnel in analytical techniques for measuring satisfactory progress toward the program objectives—progress, for example, toward removing blight and advancing from poverty.

Such adaptations of formula and other federal rules will tend to violate a major principle in grant design, i.e., simplicity. In differentiating among state and local governments, grant formulas will tend to become more, rather than less, complex.

The gains that come about through substituting differential grant rules for uniform rules must be weighed against the costs of such substitution for each major categorical program. And the imprecision of statistical indicators must be weighed against the costs of the case-by-case granting method. These indicators, despite their inadequacies, involve one of the questions that Congress must answer: Is it not possible that the indicators may better serve than administrative discretion presently does through the project grant route, in placing federal assistance where it is most required?

One by-product of a differential grant-in-aid may be a certain amount of dampening of the recently reheated conflict regarding federal grants directly to cities and the bypassing of states. Objective criteria subject to measurement can be developed that would help determine for each particular program whether federal assistance appropriately goes to the state government or to localities within the state, and in what combination to state and to eligible localities.

Among the criteria that could be used are:

1. The incremental costs of administration, taking account of existing public program responsibilities
2. The incremental costs of provision of the service, taking account of these existing public program responsibilities and economies of scale

---

[12] Sec. 101, Declaration of Policy, Title I of the Elementary and Secondary Education Act of 1965.

3. The willingness and capacity of the government to carry out the national purpose of the grant as evidenced by prior performance
4. The responsiveness of the government to the demands of the particular clientele group for which the federal assistance is provided as evidenced by prior performance
5. The relative effectiveness or benefits from the public service when administered and produced at different governmental levels (taking account of geographic externalities of the service and costs associated with gaps in the service)
6. The interaction of the specific program that is being considered with other public services provided by the several governmental levels.

Variations in assignment between state and community of administrative responsibility for the several categories of public services thus could be taken into account by formula. Again, we can interpret Title I of the Elementary and Secondary Education Act as a precedent. Grants under this program are made to local school districts, but when a state government operates schools and produces the service, the federal assistance goes to that state government. Moreover, in the additional supplements to Title I for special education—e.g., provision of educational services for the blind or for children of migrants—the portion of the funds that is granted for these supplements goes to state government agencies that produce the special educational services.

Application of the criteria suggested could possibly freeze undesirable patterns of local government. The grant differentiation actually need not impose an insuperable barrier to reducing fragmentation. States could redefine the division of responsibility between the localities and state governments, and the localities could combine or cooperate in providing the service through interjurisdictional agreements. These changes would be reflected in subsequent distributions of federal funds.

Unless some such steps are taken toward differential formulas, single rules will continue to be applied to diverse situations, with resultant undue expenditure of funds for overlapping governmental administration and, in some cases, inefficiency in public production by fragmented local governments. Exclusive federal grants to states for services that could be best provided by local neighborhoods, or exclusive federal grants to local communities when states have already assumed important responsibilities fall short of the best grant design that our information base and technology permits.

For two reasons, the possibility of such differentiated grant design is directly of concern in assessing block grant proposals. First, the recent public discussion of block grants has essentially turned on the question of direct federal assistance to cities or exclusive federal assistance to states. Second, the broader the federally aided program is, the less adaptable is the concept of grant differentiation. As indicated earlier, the assistance, if provided in a large block, tends to take on the characteristics of a general support, or fiscal, grant rather than the specific carrot which is intended to stimulate state or local program development in accord with the national purpose.

IMPROVING STATE AND LOCAL PROGRAM OPERATIONS

A complementary step in the move toward simplifying grant-in-aid procedures is to reduce, where possible, federal control and direction of the specific means by which problems are attacked. This, however, requires that other ways be sought to promote effectiveness in the use of program resources.

An increasingly popular approach requires a state (or a locality) to produce a plan for use of the funds within the defined limits of the purpose of the grant.

The potential recipient government would need federal approval of the plan before funds are made available. This approach has merit for a number of program areas; it also has several serious drawbacks. First, the requirement of detailed federal approval of plans prior to action will most certainly add to the lead time for moving against acute problems. Second, the requirement for planning in many separate functional areas, often overlapping, is likely to lead to an unsubstantive paper exercise on the part of states and localities. Third, there is frequently little reason to believe that the federal officials administering the grants are in a position to provide any better judgment on the adequacy of plans than are state and local government officials. Thus, there is danger that much energy will be dissipated on "red tape" matters that have little to do with the effectiveness of programs. There are, of course, program areas of such a nature that the development of formal state plans would be useful and could work quite well. For example, the development of a long-range plan for highway safety, tieing together the activities of all of the relevant state and local agencies, could provide a good framework for specific project decisions.

A more appealing approach, in the longer run, is to promote the development of state and local capacity to do effective program planning and evaluation. This approach could be advanced through specific categorical grants for planning to general government. One would hope that the development of this capacity in states and localities could eventually almost eliminate the felt need for "preauditing" expenditure of federal funds. Primary attention at the federal level could then be focused on the more important problems of ascertaining the status of national problems and reviewing progress toward their alleviation.

Part of the price of a federal system is inevitably some reduction in the efficiency (as seen from the national perspective) with which resources can be directed toward alleviation of the problems with highest national priority. In the light of the real costs of overcontrol and bureaucratic red tape, the national government must set its own priorities on what facets of resource allocation it wishes to control. There is no single pat solution to this. Rather, a variety of tools must be explored, to discover which combination of them will allow reasonable guidance by the federal government and at the same time permit state and local government initiative.

General support or overhead grants

THE DISCUSSION OF GRANT-IN-AID design in Chapter 3 indicated that a combination of grants is required if multiple national objectives are to be efficiently pursued within an aid system. A block grant or a general support grant cannot be realistically considered as a substitute for categorical aids without the sacrifice of certain goals; rather, these grant mechanisms should be viewed as a complement to other grant instruments within one system. Two different packages of grants directed toward the achievement of two sets of objectives were outlined in Chapter 3. In each of these packages a general support or overhead grant was regarded as a key element.

The functions that the general support grant might have in a system of grants-in-aid are summarized below. The general support grant could:

1. Improve the balance of public and private expenditures in states and localities, which is now distorted by such factors as tax competition and, especially in cities, by the differences in perspective between those who pay the taxes and those who receive the benefits from the expenditures.
2. Provide increased equalization of available public revenues among the states and localities.
3. Reduce the likelihood that specific categorical matching grants will distort state and local budgets by inducing the states and localities to forgo other public expenditures to obtain the federal grant dollars.
4. Provide an unrestricted source of funds that will permit the states and localities to fill the gaps between specific categorical aid programs, since such gaps are inevitable in the formulation of nationwide programs;
5. Provide an additional fiscal tool which the federal government can use to effect economic stabilization.

The pursuit of each of these objectives carries implications for the design of a general support or overhead grant. Each must be balanced against the other and against the difficulties of administering the grant and the political factors affecting the grant's acceptance. It is to these topics that the present chapter is addressed.

THE HELLER-PECHMAN PLAN

An unconditional grant—one with no strings attached—has been the subject of much political and economic discussion. Debate was initiated in 1964 with the Heller-Pechman proposal for "tax sharing." [1]

The plan essentially called for: (1) federal grants to states to be made in uniform per capita amounts; (2) financing of these grants through continuing permanent appropriation into a trust fund of an earmarked amount equal to 2 percent of income taxable under the federal tax; (3) a possible set-aside of a proportion of the trust fund monies for additional allocations to states with low per capita income.

The proposal was offered as a fiscal instrument for directing the economic growth and stability of the national economy within the purposes of the Employment Act of 1946. It was suggested as a second round of fiscal adjustments in the "new economics," which had proved its effectiveness through the 1964 tax reduction. That tax action had increased consumer demand, reduced unemployment, and pointed a dragging economy upward.[2] Prior to the heating up of the Vietnam conflict in late 1965, a next round of fiscal readjustments seemed likely through one or more of several alternative methods: (1) more federal tax reductions of the 1964 sort; (2) stimulation of state and local spending; (3) effective reduction of state and local taxes; or (4) reduction of social insurance taxes. As a consequence of the earlier tax reduction, it became clearer that unless there was a demand offset to the "dividend" produced by the federal tax structure, a growing economy would produce less than its capacity permitted and unemployment would continue at the 4 to 5 percent rate.

The report of a task force set up by Walter Heller to assess methods of strengthening state-local finances was not published, but the publicity given to the general proposal outlined in the task force report had considerable impact on intergovernmental fiscal relations. For the immediate period, it had the effect of consolidating the opposition of the functional groups and of the cities to a general grant into a united front in favor of categorical aids for education, community health services, neighborhood facilities, and so forth. Perhaps more importantly, through the continuing publicity given to the possibility of a general grant of $3, $4, or $5 billion or more to the states, the proposal led to enlarged requests for dollar authorizations for categorical grants.

Cautious proposals on categorical grants were converted to substantial requests for grant authorizations; and these proposed authorizations in some instances were enlarged further by the Congress. If the economy required a large additional injection of demand (private or public), there was clearly important public work to do. The agencies, public and private, concerned with clean water, better education, prevention of poverty, improvement of health, decent housing for all citizens, and revitalization of central cities had a long shopping list of needed items to purchase on behalf of the public. This list was not hastily drawn up for a spending spree; rather, it had been laboriously developed out of twenty years of hard program evaluation and congressional debate.

Additional categorical aids and a general fiscal grant were interpreted as competing, not complementary, proposals. We can perhaps most directly illustrate the validity of this competition by asking what the congressional fate of the Great Society programs would have been had the Heller-Pechman proposal

---

[1] The magnitude of the discussion regarding this proposal is only partially suggested by the compilation, *Revenue Sharing and Its Alternatives: What Future for Fiscal Federalism?*, Prepared for the Subcommittee on Fiscal Policy of the Joint Economic Committee, U.S. Congress, 3 vols. (Government Printing Office, 1967).

[2] See Walter W. Heller, *New Dimensions of Political Economy* (Harvard University Press, 1966).

been endorsed by the Administration in 1964. The query is put in this way to suggest that the Great Society program aids to the states and localities could not have gained congressional approval had the Administration at the same time been urging a large general fiscal grant. And, in fact, these two directions of national action were so opposed that they were not offered to the Congress at the same time. Furthermore, one important justification for the Heller-Pechman proposal in the early fall of 1964 was that Congress had not, over the preceding two or more decades, adopted a substantial program of national aid for education; general fiscal aid was thought to be a substitute.

We have already noted the impact of the discussion of the Heller proposal on the enactment of national aids to states and localities. The proposal thus contributed to the adoption of categorical grants that raised the amount of aids from the $10 billion total in 1964 to more than double that amount for fiscal 1969. With these new grants as a part of the federal package of aids, new interest attaches to the design of a complementary set of categorical and general support grants.

LEGISLATIVE PROPOSALS

Legislative proposals for revenue sharing modeled more or less on the Heller-Pechman proposal are numerous. By mid-March 1967, upward of seventy-six bills providing some form of revenue sharing had been introduced in the 90th Congress. Of the seventy bills introduced in the House, forty-nine were identical, except for provisions relating the tax sharing to categorical aids. All of the forty-nine were modeled on the bill introduced by Representative Charles E. Goodell; thirty-two of these called for the financing of the revenue sharing by a cutback in the categorical aids.

Revenue sharing plans differ depending upon the decision about (1) the amount of the grant (or of revenue sharing); (2) the annual changes in amounts of sharing; (3) appropriation arrangements for the shared amounts; (4) the conditions under which grants are to be made available; and (5) the basis for allocation of shared revenues among eligible jurisdictions.

Appropriation amount and annual change. In the legislative proposals, with the single exception of the Reuss bill (H.R. 1166), which called for an annual appropriation authorization of $5 billion, the amount of revenue sharing was not specified as a fixed appropriation level. The bills generally specified a percentage of either taxable income or federal tax collections as the magnitude of the grant, with most bills calling for return of a specified percent (ranging from 1 to 10 percent) of federal tax collections to the states, usually collections from the federal income tax.

Variations of the percentage-of-tax-collection proposals were: (1) percent of individual income taxes collected; (2) percent of individual and corporate income taxes collected; (3) percent of net tax revenue after deduction of expenditures for national defense and servicing and interest on the public debt, plus any extra amounts Congress might appropriate; (4) percent of income taxes, estate and gift taxes, and all custom duties collected.

The proportion of federal revenues proposed for sharing ranged widely from 1 to 5 percent at the outset, and some proposals called for a step-up from 1 percent to 5 percent. The size of revenue-sharing grants, depending upon the taxes designated for sharing and the rates, would range from less than $0.5 billion to more than $5 billion. Alternatively, some proposals called for appropriation of an amount determined by a statutory percentage of aggregate income taxable under the federal individual income tax. These proposals specify an amount equal to 1 or 2 percent of this tax base, which, in the immediate period ahead, is the equivalent of $3.5 to $7.0 billion.

When appropriations are determined as a share of tax receipts, the amount of the support grant would increase in the same percentage as the collections on which they are based. However, the following types of problems are raised by the proposals that relate the amount to be shared to a percentage of tax collections:

1. Tax collections fluctuate with changes in business activity and, accordingly, stability in the support grant to qualifying jurisdictions could only be achieved by some special provisions. For example, the majority of the bills call for annual appropriations of not less than those made available in the preceding year.
2. Fiscal policies may require that federal taxes be raised or lowered; unless there is a supplementary provision that "unties" the link between the support grant and federal collections, state and community concern about stability in federal aids would become an additional barrier to achieving a flexible fiscal policy.

The average long-term growth of federal income tax collections in response to national economic growth (without statutory rate or base changes) is larger than the growth in the base of the income tax. This is so because, as the economy expands, more taxpayers have higher incomes and become subject to higher income tax rates. Accordingly, proposals that seek to accelerate the amount of revenue sharing link the appropriation amount to income tax collections rather than the amount of taxable income. Federal revenues, with stable growth at high employment, tend to increase at about 1.2 percent for each 1 percent growth in the gross national product; federal individual income taxes are projected to grow under the same conditions, about 1.5 percent for each 1 percent increase in the gross national product. Thus, with a 6 percent annual growth in the GNP, the taxable income grows 7.2 percent and tax revenue from the individual income tax grows 9 percent.

Setting a grant as a percentage of aggregate taxable income permits the grant amount to rise automatically with the overall growth in income. Such a grant would fluctuate less widely than a grant based on federal tax collections, and would tend not to stand in the way of congressional action to stabilize the national economy by tax rate changes. The changes from year to year in taxable income and in net income tax receipts are shown in Table 9-1.

Special trust fund arrangement. In a number of the bills a trust fund arrangement was proposed. Under this type of provision, a percentage of tax collections, or of the tax base, would be permanently appropriated into a trust fund earmarked for distribution among the states. The purposes of such a provision furnish the arguments in favor of it; these purposes are: to assure continuity of the program; to assure that appropriations are in the full amount of the assigned federal revenues so that states and localities may plan with greater certainty of federal funding; and to facilitate maintenance of contingency reserves to achieve a stability in federal assistance.

Prior to the change in the budget that began with fiscal year 1969, such trust fund arrangements were also intended to remove the grant expenditures from the national administrative budget and thus to insulate it from pressures to lower federal spending. The arguments against such an arrangement are the obverse of those in favor, namely:

1. Congressional control over the appropriations is weakened.
2. Adjustment of the support grants in the light of changing circumstances is impaired.

Table 9-1. **SHARING OF THE INDIVIDUAL INCOME TAX BASE OR COLLECTIONS**

	Income tax base			Net income tax receipts	
Calendar year	Amount in billions	Percent increase from previous year	Fiscal year	Amount in billions	Percent increase from previous year
1952	$107.4	8.0%			
1953	115.4	7.4	1953	$30.1	7.9%
1954	115.3	−0.1	1954	29.5	−1.9
1955	128.0	11.0	1955	28.7	−2.7
1956	141.5	10.5	1956	32.2	12.0
1957	149.4	5.6	1957	35.6	10.7
1958	149.3	−0.1	1958	34.7	−2.5
1959	166.5	11.5	1959	36.7	5.7
1960	171.6	3.1	1960	40.7	10.9
1961	181.8	5.9	1961	41.3	1.5
1962	195.3	7.4	1962	45.6	10.2
1963	209.1	7.1	1963	47.6	4.4
1964	229.9	9.9	1964	48.7	2.3
1965	255.1	11.0	1965	48.8	0.2
1966	286.3	12.2	1966	55.4	13.6
1967[a]	318.0	11.1	1967	61.5	11.0
1968[a]	350.0	10.1	1968[a]	67.7	10.1
1969[a]	375.0	7.1	1969[a]	80.9	19.5

[a] Estimated.
Source: Compiled from Internal Revenue Service data.

3. Support grants can be stabilized by other methods without the rigidity of trust fund financing.

Only one of the many bills introduced in the first months of the 90th Congress called for annual authorization of the amount to be shared, leaving room for annual adjustment of the statutory ceiling.

Conditions of an unconditional grant. Although the general notion of the support grant is that no strings are attached, certain types of conditions were incorporated into many of the bills. For example, state compliance with fair employment provisions and civil rights legislation was often required. Complementary state planning efforts were a condition of the Reuss bill, and the Javits bill called for expenditures for health, education, and welfare purposes, i.e., a type of modified "block" grant.

Some of the proposals required a pass-through to local governments of a specified proportion of the grant, but differed markedly in the extent of the specification. Several left to the discretion of the states the reallocation of the additional federal funds; one required that the states must distribute to their local governments an equitable proportion of the added federal funds, with the ratio in each state to be no less than the average of the state's distribution of its own revenues to local governments in a preceding period. Others called for each state to reallocate a designated proportion of the added amount of federal tax shared—e.g., 50 percent—to localities. And another would require that states submit plans for the allocation of a part of the added federal grants among local governments.

A uniform rule for all the states on the proportion of the amount of the shared

Table 9-2. **FEDERAL AID TO STATES IN RELATION TO STATE AID TO LOCALITIES AND STATE DIRECT GENERAL EXPENDITURES, FISCAL 1966** *(In percent)*

State and region	State aid to localities as percent of federal aid to state	Federal aid to state as percent of direct general expenditure by state	Federal aid to state as percent of state direct general expenditures plus state aid to localities
UNITED STATES	143.5%	34.3%	23.0%
New England	116.4	27.4	20.8
Maine	53.9	30.0	25.8
New Hampshire	34.7	21.7	20.2
Vermont	42.6	36.9	31.9
Massachusetts	173.9	30.7	20.0
Rhode Island	83.7	23.9	19.9
Connecticut	96.6	22.2	18.3
Mideast	249.3	25.7	15.6
New York	361.7	26.1	13.4
New Jersey	132.6	27.4	20.1
Pennsylvania	145.6	23.8	17.7
Delaware	148.7	24.3	17.9
Maryland	250.3	28.4	16.6
Great Lakes	172.8	29.6	19.6
Michigan	206.3	27.7	17.6
Ohio	144.6	29.6	20.7
Indiana	185.2	30.7	19.6
Illinois	108.8	30.6	23.0
Wisconsin	314.1	30.1	15.5
Plains	104.7	40.3	28.4
Minnesota	147.6	45.7	27.3
Iowa	111.8	32.3	23.7
Missouri	72.2	45.4	34.2
North Dakota	73.0	32.0	26.0
South Dakota	43.4	39.6	33.8
Nebraska	81.4	39.1	29.7
Kansas	140.4	38.3	24.9
Southeast	112.8	39.2	27.2
Virginia	99.5	30.4	23.4
West Virginia	68.0	36.5	29.3
Kentucky	77.6	37.3	28.9
Tennessee	103.9	42.5	29.5
North Carolina	192.8	39.6	22.4
South Carolina	133.8	35.1	23.9
Georgia	121.3	44.4	28.9
Florida	138.5	33.0	22.6
Alabama	91.2	45.8	32.3
Mississippi	110.9	49.4	31.9
Louisiana	115.3	38.7	26.7
Arkansas	79.2	49.6	35.6
Southwest	103.4	41.5	29.0
Oklahoma	82.2	40.3	30.3
Texas	112.9	40.9	28.0
New Mexico	88.0	48.2	33.8
Arizona	113.9	40.0	27.5
Rocky Mountain	82.4	42.2	31.3
Montana	40.8	39.9	34.3
Idaho	86.8	36.0	27.5
Wyoming	51.2	51.7	40.9
Colorado	110.6	45.4	30.2
Utah	84.4	38.2	28.9
Far West	148.3	37.9	24.3
Washington	129.4	29.9	21.6
Oregon	84.0	36.5	28.0
Nevada	79.0	38.0	29.2
California	160.6	39.7	24.2
Alaska	28.9	55.2	47.6
Hawaii	28.9	25.7	23.9

federal taxes that should go to localities is deemed inappropriate, because of the wide variations among states in the relative sharing of responsibilities for major governmental functions. In some states, welfare programs are state programs financed out of state funds; in others, localities help finance the program. Arrangements for sharing educational expenditures differ markedly. In a few states the major educational expenditures are state financed; in a few at the other extreme, state financing is very restricted.

In the aggregate, in fiscal 1966, the states collected 41.6 percent of the $83 billion state and local general revenues and spent directly only 35.2 percent of the general expenditures of states and localities. But within these aggregates there is wide variation in the state-local revenue and expenditure relationships and in state aids to localities. In some states grants to localities account for over 50 percent of state general expenditures; in a few they account for less than 15 percent.

The wide differences among the states, both in allocation of program responsibility between state and local governments and in state aid practices, hamper the design of a uniform formula and make it difficult to specify a uniform nationwide rule for reserving funds for local use (Table 9-2).

In view of these variations it has been urged that a minimum percentage be set, such as 40 percent, as a floor on the amounts of federal funds shared with localities—a percentage higher than the existing nationwide average. While due recognition has been given to the possible conversion of such a requirement to a maximum share of state financial aid, the setting of the proportionate share at a sufficiently higher percentage, it has been argued, would offset any undesirable consequences for local finances.

A statutory provision requiring each state to share a specified fraction of its additional federal revenue with localities is not adequate to safeguard funds for cities. All local governments and, indeed, local functional agencies (such as educational agencies) become appropriate recipients of federal funds received by the state. Of the total amount of state aids now made available to local governments, less than 10 percent comes in the form of general aid. The more than 90 percent remainder is tied to specific functional programs.

Grant allocation among states. Allocations among jurisdictions in legislative proposals include a number of different factors, such as amounts of federal taxes paid in the jurisdiction; population (a uniform per capita amount); population combined with tax effort indexes; population coupled with tax effort indexes, and a set-aside for the poorer states; population adjusted to give larger sums to the poorer states (with or without a tax effort index). Some representative allotment formulas in bills that were before the U.S. Congress are cited below.

1. *H.R. 3127*—Fascell (D), (General)

   Allotment to a state would equal three percent of the federal taxes collected on individual income in the state.

2. *S. 694*—Scott (R), (General)

   Allotment to a state would equal the product of the total appropriation times the ratio of state's population to total national population.

3. *H.R. 5507*—Tunney (D), (General)

   Allotment to a state would equal the product of eighty-five percent of the total appropriation times the ratio of state's population to total national population. For the 17 states lowest in per capita income, there would be an additional allotment equal to the product of fifteen percent of the total appropriation times the ratio of the state's population to the total population in the aforementioned 17 states.

4. *H.R. 4070*—Goodell (R), (General)

Allotment to a state would equal the product of ninety percent of the total appropriation times the ratio of the state's population weighted by tax effort to the sum of all states' population each weighted by tax efforts. For the 17 states with lowest per capita income there would be an additional allotment equal to ten percent of the total appropriation times the ratio of the state's population weighted by per capita income to the sum of all states' population each weighted by per capita income.

5. *S. 482*—Javits (R), (Health, Education, and Welfare)

Allotment to a state would equal the product of three factors: eighty-five percent of the total appropriation, the ratio of the state's population to total national population, and the ratio of the state's tax effort to the average state tax effort. For those states with per capita income below the average of state per capita incomes, there would be an additional allotment equal to the product of fifteen percent of the total appropriation times the ratio of the difference between the average state per capita income and the state's income to the sum of such differences for all states with below average per capita income.

6. *S. 673*—Tydings (D), (General)

Allotment to the state would equal the product of the total appropriation times the ratio of the state's population to the total national population all weighted by the ratio of the state's tax effort to the average of all states' tax efforts if the state's tax effort is below this average. Metropolitan areas of population greater than 1,500,000 would qualify for direct grants equal to the product of the allotment to the surrounding state times the ratio of the population within the metropolitan area to the total population in the state. If a metropolitan area receives a grant, the surrounding state would have two-fifths of this amount deducted from its allotment. For interstate metropolitan areas, this formula (with the exception of the total population requirement of 1,500,000) would be applied to each portion of the metropolitan area separately.

7. *S. 1236*—Baker (R), (General)

Allotment to a state would be the product of three factors: the total amount appropriated; the ratio of the state's tax effort to the average of all states' tax efforts; and the arithmetic average of the ratio of the state's population to total national population and the ratio of the state's population (weighted by the ratio of average national per capita income to the state's per capita income) to the total of all states' population (each weighted by the ratio of average national per capita income to the state's per capita income).

ALLOCATION INDEXES AND ISSUES

Certain problems are characteristic of a support grant to states in relation to taxes collected. Place of tax payment has no necessary relation to need for funds and for public services. The "place" is ambiguous, since federal regulations do not require taxes to be filed or paid in the place of residence. For individual income taxes the place of payment may be the headquarters of the employing firm, the specific place of employment of the individual, the place of residence, or place of domicile of the taxpayer. Each of these "places" may be in a different state. Corporation taxes may be filed and paid from corporation headquarters rather than state of production, distribution, or employment. Customs are collected at ports without regard to the state of domicile or residence of the customs payer.

To attempt to go beyond collection of taxes to the final tax burden raises even more problems. For many of the taxes there is no single fully accepted incidence theory that could be used as a basis for measuring "place of tax burden." A number of estimates have been prepared from time to time of tax incidence by state. For purposes of general information these study findings are useful, but for purposes of payment of grants to states they are not sufficiently precise.

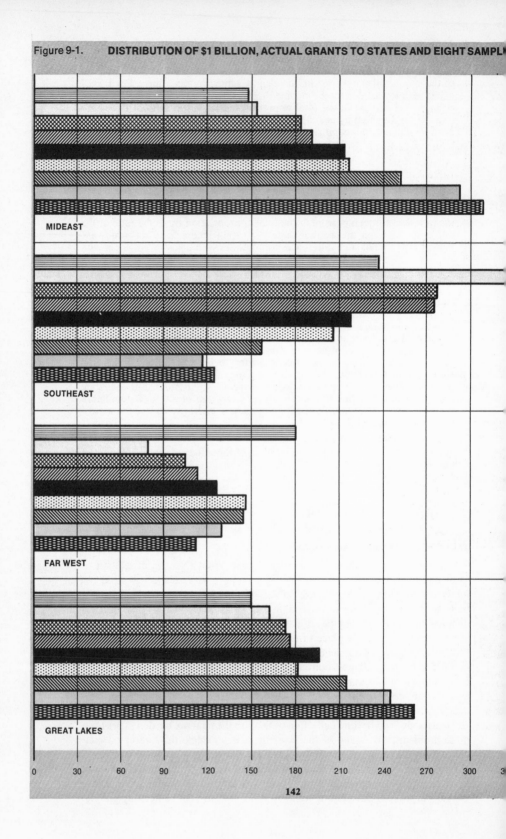

Figure 9-1.   DISTRIBUTION OF $1 BILLION, ACTUAL GRANTS TO STATES AND EIGHT SAMPL

MIDEAST

SOUTHEAST

FAR WEST

GREAT LAKES

0   30   60   90   120   150   180   210   240   270   300   3

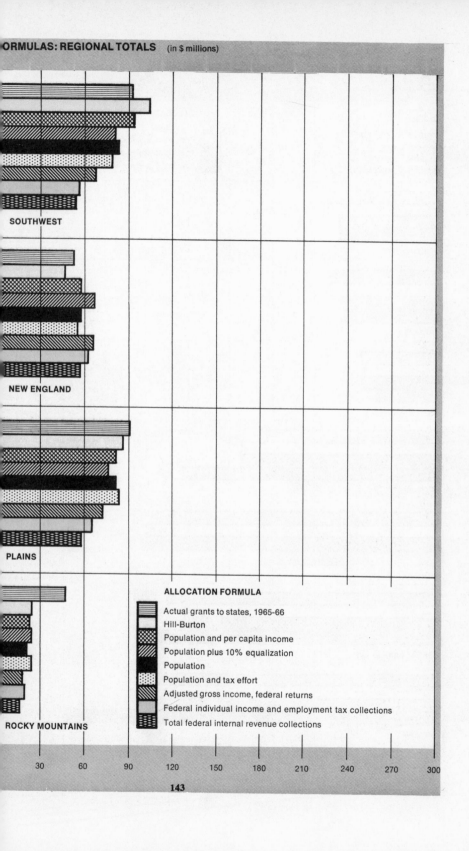

SOUTHWEST

NEW ENGLAND

PLAINS

ALLOCATION FORMULA

Actual grants to states, 1965-66
Hill-Burton
Population and per capita income
Population plus 10% equalization
Population
Population and tax effort
Adjusted gross income, federal returns
Federal individual income and employment tax collections
Total federal internal revenue collections

ROCKY MOUNTAINS

30 60 90 120 150 180 210 240 270 300

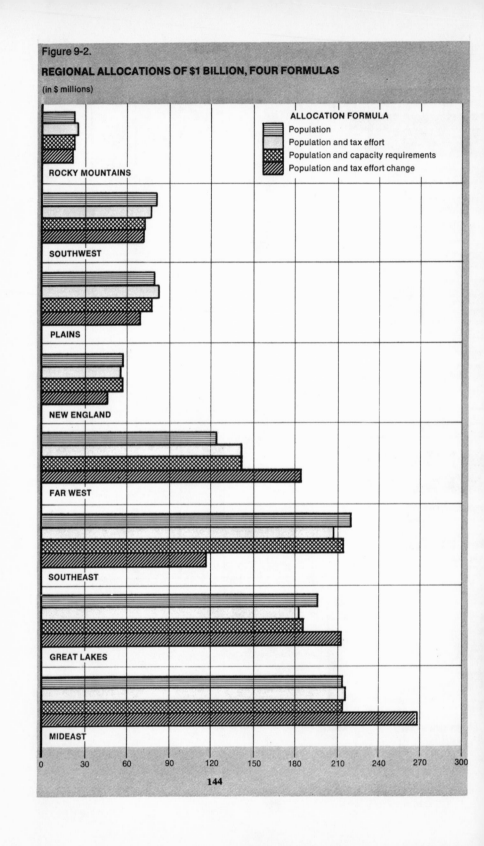

Figure 9-2.

REGIONAL ALLOCATIONS OF $1 BILLION, FOUR FORMULAS

(in $ millions)

ALLOCATION FORMULA
Population
Population and tax effort
Population and capacity requirements
Population and tax effort change

ROCKY MOUNTAINS

SOUTHWEST

PLAINS

NEW ENGLAND

FAR WEST

SOUTHEAST

GREAT LAKES

MIDEAST

0   30   60   90   120   150   180   210   240   270   300

Population serves as a general indicator of fiscal need. However, when taken alone as a measure of requirements for funds it has severe drawbacks, as indicated in Chapter 5. Population in combination with other indexes can provide allocation formulas serving various possible objectives for a general support grant. When used with a measure of tax effort, it acts to place monies in those states which have demonstrated a willingness to fund their public service needs. Use of a tax effort index tends to penalize those states where citizens have not chosen taxation levels commensurate with the nationwide average rate of state and local taxation.

Formulas for allocation of a general support grant which combine with population a measure of income per capita tend to equalize public revenues by providing larger than proportionate grants to states whose income per capita is relatively low. Alternative measures of fiscal capacity were discussed in Chapter 5. Recent research indicates (as described in that chapter) that personal income per capita no longer acts as a wholly adequate proxy for fiscal needs of the states. Requirements for public service seem to increase with urbanization; where higher average incomes are found, poverty and a backlog of needs are also found.

A general support grant can be allocated among states by other measures than those described above. A capacity requirements index such as that developed in Chapter 5 can be combined with population to place funds where heavy demands for expenditure occur, relative to the income available for tax payment. Or such indexes could be further modified by an additional index. For example, changes in tax effort might be a factor in the allocation of funds among jurisdictions. This would serve two purposes: it would reward those jurisdictions which are demonstrating their willingness to invest their own resources in the public interest, and it would bolster programs in those states where a marked effort is already being made to improve public services.

Figures 9-1 and 9-2 show the relative amounts that would be allocated to each of the regions of the United States using different grant formulas. They are arranged by distributive impact, with the exception of the regional distribution of actual categorical grants-in-aid. The regional division on a straight per capita grant distribution may be taken as a norm, and other distributions considered in relation to it. There are three measures with "equalization" formulas using some inverse function of income per capita which provide more funds to low-income states than a per capita grant. Allocations based on combinations of population and (1) tax effort level, (2) tax effort changes, (3) capacity requirements, and on three measures related to federal taxes, would provide less by way of a general support aid to low income states than would a per capita grant.

The relative amounts received by some regions diverge by as much as 40 or 50 percent from the apportionment on a straight population basis. The allotment is most sensitive to the choice of a grant formula in the Southeast, Mideast, Far West, and Great Lakes Regions. The formulas more favorable for each of these regions vary. For the Mideast, the six formulas that do not seek to equalize public revenues would provide larger shares than would a per capita formula; the most favorable formulas would be those calling for a return of total federal revenues, or a distribution based on population and incremental tax effort. Five of these same six formulas allocate a larger share of the support grant for the Far West than a per capita formula. The largest share is allocated for this region by population weighted by the "change" in tax effort formula, with a formula based on adjusted gross income, as defined for federal individual income taxes, giving the next largest share. For both Great Lakes and New England, four of these same six formulas would provide a higher federal sharing than would a per capita distribution; the largest relative share would come from formulas related to federal taxes.

For the Plains and Rocky Mountains, a formula combining population and tax effort level would yield a higher allocation than a per capita distribution. All of the three so-called equalizing formulas provide more funds for the Plains, and two of the three do so for the Rocky Mountains. However, both of these regions receive a larger relative share of actual federal grants than under any of these hypothetical allocations. For the Southeast and Southwest regions, actual grants and the "equalizing formulas" allocate a larger share of a general grant than would a per capita distribution. The formulas relating to tax effort, capacity requirements, or federal taxes would provide smaller shares than would a formula based on population alone. The largest relative share in a grant for each of these regions is provided by the Hill-Burton type formula.

Thus, at one extreme is the distribution among states and regions based on federal income taxes collected. At the other, is an equalization formula such as that applied in the Hill-Burton hospital construction grant. More per capita would go to the New England and Mideast states if income taxes were used as allocators. If the Hill-Burton type of allocation were applied in a general support grant, the per capita amounts to the Southeast states would be substantially above those to the New England and Mideast states.

UNCONDITIONAL SUPPORT GRANT FOR CITIES

Of the many bills dealing with federal grants that were introduced in the 1st session of the 90th Congress, only the Tydings bill called for direct grants to cities. Nevertheless, the urgency of enlarging public services in cities is presently disputed by very few people. The case for a massive attack on problems in the cities was strongly set forth in a staff report prepared for the Committee on State and Local Revenue of the 59th National Governors' Conference.

The National Governors' Conference recognizes the urgency of a massive attack on the critical problems that exist in our society today. Symptoms of those problems are the recent outbreaks in our core cities. The explosions in the cities have served as a warning that the American people cannot afford complacency, that remedies must be found now. There is no panacea; there is no simple solution to this crisis. This much is clear—there must be a vast enlargement in the amount of resources channeled toward alleviation of these problems. The marshaling of resources must be carried out through all levels of government and through the private sector as well. . . .

Rural inmigrants have flooded into core cities in search of employment. They have come without the prior educational and other experience that would equip them for living in complex metropolitan areas. They have come to the cities in a period of occupational transition in which private employment opportunities for those with little or no education are closing up and, at the same time, shortages are becoming more acute for the highly trained technician and professional worker. Unemployment, underemployment, low income problems are developing as a consequence of national labor market trends. . . .

Inmigrants have come without ties to the community in which they now live, with no deep sense of community participation, or of being a part of that community. While awareness of community is growing, local taxation to provide the needed services is not a feasible solution. A Welfare Administration study in Sacramento showed that blighted areas of that city accounted for 8 percent of the city's taxes. The share of items in the city's budget claimed—for health, police, and fire—was far out of proportion to taxes from the area or population there.

Neglect of services in the past needs to be compensated by more than equality of treatment now. And in many communities there is less than equality—roads in poorer neighborhoods are often deficient, as are sanitation, schools, and mass transportation services.

Unprecedented numbers and proportions of new inmigrants confronted city services with problems that were unfamiliar and required the injection of resources of a very different order of magnitude than the capabilities of the cities permit and their taxpayers would sanction. In the period ahead, a marked shift in patterns of spending is required, with even more emphasis on services for the poor. Many public activities that cities are asked to undertake are essentially new, such as producing jobs and giving assistance.

These new demands for public goods come at the time when resistances to property taxation have accumulated, pointing to alternative methods of financing.[a]

As this excerpt from the report indicates, there has been a substantial spill-in of costs to the core cities, due to long neglect. Fundamentally, these costs were not and should not be the responsibility of the cities. Massive federal aid seems required, in a variety of forms—categorical aids directed at specific problems, supplemented by general fiscal grants or combinations of categorical aids (as in Model Cities) to allow a multipronged attack on the highly interrelated problems in the core cities. To the extent that cost spill-ins continue to occur, and one expects that they will, there should be maintenance of federal support to the core cities.

The pressures on the property tax and on other taxes available to the cities are very great, to the point that the financially able citizen is fleeing to the suburbs, leaving the core city less able to cope with its mounting problems. Cities, burdened with both their traditional and newer responsibilities for services and constrained by the fragmented structure of local government and provisions of state constitutions, may possibly no longer be economically viable units. The problem was summarized in the Governors' Conference staff report as follows:

There are huge disparities within the metropolitan area in the distribution of taxable resources, on the one hand, and public problems, on the other. Despite relatively high tax burdens cities have been unable to meet the prbolems within their boundaries. Governmental fragmentation within and across state lines, special interests, and heavy suburban representation in state legislatures further inhibit the redressing of these disparities. The national government can use its revenue system to channel the large resources of the suburbs into areas where they are most urgently needed.[1]

In short, there is an argument for national action on the nation's problems in cities. We value our cities as socioeconomic units, yet the present system seems to dictate that, without assistance, such units will decay. A number of potential solutions exist, including major restructuring of financial arrangements for public services and the taking over of certain public services, such as education and welfare, by more comprehensive units of government (state and federal). Another possible remedy lies in unconditional support grants for the cities, either passed through the state or made directly.

Specifications for a Support Grant to Cities. There is no perfect definition of eligible local jurisdictions for a support grant. Nor is there a perfect formula for allocating funds, which takes appropriate account of public service requirements and resources available. Nevertheless, the question—is it possible to develop a workable formula for national support grants to cities?—has been answered in the affirmative.

There are many different formulas that can be used. For example, the Hartke bill (S. 3966), introduced in the summer of 1968, would provide for grants to incorporated municipalities with populations of 10,000 and over; the amounts would be determined by population. Necessarily, the definition of an eligible jurisdiction is somewhat arbitrary. Possibly all cities, regardless of size, should be eligible for a statutory allocation of federal support grant funds. Perhaps, however, only middle-size and large cities with their higher expenditures per capita should qualify. All local units of a specified or greater size could

---

[a] *New Directions in Federal-Aid Policy,* A Staff Study prepared by the State-Local Finances Project of The George Washington University for the Committee on State and Local Revenue to the 59th National Governors' Conference (October 1967), pp. 4-8.

[1] *Ibid.,* p. 9.

receive funds, or perhaps just local units representing general government rather than special districts. The arbitrariness, whatever definition and cutoff points are selected, raises obvious problems.

The possibilities range somewhat as follows:

1. Incorporated municipalities with populations 10,000 or more, 25,000 or more (50,000 or more, 100,000 or more, etc.).
2. Incorporated municipalities and counties with populations of 50,000 or more (100,000, or 200,000, or more, etc.).
3. Incorporated municipalities and urban counties, with urban counties defined either in terms of counties of specified size within standard metropolitan areas, or counties of specified size having at least some designated percentage of their population living in urban places.

The distribution of municipal expenditures per capita, by size of municipality, suggests a marked difference in outlays per capita between places with a population of under 50,000 and those with populations of 50,000 or over. The general expenditures per capita of municipalities having a 1960 population of less than 50,000 and those of greater population size, ranging to 1 million and over, are shown in Table 9-3.

Table 9–3. **PER CAPITA EXPENDITURES OF CITIES BY POPULATION-SIZE GROUPS, 1965–66.**

Municipalities having a 1960 population of	Per capita expenditures
ALL MUNICIPALITIES	$149.55
1,000,000 or more	287.01
500,000 to 999,999	209.37
300,000 to 499,999	155.16
200,000 to 299,999	143.05
100,000 to 199,999	159.34
50,000 to 99,999	145.70
Less than 50,000	89.81

The present fragmentation of the metropolitan economy into a multitude of separately responsible governments creates a need for intra-metropolitan jurisdictional cooperation. A grant made directly to qualifying cities may serve merely to prop up an outmoded and inefficient institutional arrangement and to impair, rather than strengthen, regional forms of financing that attempt to cope on a broader base with metropolitan problems. Any measure dealing with the problems of the cities should include incentives for intergovernmental cooperation within metropolitan areas and not the reverse.

One proposal has been advanced to permit jurisdictions within metropolitan areas of a size below the specified qualifying size for statutory eligibility to qualify nevertheless for federal aid when they join together, to provide particularized governmental activities, or a broad range of functions. Depending upon the specific allocation formulas, local intergovernmental cooperation can thus be encouraged by the designation of eligible jurisdictions in a way that permits a joining together of governments for the carrying out of specific functions. Whatever the allocation formula, it should not freeze undesirable governmental patterns and create a barrier to consolidation of governments or to interjurisdictional cooperation.

Functions are allocated by states between cities and county governments in a variety of ways throughout the United States, and, in some areas, to townships in lieu of counties. The inclusion of urban counties as eligible jurisdictions as well as incorporated municipalities poses separate issues; for example, it would tend to place a share of the funds made available by the federal government in wealthy suburban areas. Such allocations to the wealthy suburbs could be justified in part as providing the financial underpinnings for eliminating housing restrictions; this would help to open up the suburbs and spread some of the core city problems geographically within the metropolitan area. However, the intent of the support is to correct some of the disparities of suburban and central city jurisdictions. Distributions to wealthy suburbs would offset this intent.

There are a series of indexes, the simplest of which is population, on which allocations may be based. In addition to the more general limitations of population as a measure of need or of requirements for public services examined earlier, there is the problem of the wide variations among cities in the scope of their responsibility under state law. A closer approximation of "need" may be obtained, for example, by taking account of (1) population characteristics such as the number of low-income families, the number of unemployed, or the number of nonwhites, as well as population density, or (2) the pressures that are engendered for public services by high crime rates, numbers of substandard dwelling units, numbers of public assistance recipients, or obsolescence of schools and other public facilities. A weighting system can be designed to reflect the presence or absence of expenditures such as those for education, for health and hospitals, and for public assistance payments.

More specifically, plans requiring assurance of funds to local jurisdictions may incorporate indexes such as the following in their allocation formula:

1. Taxes collected within the jurisdiction.
2. Expenditures for all of selected public services; for example, total expenditures less educational outlays.
3. Total population of the jurisdiction, or population in specified income or age groups.
4. Unemployment and subemployment rates.
5. Population density.
6. Substandard housing units.

A formula can be designed that is neither as simple as a per capita distribution nor as complex as a multifactor allocation: for example, population of the jurisdiction in excess of a specified number (e.g., 25,000) and local tax effort may be combined; or population may be combined with such tax effort indexes and also with indexes of incremental tax effort.

The data for use in an objective grant formula are not at present wholly adequate. Even local population data are not recurringly available; tax effort indexes could be constructed, but no national agency is responsible for doing so, as for example, the U.S. Department of Commerce is responsible for providing state income estimates. Data on low-income families, unemployment rates, and so forth are even more deficient on a citywide basis. A decision to apply such indexes in a support grant would help identify the information, now lacking, that would be useful for a wide variety of public purposes and also facilitate the necessary collection of data.

SUPPORT AND CATEGORICAL GRANTS IN A SYSTEM OF AIDS

The majority of legislative proposals for the general support grant view it as a substitute for categorical aids. The identified separate purposes of categorical grants, whether compensation for benefit spillouts or achievement of national minimum services as a birthright for citizens, would not be served by substitution.

Increasingly greater significance attaches to the question of how the vital purposes of categorical grants are to be preserved within a federal grant system that includes general support aid. More and more criticism has been focused on the proliferation and overlapping of existing grants. The Council of Economic Advisers in its 1967 Annual Report indicated one route to assuring categorical grants within such a system:

> Under some proposed compromise arrangements, a fixed level would be established for total Federal financial aid to State and local government, designed to cover both categorical grants and general support. Categorical grants would continue to be appropriated as at present; and the balance of the support would take the form of untied grants going to cities as well as States. The untied portion would serve as an "overhead" payment to be used by States and cities to strengthen their own programs and their planning. Such a compromise is intended to provide some assurance of continued Federal support for categorical grant programs which have established their merit, while enlarging opportunities for State and local initiative and responsibility.[5]

Other but similar devices can be used. Appropriations for general support to states can be set as a percentage of categorical aids, or can be limited to a statutory percentage of such aid as a maximum. Allocations among states can also be based on the amount of categorical grants, to underscore or give emphasis to the overhead character of the general grant to the states. Thus, in one form or another, a tie between categorical aids and general support grants is essential, (1) to help give new direction to the federal grant system and (2) to achieve an overall design that is appropriate to the several parts of that system and the purposes of each part.

In combination, these two major purposes of introducing a support grant as a new fiscal tool suggest federal general support funds for both cities and states; they also suggest such general support grants as being complementary to categorical grants. The problem of additional federal support to, or additional federal revenue sharing with, states and cities is thus posed in a form and context different from those outlined in the Heller-Pechman proposal. The Heller-Pechman proposal raised the question of whether or not to have a statutory pass-through provision; the form and concept of a general support grant as we have presented it here assure that funds go to cities, whether directly or via some nondiscretionary pass-through.

Walter Heller, in his study on revenue sharing, concluded his remarks on the problem of the return route of federal taxes by saying:

> The pass-through issue is a perplexing one. Seemingly persuasive considerations can be brought to bear on both sides of the question. How to give special weight to the claims of central cities and metropolitan areas, yet not freight the formula with too many conditions, remains a challenge to ingenuity.[6]

As we have indicated here, funds for cities may be provided in a number of different ways, although no one of them is perfect. Some of the options are spelled out as plan specifications later in this chapter. The specifications also suggest a possible way to tie categorical and general support grants.

ACHIEVING THE AIMS OF A FEDERAL GRANT-IN-AID SYSTEM

Essentially, the decisions as to which jurisdictions are to be eligible for a general support grant and which formula is to be used in allocating funds depend on the functions of an unconditional support grant within a federal grant-in-aid sys-

---

[5] *Economic Report of the President, Together with the Annual Report of the Council of Economic Advisers* (Government Printing Office, 1967), p. 165.

[6] Walter W. Heller, *op. cit.*, pp. 161-62.

tem. At the beginning of this chapter we summarized some of the possible functions of these grants: (1) to adjust and improve the balance between the public and private sectors; (2) to overcome budgetary distortion regarding nonaided expenditures produced by categorical grants; (3) to facilitate bridging the gaps in categorical grants; and (4) to enlarge the use of federal revenue sources for economic stabilization and equity purposes.

Public-private balance. Achievement of this first function, along with enlargement of the public sector to serve vital public requirements, points to support for governments that have evidenced their willingness to respond to public demand with more and better public products. We have some indexes of willingness, including past performance on public expenditure policy and on tax effort; willingness is also evidenced by changes made in effective state and local tax rates. In general, as indicated in Chapter 5, it is the major industrial states and the larger cities that have responded to the growing public service demands and to the critical urban problems. It may be noted that formulas using such indexes of willingness would give more funds to the urban states, which, by the traditional yardstick of personal income per capita, are the richer states.

Enlargement of the public sector will result from additional federal support for cities only if the state governments take counterpart, and not offsetting, action on state aids to cities. The importance of state decisions on revenue distributions to cities for successful augmentation of the public sector is illustrated by the $3.2 billion out of a total $19 billion of state aid to localities in 1967 that went to municipalities; the remainder went to school districts, counties, and other governmental units as follows: [7]

TOTAL	100.0%
School districts	48.4
Counties	24.9
Municipalities	17.0
Townships	1.6
Special districts	0.5
Other	7.7

Grants represent a larger proportion of expenditures outside of central cities than they do inside. Less than 27 cents of each $1 of central city expenditures is financed by aid, whereas the average expenditure outside of central cities was more than 30 cents per dollar.[8] The total of state aid shown above includes federal funds received by states and shared with local governments. Combined state and federal aids are almost identical in central cities and outside, despite the deep current concern about the special financial problems of core cities. Larger cities receive concentrations of federal aids for housing and urban renewal, which makes the central city grant total look more favorable than it is.

Federal general support grants of $2 or $3.5 billion may be compared to the $3.2 billion in current state grants to cities. The added federal support would be intended as complementary to and supportive of state aid, but could be offset by state aid policies. If the states elect to reduce their own grants to cities as a consequence of any new federal grants to cities, little will be gained in achieving a better balance between public and private sectors. State use of a general support grant for city aids, unless such aids are earmarked and safeguarded by federal legislation, is not assured. State legislative biases against

---

[7] U.S. Bureau of the Census, *State Government Finances in 1967*, Series GS 67, No. 1 (Government Printing Office, 1968).

[8] Advisory Commission on Intergovernmental Relations, *Draft Report on Fiscal Balance in the American Federal System* (October 1967).

large cities now bar state legislative authority for special taxing or borrowing by cities and limit state or special aid to cities out of state funds in a number of states.

Nullifying or offsetting action by states to a federal direct grant to cities cannot be avoided within a federal system; however, this is not an argument for direct and exclusive grants to states. On the contrary, states that are responsive to city problems will buttress such added federal aid with their own tax funds. For example, some states have recently established offices of community affairs and are undertaking to help cities cope with the problems within their boundaries. In such cases, the additional federal grants to cities and the augmented state aid will facilitate revitalization of the cities and help bring about the necessary development of their human resources.

Relief of budgetary distortions. The second function, that of overcoming distorting pressures of categorical grants on state budgets, points primarily to additional aid to states. The major share of categorical grants, about $9 out of each $10, now goes to state governments (see Chapter 1). The general support grant would be designed to avoid the effects of reduction in unaided programs, including tax reduction. Such a purpose requires that the general support grant be given to states in proportion to the outlays (or tax reduction) which they have sacrificed by matching categorical grants. A direct measure of the distortion and its costs is not available, but figures on matching required for categorical aid may serve as a rough proxy. Although information on required matching is not routinely compiled, a 1964 study by the Advisory Commission on Intergovernmental Relations provided such estimates for the year 1962.[9]

Bridging program gaps. The function of achieving maximum program effectiveness suggests the provision of a substantial source of funds. General support grants, by filling in the gaps of categorical grants, allow states and localities to tailor categorical programs to their needs and facilitate expansion of the programs which have been recognized as of great significance but which place new demands on revenues. Thus the general support grant gives the states and localities the flexibility to develop a balanced total governmental program directed at maximizing effectiveness in moving toward its goals.

Stabilization and equity. The several additional functions of support grants depend on which concept of a grant-in-aid system is adopted. In one system, such grants are intended to facilitate greater equalization of public service levels; in another, to achieve greater equity in tax sources used for state and local programs. If the primary purpose is equalization of public service levels, the formula would be weighted to give more funds per capita to the low-income states. Greater equity in taxation would suggest a larger federal payment to jurisdictions whose tax burdens are greatest and more regressive.

A larger question is: how much federal revenue should go for outlays administered by states and localities? The question does not arise in the same form for the categorical grant programs, since the relative sharing of categorical aids is determined by the purpose of each category and by the price reduction required to achieve national program standards or efficient resource allocation. The sum of the categorical aids sets a sharing ratio without a deliberate decision on the size of the total of grants-in-aid or federal revenues shared with states and communities.

---

[9] Advisory Commission on Intergovernmental Relations, *The Role of Equalization in Federal Grants* (January 1964).

Revenue sharing through general support grants that are intended as an economic stabilization or a fiscal policy device calls for deliberate decision on the total or the incremental amount of federal taxes for state and local purposes. One guide that can be applied in determining the appropriate share is the long-range "offset" required to prevent a drag of the federal income tax collections on the national economy. The share may be set so as to channel into state and local public services the full amount of this "offset" or some part of it. Focusing on the offset necessarily places the emphasis on increments to federal sharing rather than on the overall percentage of federal taxes or of state and local expenditures to be shared.

Federal revenues now tend to rise about $2 billion with each 1 percent increase in gross national product. With a 4 percent per annum growth in gross national product in real terms and a 6 percent growth in dollar terms, federal revenues will rise about $12 billion per year (without a change in tax laws). As the income tax base expands over time, the amount of fiscal dividend produced by the growth in federal income taxes will tend to become larger. One estimate places the fiscal dividend by 1975 at about $18 billion per year.[10]

From 1960 to 1965, revenues of the federal government at constant tax rates tended to rise between 35 and 40 percent—or $35 to $40 billion. During this period, federal revenues tended to outrun actual federal outlays. Such excess revenues would, if realized, reduce demand and trigger a decline in business activity and, along with it, a reduction in federal tax collections. As pointed out earlier, tax reductions were made during this period to prevent the decline in demand for goods and services. For the period ahead, the question of stabilization policy is explicitly related to Vietnam commitments. If these commitments and the United States' financial obligations for war purposes are reduced, fiscal action will be required to offset the potential drag on demand of the growing federal income tax yield plus the reduced defense obligations.

What proportion of this "offset" to a threatened reduction in market demand should take the form of encouragement to state and local spending? There is no single answer.

Still another way of assessing the aggregate amount of federal grants within a system of aids is to ask what type of distribution of tax burdens among the income groups appears desirable in terms of national values and concepts of equity and fairness. The target of federal revenue sharing can be set so as to achieve the distribution of tax burdens for public services administered by states and localities which is considered appropriate to the national interest.

CRITERIA AND SPECIFICATIONS FOR SUPPORT GRANTS

The hurdles to adoption of a general support grant, despite the number of legislative proposals, have included: the inflationary trends in the economy following escalation of the Vietnam conflict; the failure to assure funds to cities; the lack of safeguards for categorical grants.

Public reaction on the Vietnam war may be attributed in part to a seeming conflict between public spending for that war and spending to combat poverty at home. Whatever the underlying reasons, inflationary pressures since the acceleration of the United States' commitment in Vietnam have made adoption of any large addition to federal grants-in-aid untimely. Unless offset by counterpart increases in taxes, inflationary pressures would be intensified. The question for consideration thus became: should action be taken ahead of the termination of hostilities to authorize general support grants that would go into effect

---

[10] Estimate prepared by Henry Aaron of the University of Maryland.

at a later and indefinite date?

Several proposals have been advanced for immediate authorization. One such proposal, set forth in the staff report for the Committee on State and Local Revenue of the 59th National Governors' Conference, looked to immediate authorization providing augmented grants, which, at the option of the Congress, would take the form of federal non-negotiable securities during inflationary periods. The proposal draws on the experience during World War II when large accumulated reserves in the states contributed importantly to the ability of the states to achieve a large expansion in state and local activities. For the immediate period of the Vietnam war, reserves could be accumulated only by national grants that would be made, not in cash, but in non-negotiable securities, to become payable after a designated period (this period could be extended at the option of the Congress).

An immediate grant, even if made in the form of federal non-negotiable securities, would permit states and communities to begin the planning required for program expansion. They would have the assurance of funds for implementation of their plans.[11]

Provision for payment to states and cities in the form of non-negotiable securities would serve a continuing purpose: it would strengthen the tools available to the national government for implementing a fiscal policy that can help achieve economic stability and growth. Annual increments to any support grant could be set aside for payment in non-negotiable securities in later years.

The two major barriers to enactment of a general support grant—the lack of assurances (1) to cities and (2) to groups concerned with specific categorical programs—we have discussed earlier. To overcome these barriers, a dialogue was initiated by Governor George Romney of Michigan between the cities and states to hammer out a preferred plan, which would have sufficient flexibility to adapt to changing circumstances. One step in this process was the formulation of criteria for a general support or overhead grant, as set forth below.

1. Any allocation formula for revenue sharing should be simple, understandable, and be acceptable as equitable.
2. The plan should *assure* substantial additional federal financial resources to urban communities as well as states.
3. Revenue sharing for municipalities *should not encourage present barriers to more effective structure* of local government in accord with the scope of their public service responsibilities. As a minimum, the plan should deter further geographical fragmentation of local government.
4. The revenue sharing plan should be designed to *supplement state and community funds* rather than substitute for state and local tax effort.
5. The revenue sharing plan *should not weaken any categorical federal grant designed to serve national priorities and national purposes.*
6. The procedures for federal revenue sharing should be flexible enough to support fiscal policy for a stable and growing economy, without impairing orderly planning in states and communities.

The National League of Cities, at its annual meeting in July 1967, adopted a set of criteria similar to those above. In July 1968, the criteria were adopted also by the National Governors' Conference.

Several illustrative plans were developed on behalf of the Committee on State and Local Revenue of the National Governors' Conference for consideration by the governors and mayors. Addendum A, which follows, presents descriptions of these plans, together with illustrative tables showing the differences in allotments among states. Additional illustrative materials compare the dis-

---

[11] *New Directions in Federal-Aid Policy, op. cit.,* p. 51.

tribution of $1 billion allotment among states, computed by applying various indexes to population including incremental tax effort. The amounts that would go to selected large cities, assuming a separate allocation to such cities under one formula, are also shown. Addendum B details the sources used in computing the illustrative materials shown in Addendum A.[12]

Other formulas have been advanced that are not included among the illustrative plans. One such formula seeks to encourage states either to take over some public service responsibilities from urban areas or to enlarge their state aid to cities. These incentive grants to states are combined with federal urban support grants that vary with the city's own revenue effort above some norm such as effort in excess of 80 percent of the nationwide city average—e.g., $5 per capita for 1 percent of own revenue effort above the norm. Reductions in federal aid to cities resulting from enlarged state aid would be compensated by higher grants to the state.

The social-engineering type of research that has been done on a general support grant points to a range of specification choices, with the criteria for choosing resting heavily on the concept of a grant-in-aid system. While there is no perfect grant formula, there are many workable formulas that can remove the major hurdles to adoption which have been identified in the course of public discussion on the Heller-Pechman plan. Of immediate urgency is augmentation of the financial resources of the cities.

---

[12] The emphasis in the illustrative plans on noneducational services derives from the analyses presented in Chapters 3 and 5. These analyses suggested that educational outputs required from the perspective of the nation (or, more specifically, educational achievement levels) can be best obtained by directed categorical aid for education to states and central cities with concentration of low educational achievers.

Illustrative plan specifications for a federal support grant

ALTERNATIVE PLAN 1.

Tied to categorical aid

(a) **Appropriation Authorization:** For Overhead Grants there would be authorized to be appropriated for the fiscal years 1969 and thereafter a sum equal to 25 percent of the appropriations for categorical grants-in-aid in the preceding fiscal year (not excluding highway grants). (Based on 1968 Budget request, $4.4 billion.)

Per capita plus effort

(b) **Allocations to States:** The sums appropriated would be allocated among the states on the basis of the population in each state and the tax effort index of that state. In measuring the tax effort index, both state and local taxes would be included.

Per capita pass through to cities

(c) **Allocations to Cities:** From the Overhead Grant made available to each state, the state would be required to pay an amount to each city with a population of 50,000 and over, determined as follows: The population of the city multiplied by the per capita amount allocated to the state under item (b).

Other jurisdictions

(d) **Payments to Counties and Other Municipalities:** The equitable share to be paid to other jurisdictions within its boundaries would be determined by the state.

Limit on pass through aid

(e) **Limitations on Urban Support Grants:** In no case would an Overhead Grant to a city exceed one-third of the total general revenues of the city.

Optional form of payment

(f) **Payment in Non-Negotiable Securities** (optional provision): The statute might provide that payment for the fiscal years 1969 and 1970 be made in the form of non-negotiable Treasury securities (non-interest-bearing), becoming due 18 months after the date of issue. On the due date jurisdictions receiving non-negotiable securities could elect to cash such securities or convert such securities to interest-bearing Treasury obligations. For the years beginning with the fiscal year 1971, *increments* in support grants might be made in the form of non-negotiable Treasury securities (non-interest bearing).

ALTERNATIVE PLAN 2.

(a) **Appropriation Authorization:** For Overhead Grants there would be authorized to be appropriated for the fiscal years 1969

	and thereafter a sum equal to 25 percent of the appropriations
Tied to *categorical aid*	for categorical grants-in-aid in the preceding fiscal year (not excluding highway grants). (Based on 1968 request, $4.4 billion.)

Tied to
categorical aid

and thereafter a sum equal to 25 percent of the appropriations for categorical grants-in-aid in the preceding fiscal year (not excluding highway grants). (Based on 1968 request, $4.4 billion.)

(b) **Two-Part Grant Authorization:** Appropriations for Overhead Grants would be divided into two equal funds; Fund A for allocation to states; Fund B for allocation to cities.

Two funds

(c) **Allocation to States:** State funds would be allocated among the states on the basis of the population of each state and the tax effort index of that state. In measuring the tax effort index, both state and local taxes would be included.

Per capita
plus effort
for states

(d) **Allocation to Cities:** The city fund would be allocated among the cities of the United States on the basis of their relative population. "City" for this purpose would be defined as an incorporated municipality with a population of 200,000 or more [100,000 or more; 50,000 or more].

Per capita
for cities

(e) **Limitation on Urban Support Grants:** In no case would the Urban Overhead Grant exceed one-third of the total general revenues of the eligible urban jurisdiction, or in the case of combinations of municipalities, one-third of the total local revenues devoted by them to the provision of public services specified in the agreement of cooperation.

Limit on
pass through aid

(f) **Payments to Counties and Other Municipalities:** The equitable share to be paid to jurisdictions other than cities as defined in item (d) within the boundaries of each state would be determined by the state.

Other
jurisdictions

(g) **Payment in Non-Negotiable Securities** (optional provision): The statute might provide that payment for the fiscal years 1969 and 1970 be made in the form of non-negotiable Treasury securities (non-interest-bearing), becoming due 18 months after the date of issue. On the due date jurisdictions receiving non-negotiable securities could elect to cash such securities or convert such securities to interest-bearing Treasury obligations. For the years beginning with the fiscal year 1971, *increments* in support grants might be made in the form of non-negotiable Treasury securities (non-interest bearing).

Optional
form of
payment

ALTERNATIVE PLAN 3.

(a) **Appropriation Authorization:** For Overhead grants there would be authorized to be appropriated for the fiscal year 1969 and thereafter an amount equal to 2 percent of taxable income as defined for individual income tax purposes and reported by the Bureau of Internal Revenue for the latest year for which such data are available, but in no case more than an amount equal to 25 percent of the categorical grants for the same year (not excluding highway grants). (Approximately $5.6 billion for the fiscal year 1969 based on 1966 individual income tax data; reduced to $4.4 billion by the limitation of 25 percent of categorical grants.)

Tied to
taxable income
and
categorical aid

(b) **Payments to States and Localities:** From the sums appropriated there would be paid to each state an amount for its own use and that of its localities based on the population of the state and the tax effort index of that state. In measuring the tax effort index, both state and local taxes would be included.

Per capita
plus effort

(c) **Allocation to Incorporated Urban Municipalities:** From the Overhead Grants made available to each state, the state would be required to pay an amount to each city with a population of 50,000 and over, or to pay out in behalf of combinations of incorporated municipalities whose combined populations exceed 50,000 in accordance with agreements for the cooperative provision of specified non-educational public services, an

Pass through
to cities

157

amount determined as the average of (1) the ratio of population of the city to total state population, and (2) the ratio of the amount the city spends out of local sources for non-educational purposes to the total amount the state government and local governments in that state spend out of own sources for non-educational purposes.

(d) **Limitation on Urban Support Grants:** In no case would the Urban Overhead Grant exceed one-third of the total general revenues of the eligible urban jurisdiction, or in the case of combinations of municipalities, one-third of the total local revenues devoted by them to the provision of public services specified in the agreement of cooperation.

Limit on pass through aid

(e) **Payments to Counties and Other Municipalities:** The equitable share to be paid to jurisdictions other than cities as defined in item (c) within the boundaries of each state would be determined by the state.

Other jurisdictions

(f) **Payment in Non-Negotiable Securities** (optional provision): The statute might provide that payment for the fiscal years 1969 and 1970 be made in the form of non-negotiable Treasury securities (non-interest bearing), becoming due 18 months after date of issue. On the due date jurisdictions receiving non-negotiable securities could elect to cash such securities, or to convert such securities to interest-bearing special Treasury obligations. For the years beginning with the fiscal year 1971, *increments* in support grants might be made in the form of non-negotiable Treasury securities (non-interest bearing).

Optional form of payment

ALTERNATIVE PLAN 4.

(a) **Appropriation Authorization:** For Overhead Grants there would be authorized to be appropriated for the fiscal year 1969 and thereafter an amount equal to 2 percent of taxable income as defined for individual income tax purposes and reported by the Bureau of Internal Revenue for the latest year for which such data are available, but in no case more than an amount equal to 25 percent of the categorical grants for the same year (not excluding highway grants). (Approximately $5.6 billion for the fiscal year 1969 based on 1966 individual income tax data; reduced to $4.4 billion by the limitation of 25 percent of categorical grants.)

Tied to taxable income and categorical aid

(b) **Payments to States and Localities:** From the sums appropriated there would be paid to each state an amount for its own use and that of its localities based on the population of the state and the tax effort index of that state. In measuring the tax effort index, both state and local taxes would be included.

Per capita plus effort

(c) **Assurance to Urban Counties and Incorporated Municipalities:** From the Overhead Grants made available to each state the state would be required to pay an amount to each city and urban county with a population of 50,000 and over, or to pay out in behalf of combinations of incorporated municipalities whose combined populations exceed 50,000, in accordance with agreements for the cooperative provision of specified non-educational public services, an amount determined as the average of (1) the ratio of the population of the city or county to total state population, and (2) the ratio of the amount the city or county spends out of local sources for non-educational purposes to the total amount the state government and local governments in the state spend out of own sources for non-educational purposes. In areas in which eligible city and county jurisdictions overlap the total to be allocated to the cities and counties within the area would be based on the average of (1) the percentage of total state population residing within the area and (2) the percentage of all city and county non-educational expenditures

Pass through to cities and urban counties

from own sources within the state that are made by the eligible city and county governments within the area. Allocations among eligible jurisdictions within the area would be made on the basis of their shares of area non-educational expenditures from own sources.

Limit on pass through aid

(d) **Limitation on Urban Support Grants:** In no case would the Urban Overhead Grant exceed one-third of the total general revenues of the eligible urban jurisdiction, or in the case of combinations of municipalities, one-third of the total local revenues devoted by them to the provision of public services specified in the agreement of cooperation.

Other jurisdictions

(e) **Payments to Other Counties and Municipalities:** The equitable share to be paid to other jurisdictions within its boundaries would be determined by the state. This money could be used for improvement of the structure of local government.

Optional form of payment

(f) **Payment in Non-Negotiable Securities** (optional provision): The statute might provide that payment for the fiscal years 1969 and 1970 be made in the form of non-negotiable Treasury securities (non-interest bearing), becoming due 18 months after date of issue. On the due date jurisdictions receiving non-negotiable securities could elect to cash such securities, or to convert such securities to interest-bearing special Treasury obligations. For the years beginning with the fiscal year 1971, *increments* in support grants might be made in the form of non-negotiable Treasury securities (non-interest bearing).

Table 9-A. **ILLUSTRATIVE ALLOCATIONS OF $1 BILLION UNDER VARIOUS ALLOTMENT FORMULAS: GENERAL SUPPORT GRANT** *(In thousands)*

	Factors determining allocations			
	Population	*Population plus 10% equalization*	*Population and per capita income*	*Population and tax effort*
UNITED STATES	$1,000,000	$1,000,000	$1,000,000	$1,000,000
New England	57,312	54,050	51,447	56,467
Maine	5,019	6,987	5,867	5,363
New Hampshire	3,477	3,129	3,589	3,090
Vermont	2,068	1,861	2,277	2,563
Massachusetts	27,484	24,736	23,951	28,008
Rhode Island	4,585	4,126	4,386	4,395
Connecticut	14,679	13,211	11,377	13,048
Mideast	212,762	191,486	184,279	215,848
New York	93,221	83,899	76,359	108,917
New Jersey	35,220	31,698	29,412	30,241
Pennsylvania	59,135	53,222	57,126	54,355
Delaware	2,614	2,353	2,089	2,456
Maryland	18,447	16,602	16,332	16,583
District of Columbia	4,125	3,712	2,961	3,296
Great Lakes	196,470	176,823	175,887	181,729
Michigan	42,756	38,480	37,863	42,707
Ohio	52,615	47,354	49,551	43,638
Indiana	25,110	22,599	23,387	23,841
Illinois	54,744	49,270	44,452	46,507
Wisconsin	21,245	19,120	20,634	25,036
Plains	81,024	76,267	82,146	83,472
Minnesota	18,258	16,432	18,129	21,516
Iowa	14,026	12,623	13,644	15,270
Missouri	23,017	20,715	23,065	19,996
North Dakota	3,319	4,620	3,941	3,848
South Dakota	3,482	4,847	4,213	4,139
Nebraska	7,434	6,691	7,515	6,533
Kansas	11,488	10,339	11,639	12,170
Southeast	218,298	277,634	278,616	206,592
Virginia	23,012	20,711	25,417	18,621
West Virginia	9,160	12,751	11,897	8,965
Kentucky	16,252	22,624	21,011	14,446
Tennessee	19,826	27,598	25,704	18,223
North Carolina	25,529	35,538	32,561	24,238
South Carolina	13,204	18,381	18,570	12,004
Georgia	22,767	31,693	28,085	20,927
Florida	30,333	27,300	33,566	30,299
Alabama	17,957	24,997	25,105	16,324
Mississippi	11,881	16,539	19,342	13,174
Louisiana	18,396	25,608	23,234	20,398
Arkansas	9,981	13,894	14,124	8,973
Southwest	80,926	81,576	92,642	78,652
Oklahoma	12,550	17,470	14,565	12,409
Texas	54,897	49,407	62,319	50,459
New Mexico	5,218	7,264	6,441	6,049
Arizona	8,261	7,435	9,317	9,735
Rocky Mountain	24,048	25,920	25,714	26,802
Montana	3,584	3,226	3,906	4,046
Idaho	3,543	4,932	4,139	3,857
Wyoming	1,680	1,512	1,782	1,897
Colorado	10,094	9,085	10,020	11,294
Utah	5,147	7,165	5,867	5,708
Far West	124,106	111,696	104,727	145,454
Washington	15,215	13,694	13,223	15,966
Oregon	9,982	8,984	9,684	10,373
Nevada	2,318	2,086	1,985	2,362
California	96,591	86,932	79,835	116,753
Alaska	1,389	1,250	1,213	1,067
Hawaii	3,666	3,299	3,327	3,917

Table 9-B. **FURTHER ILLUSTRATIVE ALLOCATIONS OF $1 BILLION:**
GENERAL SUPPORT GRANT *(In thousands)*

		Factors determining allocations		
	Hill-Burton	*Adjusted gross income*	*Total internal revenue collections*	*Total individual income and employment taxes*
UNITED STATES	$1,000,000	$1,000,000	$1,000,000	$1,000,000
New England	46,211	64,833	57,942	64,106
Maine	6,814	4,320	2,458	2,963
New Hampshire	3,784	3,378	2,215	2,735
Vermont	2,749	1,749	1,084	1,302
Massachusetts	20,705	31,679	27,973	30,822
Rhode Island	4,222	4,797	4,490	4,949
Connecticut	7,937	18,910	19,722	21,335
Mideast	154,858	251,995	308,083	293,543
New York	57,010	117,010	176,785	156,025
New Jersey	22,350	42,252	35,167	36,197
Pennsylvania	57,468	62,031	62,730	65,788
Delaware	1,527	3,315	9,063	6,545
Maryland	14,723	22,495	24,338 [a]	28,988 [a]
District of Columbia	1,780	4,892		
Great Lakes	163,870	215,883	262,710	244,449
Michigan	35,447	47,791	76,843	54,078
Ohio	48,489	55,816	65,275	67,467
Indiana	23,523	25,025	22,623	24,650
Illinois	34,998	66,264	79,584	79,714
Wisconsin	21,413	20,987	18,385	18,540
Plains	88,071	73,910	61,877	67,902
Minnesota	19,125	17,188	16,167	17,533
Iowa	15,084	12,827	7,810	9,165
Missouri	24,109	21,872	24,047	24,636
North Dakota	4,592	2,487	1,083	1,464
South Dakota	5,107	2,442	1,197	1,513
Nebraska	8,154	6,722	5,409	6,186
Kansas	11,900	10,372	6,164	7,405
Southeast	329,356	156,423	124,240	118,582
Virginia	28,472	19,609	15,383	14,532
West Virginia	14,283	7,008	3,374	4,130
Kentucky	24,990	11,385	15,442	7,741
Tennessee	31,139	14,300	9,162	10,751
North Carolina	39,306	17,821	23,446	14,431
South Carolina	23,077	8,185	4,991	5,691
Georgia	33,077	17,073	13,493	14,715
Florida	36,896	25,288	17,078	20,290
Alabama	29,942	11,792	6,732	8,135
Mississippi	23,184	5,710	3,036	3,783
Louisiana	27,840	12,430	8,956	10,527
Arkansas	17,150	5,822	3,147	3,856
Southwest	103,951	65,166	52,605	54,604
Oklahoma	16,917	10,199	9,122	8,255
Texas	69,887	44,037	38,021	39,069
New Mexico	7,120	3,910	2,022	2,626
Arizona	10,027	7,020	3,440	4,654
Rocky Mountain	26,783	22,089	18,182	22,856
Montana	4,254	2,942	1,496	1,857
Idaho	4,590	2,783	2,009	2,398
Wyoming	1,790	1,616	741	949
Colorado	9,869	9,982	11,478	14,672
Utah	6,280	4,766	2,458	2,980
Far West	82,880	144,682	111,168	129,968
Washington	13,071	16,322	12,725	15,090
Oregon	9,557	10,423	6,852	8,416
Nevada	1,240	2,766	1,836	2,222
California	59,012	115,171	89,755	104,240
Alaska	920	1,299	669	930
Hawaii	3,097	3,721	2,525	3,056

[a] Maryland and District of Columbia shown together.

Table 9-C. **ILLUSTRATIVE ALLOCATIONS OF $1 BILLION BY POPULATION AND INCREMENTAL TAX EFFORT, AND BY POPULATION AND CAPACITY REQUIREMENTS** *(In thousands)*

	Population and incremental tax effort	Population and capacity requirements
UNITED STATES	$1,000,000	$1,000,000
New England	45,901	57,304
Maine	5,688	5,713
New Hampshire	1,888	3,144
Vermont	2,438	2,369
Massachusetts	14,915	27,690
Rhode Island	5,881	4,425
Connecticut	15,091	13,963
Mideast	268,896	213,846
New York	145,037	107,665
New Jersey	38,535	29,419
Pennsylvania	55,992	53,294
Delaware	7,556	2,222
Maryland	18,994	17,577
District of Columbia	2,782	3,669
Great Lakes	211,756	188,280
Michigan	47,233	47,535
Ohio	50,352	45,431
Indiana	41,269	22,676
Illinois	41,207	47,841
Wisconsin	31,695	24,797
Plains	69,154	78,933
Minnesota	20,941	20,862
Iowa	7,573	14,720
Missouri	26,911	18,678
North Dakota	220	3,783
South Dakota	1,159	3,539
Nebraska	2,961	6,165
Kansas	9,389	11,186
Southeast	116,810	214,650
Virginia	3,119	20,355
West Virginia	12,986	9,098
Kentucky	13,161	18,877
Tennessee	9,368	18,765
North Carolina	19,025	23,287
South Carolina	1,788	11,166
Georgia	9,303	21,094
Florida	18,557	29,764
Alabama	17,044	16,392
Mississippi	1,616	14,684
Louisiana	8,814	22,901
Arkansas	2,029	8,267
Southwest	73,965	74,147
Oklahoma	4,292	11,911
Texas	48,595	48,254
New Mexico	7,590	4,309
Arizona	13,488	9,673
Rocky Mountain	23,743	24,196
Montana	3,374	3,480
Idaho	3,845	3,370
Wyoming	1,733	1,594
Colorado	9,509	10,277
Utah	5,282	5,475
Far West	184,412	143,000
Washington	16,986	17,242
Oregon	1,376	10,879
Nevada	1,376	2,417
California	164,674	112,462
Alaska	2,057	987
Hawaii	3,305	4,657

Table 9-D. **ALLOCATIONS OF $1 BILLION UNDER 3 ILLUSTRATIVE PASS THROUGH PLANS** *(In thousands)*

	Total amount to each state	Amount retained by state government		
		Plan 1	Plan 3	Plan 4
UNITED STATES	$1,000,000	$642,225	$757,901	$584,047
New England	56,428	36,247	40,287	29,699
Maine	5,332	4,932	4,996	4,611
New Hampshire	3,082	2,635	2,740	2,695
Vermont	2,506	2,506	2,506	2,506
Massachusetts	28,189	15,476	17,872	11,622
Rhode Island	4,424	2,239	2,721	2,092
Connecticut	12,895	8,459	9,452	6,173
Mideast	215,642	120,443	141,285	97,179
New York	109,613	45,270	58,095	40,370
New Jersey	30,131	21,815	23,321	14,372
Pennsylvania	53,533	36,563	41,809	28,148
Delaware	2,374	1,864	2,027	1,419
Maryland	16,700	11,640	12,742	9,579
District of Columbia	3,291	3,291	3,291	3,291
Great Lakes	182,796	112,913	138,489	105,762
Michigan	42,788	25,758	32,134	23,341
Ohio	43,810	27,294	33,471	24,087
Indiana	23,830	16,657	19,350	16,028
Illinois	46,943	25,584	33,423	24,969
Wisconsin	25,425	17,620	20,111	17,337
Plains	84,045	62,038	69,723	62,748
Minnesota	21,505	15,505	17,527	14,374
Iowa	15,446	11,739	13,160	12,119
Missouri	20,058	13,018	15,164	14,247
North Dakota	3,797	3,797	3,797	3,557
South Dakota	4,174	3,777	3,928	3,828
Nebraska	6,700	4,656	5,427	5,148
Kansas	12,365	9,546	10,720	9,475
Southeast	207,351	162,503	178,387	149,677
Virginia	18,932	13,745	14,729	11,556
West Virginia	9,013	7,931	8,346	7,773
Kentucky	14,486	12,038	14,240	11,379
Tennessee	18,224	13,577	14,962	11,849
North Carolina	24,380	20,480	21,844	19,129
South Carolina	12,071	10,900	11,335	9,843
Georgia	20,768	15,763	17,570	15,021
Florida	30,537	22,139	24,918	17,577
Alabama	16,328	11,968	13,520	11,354
Mississippi	12,883	12,033	12,033	12,092
Louisiana	20,515	13,848	16,330	14,049
Arkansas	9,214	8,081	8,560	8,055
Southwest	78,337	45,797	58,578	51,979
Oklahoma	12,485	9,014	10,550	9,735
Texas	50,133	27,222	35,895	31,684
New Mexico	5,923	4,673	5,129	4,911
Arizona	9,796	4,888	7,004	5,649
Rocky Mountain	27,177	20,561	23,131	18,979
Montana	4,068	3,417	3,694	3,456
Idaho	3,939	3,939	3,939	3,592
Wyoming	1,935	1,935	1,935	1,935
Colorado	11,507	7,215	8,849	6,753
Utah	5,728	4,055	4,714	3,243
Far West	143,022	79,743	104,825	64,829
Washington	16,074	11,075	13,116	10,173
Oregon	10,347	7,864	8,816	6,788
Nevada	2,352	1,395	1,776	1,254
California	114,249	59,409	81,117	46,614
Alaska	1,123	1,123	1,123	1,123
Hawaii	4,081	857	2,073	2,072

Table 9-E **ALLOCATIONS OF $1 BILLION UNDER THREE ILLUSTRATIVE 50-50 SPLIT PLANS** *(In thousands)*

	Total amount to each state			Amount retained by
	Plan 2	*Plan 2A*	*Plan 2C*	*state government*
UNITED STATES	$1,000,000	$1,000,000	$1,000,000	$500,000
New England	39,279	48,677	50,761	28,213
Maine	2,666	2,666	2,905	2,666
New Hampshire	1,541	1,541	1,946	1,541
Vermont	1,253	1,253	1,253	1,253
Massachusetts	22,622	26,731	28,628	14,094
Rhode Island	4,750	4,279	4,580	2,212
Connecticut	6,447	12,207	11,449	6,447
Mideast	267,767	251,689	254,876	107,821
New York	163,047	148,182	151,132	54,806
New Jersey	23,400	26,663	25,378	15,066
Pennsylvania	58,652	56,307	57,291	26,767
Delaware	1,187	1,187	1,672	1,187
Maryland	19,836	17,705	17,758	8,350
District of Columbia	1,645	1,645	1,645	1,645
Great Lakes	203,422	202,140	204,396	91,399
Michigan	41,822	43,952	45,371	21,394
Ohio	55,182	51,802	51,153	21,905
Indiana	17,740	23,891	21,977	11,915
Illinois	66,898	61,134	64,049	23,472
Wisconsin	21,780	21,361	21,846	12,713
Plains	76,113	74,540	73,485	42,023
Minnesota	20,492	19,750	18,727	10,752
Iowa	10,279	9,805	11,037	7,723
Missouri	25,019	22,239	22,883	10,029
North Dakota	1,899	1,899	1,899	1,899
South Dakota	2,087	2,087	2,251	2,087
Nebraska	7,039	7,635	6,843	3,350
Kansas	9,298	11,125	9,845	6,183
Southeast	153,099	164,084	160,261	103,674
Virginia	15,885	16,971	16,720	9,466
West Virginia	4,506	4,506	5,277	4,506
Kentucky	12,021	11,135	11,093	7,243
Tennessee	15,197	18,180	16,628	9,112
North Carolina	14,655	16,497	16,177	12,190
South Carolina	6,035	6,035	6,877	6,035
Georgia	16,346	17,891	17,260	10,384
Florida	24,659	24,724	24,410	15,269
Alabama	14,814	14,919	14,216	8,164
Mississippi	6,441	7,880	7,440	6,441
Louisiana	17,933	19,665	18,828	10,257
Arkansas	4,607	5,681	5,335	4,607
Southwest	91,493	90,173	87,061	39,169
Oklahoma	13,409	12,080	11,509	6,243
Texas	59,787	61,733	60,250	25,066
New Mexico	5,423	4,966	4,562	2,962
Arizona	12,874	11,394	10,740	4,898
Rocky Mountain	19,629	20,395	20,711	13,588
Montana	2,034	2,034	2,121	2,034
Idaho	1,970	1,970	1,970	1,970
Wyoming	967	967	967	967
Colorado	11,794	10,673	11,100	5,763
Utah	2,864	4,751	4,553	2,864
Far West	140,473	140,713	141,079	71,510
Washington	14,851	16,871	15,833	8,037
Oregon	9,731	8,887	8,598	5,173
Nevada	1,176	1,176	1,344	1,176
California	114,715	113,779	115,304	57,124
Alaska	562	562	562	562
Hawaii	8,161	7,025	6,806	2,040

Table 9-F. **ILLUSTRATIVE ALLOCATION TO SELECTED CITIES UNDER PLAN 2B: 1968 AMOUNT ASSUMING $5 BILLION TOTAL GRANT**

(In thousands)

TOTAL (all cities with populations 50,000 and over)	$2,500,000
New York	307,400
Chicago	140,200
Los Angeles	97,900
Philadelphia	79,100
Detroit	66,000
Baltimore	37,100
Houston	37,000
Cleveland	34,600
Washington, D. C.	30,100
St. Louis	29,600
San Francisco	29,300
Milwaukee	29,300
Boston	27,500
Dallas	26,900
New Orleans	24,800
Pittsburgh	23,900
San Antonio	23,200
San Diego	22,600
Seattle	22,000
Buffalo	21,000
Cincinnati	19,900
Honolulu	19,800
Memphis	19,600
Denver	19,500
Atlanta	19,200
Minneapolis	19,100
Indianapolis	18,900
Kansas City, Missouri	18,800
Columbus	18,600
Phoenix	17,400
Newark	16,000

CHAPTER 9, ADDENDUM B

Illustrative allocations of general support grant: amounts and derivation

---

TABLE 9-A. ILLUSTRATIVE ALLOCATIONS OF $1 BILLION UNDER VARIOUS ALLOTMENT FORMULAS:

Column 1. Based on the state's relative share of population resident in the fifty states as estimated for July 1, 1966. Source: *Current Population Reports,* Series P-25, No. 354.

Column 2. Ninety percent allocated by the state's relative share of population resident in the fifty states as estimated for July 1, 1966; 10 percent allocated among the seventeen states with lowest per capita personal income for 1966, based on relative share of population resident in those seventeen states. Sources: *Current Population Reports,* Series P-25, No. 354; *Survey of Current Business,* April 1967.

Column 3. Based on the state's relative share of 1966 population divided by 1966 personal income per capita for the state relative to the national average personal income per capita. Sources: *Current Population Reports,* Series P-25, No. 354; *Survey of Current Business,* April 1967.

Column 4. Based on the state's relative share of 1966 population multiplied by an index of 1964-65 tax effort for the state relative to the national average tax effort. The ratio of state and local tax revenues to personal income received in the state is used to measure tax effort; an average of calendar year personal income is used for fiscal year. Sources: *Current Population Reports,* Series P-25, No. 354; *Survey of Current Business,* April 1967; *Governmental Finances in 1964-65.*

TABLE 9-B. FURTHER ILLUSTRATIVE ALLOCATIONS OF $1 BILLION:

Column 1. Based on the Hill-Burton formula as effective July 1, 1967 through June 30, 1969: the state's relative share of 1966 population multiplied by the quantity (100 percent minus one-half of the percent which personal income per capita for the state, average 1963-65, constitutes of personal income per capita, average 1963-65, for the nation) squared. Sources: *Current Population Reports,* Series P-25, No. 348; *Survey of Current Business,* August 1966.

Column 2. Based on the state's relative share of adjusted gross income reported on federal individual income tax returns for 1964. Source: *Statistics of Income 1964, Individual Income Tax Returns.*

Column 3. Based on the state's relative share of total federal internal revenue collections in 1966. Source: *Treasury Bulletin,* May 1967.

Column 4. Based on the state's relative share of federal individual income and employment tax collections in 1966. Source: *Treasury Bulletin,* May 1967.

TABLE 9-C. ILLUSTRATIVE ALLOCATIONS OF $1 BILLION BY POPULATION AND INCREMENTAL TAX EFFORT, AND BY POPULATION AND CAPACITY REQUIREMENTS:

Column 1. Based on the state's relative share of 1967 population multiplied by an index of incremental tax effort from 1957 to 1964-66. The ratio of state and local tax revenues in fiscal 1957 to personal income received in the state in fiscal 1957 is used to measure 1957 tax effort; an average of calendar year personal income is used for fiscal year. State and local tax revenue relative to personal income over the three fiscal years 1964-66 is used to measure 1964-66 tax effort. For the one state where the index of incremental tax effort for this interval is negative, a value of 0.1 was substituted; this is one-half of the incremental tax effort in the state with the next smallest tax effort change. Sources: *Current Population Reports,* Series P-25, No. 384; *Census of Governments, 1957; Governmental Finances in 1965-66; Governmental Finances in 1964-65; Governmental Finances in 1963-64; Survey of Current Business,* April 1967.

Column 2. Based on the state's relative share of population resident in the fifty states as estimated for July 1, 1967, multiplied by an index of capacity requirements in 1962. The capacity requirements index as defined in Chapter 5 is computed as the ratio of state and local general expenditures less federal grants-in-aid and fees and charges to aggregate personal income in the state. Sources: *Current Population Reports,* Series P-25, No. 384; *Census of Governments, 1962; Survey of Current Business,* April 1968.

TABLE 9-D. ALLOCATIONS OF $1 BILLION UNDER THREE ILLUSTRATIVE PASS THROUGH PLANS:

Column 1. The amount allocated to each state including funds earmarked for pass through to local governments, based on the state's relative share of 1966 population multiplied by an index of tax effort over the three fiscal years 1964-66 for the state relative to the national average tax effort. State and local tax revenue relative to personal income received in the state for the three fiscal years 1964-66 is used to measure tax effort. Sources: *Current Population Reports,* Series P-25, No. 354; *Governmental Finances in 1965-66; Governmental Finances in 1964-65; Governmental Finances in 1963-64; Survey of Current Business,* April 1967.

Column 2. Amount retained by the state government after a required pass through to each city which had in 1960 a population of 50,000 or more persons, of that proportion of the grant to the state which the 1960 population of the city constitutes of the 1960 population of the state. Source: *1960 Census of Population.*

Column 3. Amount retained by the state government after a required pass through to each city which had in 1960 a population of 50,000 or more persons, of that proportion of the grant to the state which is constituted by the average of (1) the percent of the population of the state in 1960 which resided in the city in 1960, and (2) the percent of the tax collections by the state and localities in the state in fiscal 1962 which were collected by the municipality in fiscal 1962. Sources: *1960 Census of Population; Census of Governments, 1962.*

Column 4. The amount retained by the state government after a required pass through to each municipality, county government or township government which had in 1960 a population of 50,000 or more persons and is in a Standard Metropolitan Statistical Area, certified as of May 1, 1967. Each eligible local government receives that proportion of the grant to the state which is constituted by the average of (1) the percent of the population of the state in 1960 which resided in the eligible cities, counties and townships in 1960 and (2) the percent of the tax collections by the state and localities in the state in fiscal 1962 which were collected by the eligible local government in fiscal 1962. Where eligible governments overlap geographically, persons residing in both jurisdictions are counted once: the population for percent (1) above for municipalities (or townships) is the city (or town) population, and the population for the county is the outside-city population. Sources: *1960 Census of Population; Census of Governments, 1962;* Bureau of the Budget, *Standard Metropolitan Statistical Areas.*

TABLE 9-E. ALLOCATIONS OF $1 BILLION UNDER THREE ILLUSTRATIVE 50-50 SPLIT PLANS:

Column 1. The amount allocated to each state composed of funds going directly to the state government without required pass through, and funds going directly to cities which had in 1960 a population of 200,000 or more persons. The state amount is based on the state's relative share of 1966 population multiplied by an index of tax effort over the three fiscal years 1964-66 for the state relative to the national average tax effort. (State and local tax revenue relative to personal income received in the state for the three fiscal years 1964-66 is used to measure tax effort.) The allocation to each eligible city is based on the city's relative share of 1960 population in cities of 200,000 or over. Sources: *1960 Census of Population; Current Population Reports,* Series P-25, No. 354; *Governmental Finances in 1965-66; Governmental Finances in 1964-65; Governmental Finances in 1963-64; Survey of Current Business,* April 1967.

Column 2. The amount allocated to each state composed of funds going directly to the state government without required pass through and funds going directly to cities which had in 1960 a population of 100,000 or more persons. The state amount is based on the state's relative share of 1966 population multiplied by an index of tax effort over the three fiscal years 1964-66 for the state relative to the national average tax effort. (State and local tax revenue relative to personal income received in the state for the three fiscal years 1964-66 is used to measure tax effort.) The allocation to each eligible city is based on the city's relative share of 1960 population in cities of 100,000 or over. Sources: *1960 Census of Population; Current Population Reports,* Series P-25, No. 354; *Governmental Finances in 1965-66; Governmental Finances in 1964-65; Governmental Finances in 1963-64; Survey of Current Business,* April 1967.

Column 3. The amount allocated to each state composed of funds going directly to the state government without required pass through and funds going directly to cities which had in 1960 a population of 50,000 or more persons. The state amount is based on the state's relative share of 1966 population multiplied by an index of tax effort over the three fiscal years 1964-66 for the state relative to the national average tax effort. (State and local tax revenue relative to personal income received in the state for the three fiscal years 1964-66 is used to measure tax effort.) The allocation to each eligible city is based on the number of persons in excess of 50,000 resident there in 1960, relative to the 1960 national total of residents of cities in excess of 50,000 per city. Sources: *1960 Census of Population; Current Population Reports,* Series P-25, No. 354; *Governmental Finances in 1965-66; Governmental Finances in 1964-65; Governmental Finances in 1963-64; Survey of Current Business,* April 1967.

Column 4. The amount allocated directly to each state without required pass through to local governments, based on the state's relative share of 1966 population multiplied by an index of tax effort over the three fiscal years 1964-66 for the state relative to the national average tax effort. (State and local tax revenue relative to personal income received in the state for the three fiscal years 1964-66 is used to measure tax effort.) Sources: *Current Population Reports,* Series P-25, No. 354; *Governmental Finances in 1965-66; Governmental Finances in 1964-65; Governmental Finances in 1963-64; Survey of Current Business,* April 1967.

TABLE 9-F. ILLUSTRATIVE ALLOCATION TO CITIES UNDER PLAN 2B: 1968 AMOUNT ASSUMING $5 BILLION TOTAL GRANT:

Column 1. Amount going directly to each of the 31 largest cities, without passing through the state government. The allocation to each eligible city is based on the city's relative share of 1960 population in cities of 50,000 or over. Source: *1960 Census of Population.*

CHAPTER 10

Strengthening state and local taxes

THIS REPORT HAS MAINLY FOCUSED on federal grants as a source of funding for state and local services within our federal structure. In the present chapter we review possible federal actions concerning state and local taxes to strengthen the financing of the public sector at a decentralized level. National goals with respect to state and local taxation are identified, and federal approaches to some of them are described. The more comprehensive proposals with respect to state and local government revenues, involving tax credits, are then discussed.

A NATIONAL VIEW OF STATE AND LOCAL TAXATION

When a market analogy for the public sector is applied to taxation at state and local levels, problems of national concern become evident. There is a strong resemblance between these questions on taxation, and questions related to spending by the state and local governments in our federal system. Direct and indirect effects of taxation may spill over jurisdictional lines; there are, for example, national goals relating to the equity and incidence of taxation on which action may be necessary, and there is a national interest, as well as a state and local interest, in increasing the efficiency of use of resources and in assuring the preferred balance between public and private goods.

Among the national goals that the proposals for national action are aimed at serving are:

1. Greater efficiency in net yield of revenues per dollar spent for tax administration and compliance.
2. Greater neutrality of the impact of taxation on locational decisions of persons and business firms.
3. Improved ability of governments to respond to public demands.
4. Greater compatibility of tax practices with principles of fairness in taxation.
5. Implementation of the objectives of stable economic growth as originally set forth in the Employment Act of 1946.

Over the years, views on the appropriate national action to influence state and local tax policy have differed sharply. The positions taken by two earlier study groups (1943 and 1955) on intergovernmental fiscal relations illustrate differences that have persisted.

In 1943 the Groves Committee on Federal, State, and Local Government

Fiscal Relations called attention to the responsibility of the nation in state and local taxation:

If the economic system is beset by multiple tax burdens, compliance and administrative costs, and by upsetting differentials, it is the duty of the Federal Government to remove these obstacles to economic activity and progress. It is not an impairment of State rights to create conditions under which the States will find it advantageous to cooperate and to enact and enforce desirable measures, which in the absence of such conditions do not appeal to the self-interest of the individual states.[1]

In 1955, the Kestnbaum Commission report took an opposing position:

The independent taxing powers of the States are basic in sustaining their freedom of action and governmental strength. Overlapping reflects in part the exercise of initiative and autonomy by governmental units with differing tax bases, natural resources, and political preferences.[2]

The Commission found, however, that certain federal actions directed at increased efficiency and neutrality of state and local tax systems were beneficial to the states and in keeping with their basic independence. Among these, federal-state cooperation on administrative aspects of taxation was especially emphasized.[3]

ADMINISTRATIVE COOPERATION TO IMPROVE STATE AND LOCAL TAXES

In 1961, the Advisory Commission on Intergovernmental Relations in commenting on cooperation in tax administration noted:

The Federal and State Governments have a more specific interest in the quality of each other's tax administration as well. Just as taxpayers' respect for Federal tax administration has complementary benefits for State administrations, so improved State tax enforcement eases the Federal enforcement task. The temptation to take liberties with tax laws increases with the size of the prospective "steal." Each discouragement to underreporting Federal tax liability increases the odds against underreporting to the State, and vice versa. Tight administration at one level inevitably rubs off to the benefit of the other.[4]

Extended use of the same or similar tax bases by nation, state, and city has heightened concern about methods of cooperation in keeping with economic and fiscal realities. Such administrative cooperation has addressed itself to the limited purpose of raising relative yields per dollar spent on tax collection.

Cooperation in tax enforcement developed first for alcoholic beverage taxes with principal emphasis on regulation and criminal law enforcement rather than on voluntary compliance on civil taxation. The first major effort toward cooperative administration of taxes grew out of a 1949 White House Conference, during which a pilot exchange of income tax audit information between the federal Internal Revenue Service and a selected group of states was planned. Wisconsin and North Carolina were initial participants in this demonstration; subsequently agreements on audit exchanges were made with Colorado, Kentucky, and Montana.

The Kestnbaum Commission, reviewing the pilot demonstration of audit ex-

---

[1] *Federal, State, and Local Government Fiscal Relations,* Report of the U.S. Treasury Committee on Intergovernmental Fiscal Relations, Senate Document No. 69 (1943), p. 449, as cited in James A. Maxwell, *Tax Credits and Intergovernmental Fiscal Relations* (The Brookings Institution, 1962), p. 126.

[2] Commission on Intergovernmental Relations, *A Report to the President for Transmittal to Congress* (Government Printing Office, June 1955), pp. 104, 106.

[3] *Ibid.,* pp. 106-107.

[4] Advisory Commission on Intergovernmental Relations, *Intergovernmental Cooperation in Tax Administration* (June 1961), pp. 1-2.

changes, had strongly urged extension and intensification of such efforts. Evaluation of the ongoing program by the Internal Revenue Service led to the development of a broader program of national-state cooperation. Three basic criteria were formulated by the IRS as a consequence of this assessment:

1. Each agreement with a state should fully reflect the legal and administrative facts in the contracting state.
2. Agreements should encompass all categories of taxation and not be restricted to the income tax.
3. The scope of cooperative activities should seek to attain an optimum balance between tax yields and other revenue benefits and costs of administration.

The first of the agreements using these criteria as guidelines was concluded with Minnesota in 1957. Provision was made for exchange of all information relevant to the administration of all taxes (except those on alcohol and tobacco). Since 1957, given the Minnesota experience as a backdrop and with the active support and encouragement of the National Association of Tax Administrators, agreements for cooperation on all taxes between nation and state have been worked out with a total of forty-three states, plus the District of Columbia.

The Letters of Agreement cover a wide scope "in the interest of extending mutual benefits to be derived from coordination of tax administration" by state and nation. All agreements are "open-ended" so that cooperative exchange programs may be adjusted to new tax developments. The specifics covered may be illustrated by the provisions of the agreement between the Commissioner of Internal Revenue and the Governor of the State of Alaska. Cooperation on income taxes includes provisions for exchange of audit information, avoidance of duplicate audit of returns by the state and Internal Revenue, and exchange of information on nonfilers, on location of delinquent accounts, and on large refunds. Information will also be exchanged on inheritance and estate taxes, gasoline, special motor fuel, and highway use taxes, and various excise, licensing, and occupation taxes. Data comparisons, using electronic equipment, of federal and state tax returns are to be explored. Other specific exchanges enumerated in the agreement include information on corporation filing in Alaska, on corporate formations and dissolutions, and on employer returns of withholding and liability under federal unemployment tax laws.

The cooperative program is by its design a step toward harmonization by minimizing duplication of effort at both state and federal levels. The intent is to reduce the cost of tax administration and to shore up the self-assessment system by greater efficiency in enforcement.

COMPLIANCE PROBLEMS

The multiplicity of taxing jurisdictions has compounded the confusions and costs to individuals and businesses in complying with differing tax laws. Particularly in the field of income taxation, differences in definitions of excluded income items, deductions, and exemptions and of income sources add greatly to the costs of tax compliance, unnecessarily irritate taxpayers, and inhibit the effective use of cooperative administrative arrangements in the enforcement of those taxes. Because payroll and income taxes have constituted the main areas of concern on uniformity of definition, a coordination of tax bases at the national government level has been worked through for income and payroll tax compliance. Divergencies still exist, however, between the payroll tax bases for unemployment compensation and those for federal social insurance contribution purposes.

Increasingly, states have moved toward greater uniformity with the national definition of income for personal income taxes, although varying in the extent to which they have tied their bases to the national statute. Some use the standard deduction and personal exemption as specified under federal law, and a few determine the state tax as a percent of the computed federal tax liability. The income tax states that presently do not accord with the federal definition of "adjusted gross income" have, however, moved toward making other specific statutory provisions similar to or identical with the federal law. Greater uniformity in definition of tax bases has as its main purpose easing the problems of compliance.

The business of many firms and industries is nationwide through branches and production plants in a number of states. Stockholders are located throughout the nation. The preference of many taxpayers is for nationwide uniformity of tax rules, as exemplified by national tax laws. In 1966, hearings of the so-called Willis Subcommittee of the House Judiciary Committee, in considering H.R. 11798, emphasized the tax compliance problems facing industrial, retail, and service industry firms that do business in many states and communities.[5] Compliance costs are high in a number of instances. Irritants and uncertainties in business operations are increased, hampering rather than encouraging industrial operations. If compliance costs were reduced, net revenues of states and localities could be increased at no additional cost to these taxpayers. Possibilities have been recognized at both federal and state levels for easing compliance and administrative problems.

The federal action on compliance problems was precipitated by United States Supreme Court decisions in 1959 and 1960, which affirmed the jurisdiction of a state or local government to tax a business engaged only in sales activities within such state or locality, even though it had no physical property or full-time employees in the jurisdiction. Criticism by various state officials of the proposed H.R. 11798 before the Willis Subcommittee led to other bills (H.R. 16491 and, in the 90th Congress, H.R. 2158), which eliminated some of the offending provisions. The latest bill, H.R. 2158, was passed by the House on May 22, 1968. It is intended to relieve businesses that can qualify under it of the burdens of overlapping or nonuniform taxation.

The states' own answer to this set of problems was the development of a Multistate Tax Compact. In essence, the compact (1) provides that a taxpayer may elect to report his income under the state or local law or under the Uniform Division of Income for Tax Purposes Act, which is a part of the compact; (2) permits a small taxpayer to pay an optional tax on gross sales in lieu of net income; (3) grants credit under state and local law or under the Uniform Division of Income for Tax Purposes Act; (4) grants credit for state and local sales taxes paid to other jurisdictions; (5) relieves vendors from collection of sales or use taxes, upon good-faith acceptance of an exemption certificate. A Multistate Tax Commission was established to study and recommend solutions to problems as they arise and to propose to the states the adoption of uniform rules, regulations, and forms. To settle multistate apportionment and allocation disputes, an arbitration proceeding was made available to the taxpayer. If the states so choose, a program of cooperative auditing may be undertaken.

Development of the compact was completed in December 1966. By the summer of 1968, fourteen states had adopted the compact, eleven of them during 1967 legislative sessions. The Multistate Tax Commission held its organiza-

---

[5] Subcommittee on State Taxation of Interstate Commerce, House Committee on the Judiciary, *Hearings on H.R. 11798* (January-April, 1966).

tion meeting in June 1967, and three subsequent meetings have been held. Hearings were scheduled by the Commission for September 1968, to consider recommendations for regulations and laws relating to business taxation.

FAIRNESS IN THE TAX SYSTEM

Presently, state and local governments make relatively heavy use of property and sales taxes and relatively light use of personal income taxes. The distribution of tax burdens under the federal tax system with its heavy reliance on income taxes is generally considered fairer than the distribution of the systems of states and communities. While the federal tax structure is progressive across the income distribution, the state and local structure is regressive in its impacts. And even when the present grants to states and localities from federal revenue sources are included, the incidence of the funding of state and community expenditures is still regressive (as Table 10-1 indicates).

Table 10-1. **FEDERAL, STATE, AND LOCAL TAXES AS A PERCENTAGE OF INCOME, 1965**

| Money income class (after taxes) | Federal | State and local | |
		Own revenues	Including 1967 federal aids
ALL FAMILIES	16.1%	9.6%	11.5%
Under $2,000	9.8	13.6	14.8
$2,000–2,999	10.6	11.3	12.7
$3,000–3,999	13.3	11.2	13.0
$4,000–4,999	13.2	10.4	12.1
$5,000–5,999	13.9	10.2	12.0
$6,000–7,499	14.0	9.5	11.3
$7,500–9,999	14.9	8.9	10.7
$10,000–14,999	17.8	8.5	10.5
$15,000–Over	33.2	8.4	11.6

SOURCE: Columns 1 and 2 from Tax Foundation, Inc., *Tax Burdens and Benefits of Government Expenditures by Income Class, 1961 and 1965.* (Percentages as shown in Tax Foundation Report are of total income, including value of income in kind.) Column 3 was computed from Columns 1 and 2 on the basis of the percentage of federal revenues required for federal aid to states and communities; no adjustment was made in total amount of federal taxes and in amount of money income after taxes.

States and localities make less use of the personal income tax than of sales and property taxes for a number of reasons—among them, that (1) the federal government makes heavy use of the personal income tax; [6] (2) the redistributive effects of progressive state personal income taxes can be escaped by moving to other states; and (3) the burden of the personal income tax may be more clearly felt than the burden of some other taxes.

It is possible through national action to maintain or increase the relative importance of personal income taxation in the overall nationwide tax structure even while state and local expenditures are enlarged. The action should lead to either (1) greater relative use of the national government tax system without causing offsetting reductions in the relative use of personal income taxation by states and localities, or (2) reduction of the restraints on state and local

---

[6] "Heavy federal use of the personal income tax, especially since 1940, has been the single most important deterrent to its expanded use by the States"; see Advisory Commission on Intergovernmental Relations, *Federal-State Coordination of Personal Income Taxes* (October 1965), p. 111.

use of the personal income taxes. The first of these could be achieved through the general support grant discussed in Chapter 9, the second through a tax credit that would reduce the restraints on state and local use of personal income taxes.

TAXES AND EXPENDITURES

The national interest is served by augmenting state and local tax funds so that these governments may enlarge public services and make viable our decentralized federal system. But a variety of forces are at work that tend to restrain states and localities from expanding taxes and expenditures. For example, not all taxpayers have the same preferences for public services. Essentially, group preferences are substituted for individual preferences, and this group decision making is achieved generally through a consensus that itself is likely to create a barrier against public action. Unless there is general agreement on new taxing and spending, the status quo is likely to be maintained. Especially when the groups paying the taxes are those not directly benefiting from the services, taxpayer opposition stands in the way of local financing.

The bias of consensus against action is strengthened by business opposition to taxes paid initially by firms, without corresponding direct benefits and with possible competitive disadvantage to them. A number of studies have been made of the effect of state taxation on industrial location; the findings are far from conclusive. Nevertheless, the issue of constraint is definitely present, as evidenced by the familiar comparisons of tax loads in one state with those in others, for all taxes or selected types of taxes that are levied on industry. The facts about taxation policies suggest that tax competition both within and between metropolitan areas plays a considerable part in taxing and spending decisions, leading toward considerable uniformity of effective rate patterns, despite differences in public services in different locations.

Certain offsetting factors tend to work in the direction of increased state and local taxes. Many of the taxes levied by states and localities fall, in part, as burdens outside the jurisdiction collecting the revenue. Tax exporting between localities is even more widespread than between states. A property tax levied on a public utility by one local government, for example, would be paid by the consumers of gas or electricity not only in that local jurisdiction but in the entire area served. McLure has estimated the percentage of state and local taxes, in general, and of property taxes in particular, that were exported across state boundaries in 1962.[7] Such spillover of taxes, or tax exporting, tends to encourage consumption of more public services than voters actually would be willing to pay for if they had to pay the entire cost themselves.

There is no reason for this countervailing distortion to be equal in magnitude to the forces which work to repress state and local taxing and spending in any jurisdiction. The fragmentation of government, such as exists in most metropolitan areas, serves to increase the volume of interjurisdictional flows of benefits and burdens so that the attainment of desired expenditure levels become even more unlikely. Most of the wealth and income of the United States is located in metropolitan areas. One obvious thrust, accordingly, has been to reduce the externalities both in expenditures and in taxation through areawide metropolitan financing.

In the period ahead, a marked shift in patterns of spending is required, with even more emphasis on services for the poor. Many public activities—such as

---

[7] Charles E. McLure, Jr., "The Interstate Exporting of State and Local Taxes: Estimates for 1962," *National Tax Journal,* Vol. 20 (March 1967), pp. 49-77.

producing jobs and giving job assistance—that cities are asked to undertake are essentially new. The existing tendency of taxpayers to opt in favor of "no action" might be reinforced by the divergence between those who pay the taxes and those who would benefit from the public services within a metropolitan taxing area. Reassessment of metropolitan solutions to public service problems is clearly required.

Grants-in-aid have increased as a way to counteract these tax restraints and give the citizen-consumer the services he seeks. Through the financial stimulus of a grant from the national government, the scale is weighted in favor of action rather than inaction on public programs by the reduced price to local taxpayers. More comprehensive (or less restrictive) action on state and local revenue problems is proposed through general revenue sharing. Other approaches, however, that are similarly comprehensive may be taken.

TAX CREDITS AS A FISCAL DEVICE

An alternative way to facilitate the raising of additional state and local revenue (or to encourage states to impose income taxes or to expand their use of income taxes) is through a tax credit for state and local taxes. Persons filing federal income tax returns would deduct from their federal payment part or all of their state and local taxes.[8] Credits against the federal tax for state and local taxes paid have also been proposed as an alternative to tax sharing through unconditional grants-in-aid. And as the public discussion has continued, consideration has been given to the combining of a tax credit and an unconditional grant; the specifics of the combination are left undetermined and dependent upon fiscal and economic circumstances as they emerge.

The effect of such a credit on state and local government finances is to reduce the burden on state and local taxpayers of these taxes. The credit changes the conditions under which the cost of expenditures is shared. By incurring a reduction in its income tax receipts because of the credit, the federal government, and indirectly the taxpayers of the entire nation, share in the tax burden of each individual state or locality.

Tax credit arrangements have been used for some time to encourage use by the states of certain taxes. An offset of state death taxes against federal estate taxes was introduced in 1926, in response to Florida's action amending its constitution to prohibit inheritance taxation. Every state except Nevada presently imposes a tax at least equal to the maximum permissible federal offset of 80 percent of the federal tax at 1926 rates. Death taxes collected by the states in 1966-67 amounted to $795 million, or 2.1 percent of states' own revenue. In 1935, as part of the Social Security Act, a credit was adopted against the federal unemployment tax. Employers are allowed credit up to 90 percent of the federal unemployment tax on covered payrolls, for state unemployment contributions. Every state takes full advantage of this offset.

Such credits aim at increasing state and local access to particular taxes, or at increasing the incentive to states and localities to undertake certain expenditures, in parallel fashion to a grant-in-aid. The death tax credit had as its objective continued state use of that tax in the face of a threat of competitive reductions in its use; the unemployment tax credit's intention was the same as the counterpart grant program for unemployment compensation administration, namely, introduction and support of unemployment compensation in the states.

---

[8] This differs from the present deduction for nonfederal taxes in being a proportional reduction of the actual tax liability, rather than deduction from the income on which the income tax is computed.

The recent proposals for credits against federal income taxes for state and local taxes aim (1) at encouraging personal income taxation by state and local governments (giving states greater "freedom" to use that tax) or (2) at increasing the net (after federal tax) resources of persons from which the tax revenue of state and local governments must come. They look to the following benefits:

1. Facilitating a growth in state and local spending.
2. Increasing the fairness of the state and local tax structure.
3. Giving state and local taxes greater responsiveness to economic growth.

PROPOSED TAX CREDITS

Most of the various proposed credits allow federal income taxpayers to deduct the amount of certain state and local taxes paid from their gross federal income tax liability, to some limit. They can be termed full offset credits, since each eligible dollar of state and local taxes would reduce the federal tax payment by a full dollar. The variations on a full offset credit include:

1. A fixed dollar full offset credit, which would permit the taxpayer to deduct from his federal income tax, up to some limit such as $100, all of specified state and local taxes paid.[9]
2. A proportional full offset credit, which would permit a full offset for eligible state and local taxes paid up to some proportion, such as 20 percent, of gross federal income tax liability. If gross federal income tax liability were $500, up to $100 of eligible state and local taxes paid could be credited; if $1,000, up to $200 could be credited. Had eligible state and local tax payments been $400 in the latter case, the net burden of these taxes would be $200.
3. A proportional full offset credit with the maximum defined as a declining proportion of gross federal liability, as suggested by Walter Heller in 1959.[10] Heller's graduated credit would permit an offset for state income tax payments of up to 20 percent of the first $200 of federal liability, 10 percent of the next $300, and 1 percent of the remainder. For example, a person with gross federal income tax liability of $1,000 could offset up to $75 [20% x $200 + 10% x $300 + 1% x $500] for the payment of state income taxes.

Some of the proposals more recently advanced allow an offset of a portion of state and local taxes paid. These are referred to as partial offset credits, because each eligible dollar of state and local taxes reduces the federal tax liability by only part of a dollar. They include:

1. A partial offset credit, which would permit a specified percentage of eligible state and local taxes paid as an offset to gross federal liability.
2. A partial offset credit (using as an example a credit of 40 percent), proposed by the Advisory Commission on Intergovernmental Relations in 1965. This mechanism would permit taxpayers "a choice between continuing to itemize their State income tax payments *or* to claim instead a specified percentage of such payments as a credit against their Federal tax liability. The standard deduction provisions would not be modified." [11]
Some of the congressional bills containing this proposal permit the credit to be taken for *all* state and local taxes.
3. A partial offset credit, proposed by the staff of the Committee for Economic Development, which would permit taxpayers to credit a fixed percentage of

---

[9] Such a credit for state personal income taxes paid was proposed by Robert Nathan in an address before the Philadelphia Chapter, Americans for Democratic Action, May 9, 1957.

[10] See House Committee on Ways and Means, *Tax Revision Compendium*, Vol. I (1959), pp. 425-526.

[11] Advisory Commission on Intergovernmental Relations, *op. cit.*, p. 116.

the *net cost* of their state personal income taxes.[12] From total state income tax payment would be subtracted the tax benefit from itemizing state income taxes for federal tax purposes—or the benefit for state taxes implicit in the taking of the standard deduction—before the credit is computed. For example, if $100 of state income taxes is paid, the itemization of this amount has reduced the federal tax liability of a person in the 25 percent tax bracket by $25. Therefore, the state income tax payment of $100 actually cost this taxpayer $75, and the credit would be 25 percent of this net cost of $75, or $18.75.

Although most of the recent proposals are to offset only personal income taxes, a few are concerned with the whole range of state and local taxes. The strongest case for a tax credit can be made in terms of promoting equity and income-responsiveness in state and local tax structures, and such arguments point to limiting the credit to state and local income taxes.

Federal tax credits for other state and local taxes pose equity problems, but there are other reasons also for arguing that the credit should be limited to an offset against personal income taxes. Substantially all persons who pay state or local income taxes also incur a federal tax liability against which a credit can be taken, because state government tax regulations usually permit personal exemptions higher than those permitted by the federal government. Many consumers who pay sales taxes have no federal income tax liability against which to take a credit. An equitable federal credit covering sales taxes would probably need to involve a reimbursement of low-income persons, such as would be involved in a "negative" federal tax. An equitable federal credit against property taxes would not only face the same difficulties but also might be even more difficult to apply, because persons who rent, rather than own, homes do not directly pay property taxes, although rental charges reflect these costs to landlords.

FULL OFFSET VS. PARTIAL OFFSET CREDITS

The extent to which the burden is eased on individual taxpayers in a given jurisdiction from the tax policies of that jurisdiction, and the consequent extent of the effect of a credit on state and local taxation, depend on the proportion of the burden shared by the federal government. If an additional dollar of state and local taxation leads to no increase at all in the direct net burden of the taxpayer involved—that is, if it can be fully offset against federal tax liability— there is the maximum incentive for state-local governments to pick up this additional revenue. In the case of a $100 "full offset" credit for state income taxes paid, state governments would have a large incentive to place an income tax of $100 on every person whose gross federal income tax liability is great enough (at least $100) to permit him to take full advantage of the credit.

However, with full offset credits which have a limit of any form, once a state has imposed taxes that are high enough to "pick up" the credit, there is no further encouragement for increases in state and local taxes beyond the credit limit. If taxes "picking up" this credit *already* exist, the tax credit provides only tax relief, and no incentive to enlarge the public sector. A credit limited to state personal income taxes provides even less incentive to increase taxes. The state may give its taxpayers the benefits of the federal tax credit by changing its tax structure to put greater relative emphasis on the income tax, but even this incentive would exist only if the state income tax were not already high enough to permit the taxpayers to benefit from the maximum credit. If a tax credit were

---

[12] Committee for Economic Development, *A Fiscal Program for a Balanced Federalism* (June 1967), p. 68.

to provide for a full offset against federal income taxes with *no* ceiling, state and local governments would be able to increase their revenue until all direct federal tax liabilities were wiped out. Virtually no direct cost would accrue to the taxpayers of an individual jurisdiction as a result of the tax policies of that jurisdiction. Such proposals are not put forward and clearly would not meet national objectives.

In contrast, partial offset credits would provide a lesser incentive for states and localities to increase taxing and spending, but this is an incentive which would continue to operate with no cut-off. A partial offset credit is similar to a matching grant-in-aid, in that it reduces the price to the state or local government of a given program, in this case, taxation. A credit limited to 20 or 40 percent of state income tax payments would provide a lasting incentive for states to use income taxes effectively. For the taxpayer, $1 or $2 out of each $5 paid to the state would be offset against his federal income tax including $1 or $2 out of each $5 of existing state income taxes. The underlying bases for government fiscal decisions could be changed because the direct effects of taxation on the taxpayer would alter over a continuing range. A reasonably effective credit set, say, at 20 percent would leave the states free to choose to retain their present tax structures, but also to react by placing a somewhat greater, or perhaps much greater, relative emphasis on personal income taxation, and to place a much greater, or somewhat greater, or no greater, absolute tax load on their taxpayers.

Because partial credits are open-end, like open-end grants-in-aid, they have been criticized as resulting in a potential tax loss—with an unknown upper limit —to the federal government. Whereas the maximum federal tax loss from a credit with limited per capita value, or with its value limited to a proportion of federal liability, can be calculated, a credit based on state and local tax action depends on the level of state and local tax collections and makes the federal subsidy undetermined. Any changes in the structure of state and local taxation, including those made to give the taxpayers the maximum federal tax saving from the credit, would affect the subsidy.

The Advisory Commission, with regard to its proposal, has estimated that:

The present system of itemizing State income tax payments cost the Federal Government approximately $700 million in fiscal year 1964, as compared with a potential revenue cost of $1.2 billion for an optional 40 percent credit for the same year. . . .
On the very extreme assumption that a 40 percent credit would immediately encourage every state to enact an individual income tax with a yield equivalent to 3½ percent of the adjusted gross income reported on Federal income tax returns less personal exemptions (a most unlikely assumption), the additional cost in Federal revenue foregone would approximate $4.2 billion in fiscal year 1968.[13]

With regard to the CED proposal, the staff estimated that:

A 25 percent credit . . . would have decreased United States income tax revenue in 1965 by about $700 million. . . . If we assume that the introduction of such an income tax credit would have caused all states to tax personal incomes as heavily as Oregon, which made the greatest relative personal income tax effort in 1965, the reduction in federal income tax receipts due to the tax credit would have been about $2.5 billion at the 1965 taxable income level.[14]

TAX CREDITS AND EQUITY

The distribution of tax burdens in the states and localities can be altered through a tax credit mechanism. Most of the tax credit proposals outlined

---

[13] Advisory Commission on Intergovernmental Relations, *op. cit.,* pp. 116-17.

[14] Committee for Economic Development, *op. cit.,* p. 68.

earlier have the potential for reducing the federal tax liability of low-income federal taxpayers proportionately more than the liability of high-income groups. States in which low-income taxpayers are numerous stand to gain more, relative to their present net resources, than high-income states. The effects of the various types of credits relative to federal tax liability on relatively low-income and high-income federal taxpayers are outlined below, assuming that eligible state and local taxes are already applied, but that there is no further "picking-up" of the revenue so released:

1. A fixed dollar full offset, such as $100, would fully eliminate the federal tax of a person whose gross federal liability was $100, but would only partially eliminate the federal liability of higher bracket taxpayers to an extent determined by the gross federal liability.

2. A full offset credit with a maximum of a fixed percentage of the gross federal liability would, by definition, have the potential for reducing the federal tax by a constant percentage for low- and high-income taxpayers. But the federal income tax takes a greater proportion of income from high-income groups than from low-income groups. Thus the reduction of tax liability relative to income would be greater for taxpayers of high brackets than for taxpayers in low brackets.

3. By definition, the full offset credit with the maximum defined as a declining proportion of gross federal liability would be worth proportionately more for low-income taxpayers than for high-income taxpayers.

4. The partial offset credit with alternative itemization provides substantial gains for lower-income persons who take a standard deduction, and no gain for persons in upper brackets, and some gain for persons in lower brackets who itemize. The mechanism, therefore, is of greatest aid to the lowest-income federal taxpayers and of no aid to those of the highest income.

5. The CED staff proposal provides proportional offset for taxpayers in various income brackets, which are constant in relation to eligible tax burdens *after* subtracting the value of deductibility. Because deductibility is of the greatest value to high-income persons, a constant proportion of the remaining burden is equivalent to a falling proportion of original eligible tax payments. This proposal, therefore, provides smaller proportional offsets to higher-income persons, relative to gross federal liability, than to lower-income federal taxpayers.

All of the credits outlined above tend to increase the progressivity of the federal income tax, except for Scheme 2, which has no effect on progressivity.

A credit restricted to *income* taxes may also result in an increase in the progressivity of state-local taxation, because it would encourage greater relative use of the progressive income tax and less relative use of proportional or regressive sales and property taxes.

"PICKING-UP" THE TAX CREDIT REVENUES

One of the aims of tax credit proposals is the expansion of state use of income taxes. There is a variation among credits in the ease of raising such taxes with a neutral or beneficial effect on equity.

With the full offset credit, the tailoring of a state plan to fit the taxes levied exactly to the amount of the credit, and thus to the federal subsidy, would not be easy. For one thing, many low-income groups do not have a federal tax liability. Thus, if a state wanted to take advantage of this type of credit without placing a higher total tax burden on low-income persons, it would have to place its taxes in a manner that would not affect those persons who have no federal liability. On the other end of the income spectrum, the state levy would have to be set so that it would only affect those with federal liability of less than the maximum permissible offset and only to the extent of that liability. Coordinated tax action by the state and locality would be needed to match their combined tax programs to the federal maximum offset.

Under a "proportional full offset" credit, states would all try to levy taxes on the incomes of individuals—taxes at least as large as the amount of the permissible offset against federal income tax liability. There would be similar difficulties in applying a tax that would pick up released revenues but not increase the tax burden on low-income persons. Because the maximum permissible offset would depend on federal tax liability, the latter must be known before an equitable state pick-up of credit funds can be made.

With the partial offset credit (in the Advisory Commission proposal), it would be difficult for the states to take advantage of the credit by raising their own tax rates in a manner that would be equitable for the different income groups and also equitable as between itemizers and persons who take the standard deduction. This is because the value of the credit to individuals differs, depending on tax brackets and on whether the taxpayer chooses to itemize or take the standard deduction.

The tax credit proposed by the CED staff is the only one for which it is relatively easy for other governments to pick up the tax in a manner that does not increase the total tax burden of any individual. The credit, limited to state income taxation, is essentially neutral; therefore, if the credit is for 20 percent of state income taxes, all payers of state income taxes would continue to pay an unchanged amount of combined federal and state taxes if states with income taxes raised the tax liability of each payer by 25 percent. For full pick-up, each state can raise its taxes by a percentage determined by the formula:

$$\frac{1}{1 - (\text{credit proportion})}.$$

CHAPTER 11

Summary

MANY PRESCRIPTIONS HAVE BEEN OFFERED as remedies for the present federal grant-in-aid programs. The sorting out of these remedies depends upon the concept of fiscal federalism and an assessment of the policy implications of a full-scale implementation of planning, programming, budgeting systems in nation, state, and city. Two concepts have been set forth in this report for a system of federal grants (see Chapter 3). Each of these points to a combination of categorical and unconditional federal grants.

CATEGORICAL GRANTS

Categorical conditioned grants serve important purposes through joint action of national and state and local governments. Corrective measures are needed now to reduce the complexity of the present grant programs and to meet the problems created by proliferation. The present complexity and number of separate grants could be greatly reduced by the use of optional methods for achieving the specific purposes of existing aids. Some of the options discussed in Chapters 7 and 8 of this report included:

1. Packaging of grants by state or city and a more active role of the national government in grantsmanship and joint funding.
2. Consolidating demonstration project grants into a single authorization for each department of the national government that carries out substantial intergovernmental programs. Such consolidations should authorize federal support for demonstrations of new public products and new methods of producing or delivering them, over the broad spectrum of each department's responsibilities.
3. Making more extensive use of target grants, such as the Model Cities program, to finance combinations of public services that are directed at specific national purposes, e.g., an advance from poverty, or correction of blight in inner-city neighborhoods.

These three measures retain all the encumbrances of preauditing of proposed projects. However, decentralizing or eliminating the preaudit procedure could be achieved, for example, by:

4. Converting project grants to formula aids that would place responsibility on the states for project selection, and
5. Converting project grants to "differential" formula grants. Through differential formulas, federal funds could be placed where they would be put to

effective use in accord with the responsibilities being exercised by the several levels of governments. Such grants can assist the movement away from the present pattern of grants encumbered with conditions that are applied with inflexible uniformity to diverse situations. More sophisticated (and necessarily more complex) formulas are needed to zero in on the public products sought and to direct funds to the effective producing unit or level of government so that the purposes of intergovernmental programs can be achieved.

Any of the five above measures could be made more effective by:

6. Accepting a formula planning grant to give federal support to PPB•systems in state, county, and city. Such grants would achieve their purposes if additional funds were set aside for personnel training in program analysis and for program evaluation.

GENERAL SUPPORT OR OVERHEAD GRANTS

The counterpart to these or similar options for reform of the categorical grant-in-aid is an unconditional general support or overhead grant. This concept was discussed at some length in Chapter 9, and a range of specifications for such a grant was presented. While none of the specification patterns is a perfect grant-in-aid design, each is workable and would assure the enlargement of public resources that is needed to reduce the severe constraint on public spending in cities and to overcome state budgetary distortions and program gaps resulting from categorical grants.

*   *   *   *   *

As a structure for these prescriptions, the conceptual underpinnings of the grant-in-aid system have been reviewed in this study, and we have made a beginning toward assessing the meaning of PPBS implementation for federal grant-in-aid design. Clearly, programs—some of which are optional ways of satisfying public purposes—are aided now under a great variety of grant formulas. Categorical grants viewed from the perspective of the state or city are essentially price-reduction devices that lower the costs against which to test relative utility gains from expenditures made, taking account of the augmented resources provided by the aid.

In this volume, John Cotton has built on a review of the earlier theoretical work to provide a new point of departure for further conceptual studies. The formulation he has developed keeps separate the decisions on taxing at each level of government. Such a separation appears to us more operational for allocative decisions in a PPB setting than does the combined view of fiscal federalism made explicit by Richard A. Musgrave in "Approaches to a Fiscal Theory of Political Federalism." [1]

---

[1] In A Conference of the Universities-National Bureau Committee for Economic Research, *Public Finances: Needs, Sources, and Utilization* (Princeton University Press, for the National Bureau of Economic Research, 1961), pp. 97-122.

APPENDIX

Studies on determinants of
public expenditures: a review*

THE SUBSTANTIAL AMOUNTS OF PUBLIC FINANCE DATA which were made available by the U.S. Bureau of the Census, Division of Governments, in the 1957 and 1962 *Census of Governments* stimulated a notable increase in empirical studies on public expenditure determinants. This has become an investigative area of growing importance to all researchers in fields that involve public expenditure. For example, in this present study, reference was made in Chapter 3 to determinants studies as providing an objective test for the capacity of federal matching shares to achieve minimum national standards at lowest federal tax cost. And Chapter 5 emphasized determinants research as a way of predicting relative expenditure requirements as part of an index of emerging pressures on fiscal capacity in the states.

The Census of Governments volumes of 1967 will undoubtedly stimulate further work on determinants. Therefore, we believed it would be useful to compare, contrast, criticize, and, as far as possible, synthesize the results of the statistical analyses already published. Through identification of both the strengths and limitations of their concepts and methodologies, meaningful boundaries may possibly be set for the direction of future research in this area. To this end, we compiled a listing of sixty-six studies; these include both analyses of determinants and discussions of such analyses. Some fifty of the studies were chosen for explicit comment here, but all of those on the list were part of the background of our review.* *

* By Roy W. Bahl, Fiscal Affairs Department, International Monetary Fund. The initial work on this review was completed while Professor Bahl was associated with the Regional Research Institute, West Virginia University. He notes that he is indebted to Professors Jerry Miner and Robert J. Saunders for a number of helpful comments, but he is solely responsible for the ideas expressed.

** The list of sixty-six references will be found at the end of the Appendix, in numbered alphabetical order. The number in parentheses following an author's name in the text of the review refers to that numbered order. The studies not explicitly discussed are so noted in the listing, because we believe that readers will find a full perusal of the listing rewarding for their own purposes.

We cannot, of course, claim that our list covers the complete output of existing studies up to the spring of 1967—the time when this paper was being written. Further, the volume of determinants literature has been increasing steadily since that date, and, for various reasons, it has been possible to include only a very few of the most recent contributions here.

WHY DETERMINANTS STUDIES?

One could venture several explanations (including the work noted above of the Governments Division of the U.S. Bureau of the Census) for the proliferation of determinants studies in recent years. The major explanation lies in the lack of a general theory to explain the pattern of expenditure variation among governmental units. Accordingly, research has been stimulated on the decision-making process of such units and on forecasting their needs. What the research studies are designed to do is to assist governments in estimating expenditures for periods ahead and to improve our understanding of the complex of forces and their interactions that determine how much a jurisdiction spends relative to others. The existence of large amounts of comparable published fiscal data for state and local governments has encouraged this particular approach. In addition to the 1957 and 1962 *Census of Governments* volumes, certain expenditure data are available on an annual basis in *Governmental Finances, Compendium of City Government Finances,* and *Compendium of State Government Finances*. Also, many states collect and make available extensive data on the expenditures and revenues of local units.

A third reason for the rash of determinants studies is the appeal and simplicity of the regression technique. Given the availability of a variety of suitable computer packages, a multiple regression analysis is easily carried out, and it gives the illusion of being a sophisticated quantitative technique. However, failure to take account of certain of the difficulties inherent in this statistical method has led in several cases to misleading, if not erroneous, interpretations of results.

STATISTICAL TECHNIQUES USED

The technique most often used in the studies is the cross-sectional multivariable regression. However, a difficulty with the analysis of cross-sectional data is that it enables only a static interpretation (e.g., that *differences* in per capita expenditures among governmental units are associated with *differences* in independent variables *at a single point in time*), although the objective may be to make a dynamic inference (*e.g.,* that the *change* in per capita expenditures of a governmental unit is associated with a *change* over time in the population of that unit).

To go beyond the static interpretation of cross-sectional results, Sacks-Harris (55) and Bahl-Saunders (8) have examined the stability and the size of standardized regression coefficients computed from cross-sectional analyses for different years in order to describe temporal changes in the relative importance of the independent variables. To the extent that the intercorrelations among the independent variables changed between points in time this method of estimating changes in the relative importance of the determinants does not yield accurate results.

A second method that has been used to examine the temporal dimensions of the determinants is to regress *differences* of selected independent variables on *differences* of per capita government expenditures; see Bahl and Saunders (7) and Kee (42). This approach enables description of changes in the pattern of variation among government units of per capita expenditure increments, but it falls short of describing the temporal covariability between per person spending and selected independent variables for a particular unit of analysis. That is to say, the response of per capita expenditures of some unit of government to a change in certain institutional or economic factors may not be satisfactorily explained by a cross-sectional analysis.

In a more recent study—Fredland, Hymans, and Morss (25)—both cross-section and time series data have been used to identify factors affecting the short-run expenditure decisions made by state governments. The authors first ran time series regressions on individual states and then performed a covariance analysis employing pooled data across states, and over time.

Wood (66) uses a factor analysis in examining the questions: (1) in what relevant respects do communities within a metropolitan area differ? and (2) how are expenditure patterns related to these community differences? He concludes that factor analysis is preferable to regression because the former takes into account underlying structural characteristics rather than just the measurable characteristics, or proxy variables.

In actuality the choice of a statistical technique in these studies is primarily determined by the nature of the available data; in theory, however, the cross-section and the time series analyses are not designed to answer the same kinds of questions. The cross-section regression gives a picture of the aggregate pattern, or structure, of public spending, while the time series analysis enables a measurement of the trend in public spending for an individual unit and a description of fluctuations about this trend. Accordingly, the time series approach gives little information about structure at a point in time, and the cross-section approach gives little information about temporal covariability between per capita expenditures and the explanatory factors.

Those who are dissatisfied with the regression model because it involves using proxy variables for the true underlying structural differences (or changes), or because of difficulties in identifying the separate effects of explanatory variables, have the option of turning to multivariate techniques such as factor analysis and principal components analysis, both of which are concerned with the examination of interdependencies. In any case, the high degree of correlation among independent variables used in these analyses makes a thorough examination of interdependencies a necessary prerequisite to the regression analysis.

LIMITATIONS OF DETERMINANTS STUDIES

The factors that have resulted in the popularity of determinants studies have also resulted in some of the more serious limitations of this approach. Incomparabilities and inadequacies in the data and shortcomings in the regression technique are two serious problems encountered in interpreting the results of those analyses. In addition to methodological limitations, many of the studies have been plagued by one or more of three conceptual problems: circularity in the statistical model, a blurring of the concepts of cost and expenditures, and confusion in use of the concept of economies of scale. These problems are examined in the following sections.

METHODOLOGICAL

The regression technique enables the partitioning of the total variation in the dependent variable into two components: (1) a systematic variation associated with variations in the independent variables and (2) an error term. However, investigators have attempted to measure the separate effect of the independent variables by using statistical measures such as partial correlation, beta, or elasticity coefficients. Each of these measures assumes all explanatory variables to be held constant except the one in question and then purports to discover the "sensitivity" of the dependent variable to a small change (or in the case of a cross-section, difference) in the independent variable. However, if the independent variables are intercorrelated, i.e., if they are not truly independent, the *ceteris paribus* assumption cannot be met. This problem of statistical confluence or multicollinearity renders any measures of the partial effects of the independent variables suspect.

Frisch (26) found that when there is substantial correlation among the explanatory variables, there is a tendency for the standard errors of the estimated parameters to become large. The fact that confluence is manifested by large standard errors of the parameters indicates the dangers in inferring that only variables with significant regression coefficients are important. A regression coefficient may well be nonsignificant because it contributes little to explained variation, i.e., because the explanatory factor is unrelated to the dependent variable. However, a regression coefficient may also be statistically nonsignificant if it is closely related to another of the explanatory variables, even if it is an important "explainer" of variation in the dependent variable.

Other methodological problems relate to the data that have been used. First, there are serious problems of comparability of expenditure data among governmental units. For example, in analyzing a national cross-section of municipal expenditures, one must take account of state-to-state differences in the nature of functional responsibilities; otherwise inferences may be drawn concerning expenditures *in the city area* when data relate only to expenditures *by the city* government. These difficulties are compounded as the nature and magnitude of the incomparabilities in the data change through time. For these reasons, most serious analyses of municipal expenditure patterns have focused on individual functional categories, or a grouping of expenditure functions common to all the cities in a given sample. A second data limitation is the lack of adequate time series data, a lack which negates the possibility of more extensive statistical examination of the dynamics of the public expenditure decision.

CIRCULARITY

In one sense, the inclusion of federal aid as an explanatory variable for per capita state and local government expenditures combined introduces an element of circularity since total expenditures are equal to the sum of expenditures from own sources and expenditures from intergovernmental sources. Hence, it is not surprising that if all other things are held constant, higher levels of grants are associated with higher levels of expenditures. Empirically, there would appear to be two ways of adjusting for circularity. First, one might subtract per capita intergovernmental aids from per capita total expenditures, thereby expressing the dependent variables as per capita expenditures from own sources. This does not completely eliminate the circularity problem since, for example, some federal grants carry matching requirements and therefore cause expenditures from own sources to be greater. A second approach is to omit per capita federal (or state) grants as an independent variable. However, it is important to note that this does not completely eliminate the effects of intergovernmental aids on the level of per capita expenditures because of the intercorrelation between intergovernmental aids and the explanatory variables. For example, if the variable, "percentage of families with income under $3,000," is found to be an important determinant of interstate variations in per capita public assistance payments, the effects of state aids may still be present since states with greater proportions of low income families receive greater per capita public welfare aids.

A similar problem in some determinants studies relates to the use of per capita assessed value, which is often cited as a statistically significant explanatory variable. This significance is not unexpected since higher per capita assessed value may mean higher per capita property tax revenues—which may in turn lead to higher per capita total revenue, and consequently, higher per capita expenditures. But the conclusion that revenues are a significant determinant of expenditures is of little use in constructing a positive theory of public spending.

Another way in which circularity has been introduced into these studies is by explaining variations in expenditures for a given function using the cost of inputs as an independent variable. A hypothetical example of this conceptual error would be the use of "number of policemen" and "average police officer salary" as explanatory variables. A less hypothetical example is the use of "average teacher salary" as an explainer of variations in education spending.

COST AND EXPENDITURES

A second conceptual problem relates to the use of the terms "cost" and "expenditures." Some studies purport to explain variations in the former, some in the latter, and some use the terms synonymously. One could conceptualize the total variance in per capita expenditures (σ_e^2) as having a quality component (σ_q^2) and a cost component (σ_c^2) such that

$$\sigma_e^2 = \sigma_c^2 + \sigma_q^2. \tag{1}$$

If the objective is to explain variations in per capita expenditures, a stochastic model such as

$$E = f(x_1, x_2, \ldots, x_n, u) \tag{2}$$

could be used where E is per capita expenditures, the x_i are independent variables which are proxy measures for the determinants of differentials in cost *and* quality, and u is an error term. On the other hand, if the objective is to explain the variance in *costs,* which is clearly equal to

$$\sigma_c^2 = \sigma_e^2 - \sigma_q^2, \tag{3}$$

the dependent variable in the stochastic model must be C$=$(E-Q). Hence

$$(E-Q) = f(x_1, x_2, \ldots, x_n, u), \tag{4}$$

and the independent variables are not assumed to reflect quality differences. The third case mentioned, cost and expenditures treated as being equal, $\sigma_e^2 = \sigma_c^2$, clearly assumes $\sigma_q^2 = 0$.

Since a satisfactory method of eliminating the quality component from expenditures has not been developed, the alternatives in handling the problem are to assume (1) that there is no quality difference among the units of government being analyzed; or (2) that "independent" variables reflecting only quality differentials can be included among the explanatory variables in the equation thereby netting out the effects of quality; or (c) that the independent variables account for both cost *and* quality differentials and the objective is to explain per capita expenditure variations.

The first alternative (to assume that various governmental units offer the same quality of service) is unrealistic. The second could be implemented only if one could identify independent variables that both reflect quality differentials and are not highly correlated with other explanatory variables. Hirsch (35) has attempted to include quality as an independent variable to explain per capita education expenditure variations among twenty nine St. Louis county school districts. However, his index of quality is "average teacher salary"; consequently the significance of this index as a determinant of expenditures may be due only to the effect of average teacher salary as a cost of operation.

Schmandt and Stephens (58) in examining the relationship between per capita expenditures, population, and service level for nineteen cities and villages in Milwaukee County, construct a measure of quality based on output rather than input. Their measure is derived from a breakdown of each municipal service into subfunctions. For example, police protection is broken down into sixty five categories, including foot and motorcycle patrols, criminal investigation, youth aid bureau, school crossing guards, pulmotor service, and so forth. "The service index or level for each function is then determined by adding the number of activities performed by the municipality." A total of 550 municipal subfunctions are used. Analysis of rank correlation coefficients shows that governmental units having larger populations supply residents with significantly more subfunctions of services ($r = .80$), but that no relationship exists between service level and per capita expenditures ($r = .07$).

Though an output measure such as "number of subfunctions performed" is probably a better index of quality than an input factor such as "average teacher salary," it is not suitable for use as an independent variable in the multiple regression analysis. First, even if two municipalities provide the same number of subfunctions, it does not necessarily follow that the scope or quality of performance in the two municipalities is the same. For example, two equal-size municipalities may provide summer recreational programs for youths, but on vastly different scales. A more important restriction on using this measure of service level as an independent variable in the regression equation is the degree of intercorrelation with other explanatory factors. The purpose of including a quality variable is to examine the covariability between per capita expenditures and some explanatory factor while holding constant the effects of quality; but if this measure of quality is collinear with the other independent variables, any measure of separate effect will be biased.

Having ruled out the possibility of including quality as an independent variable, one is left with the alternative of assuming that the independent variables reflect the factors of cost, quality, and ability to pay. To illustrate the problems of interpretation created by this assumption: if per capita income is found to be significantly and positively related to per capita police expenditures, it could be argued that persons with higher incomes require greater levels of police protection, or that higher-income families demand a higher quality police force, or that higher-income levels reflect a greater capacity to finance police services. It is this kind of problem which makes a thorough interdependency analysis an imperative prerequisite to any regression analysis.

ECONOMIES OF SCALE

A third point of confusion in determinants studies relates to attempts to make use of the microeconomic concept of (internal) economies of scale to explain the slope of the long-run average cost curve in the provision of a public service. Theoretically, economies of scale (declining per unit costs) exist because the expansion of the firm enables management to combine productive factors in such a way that average productivity increases. It also seems feasible that as the size (population) of the governmental unit served expands, per unit costs might be lowered. However, most empirical examinations of this question have proceeded without consideration of the nature of the underlying production functions for public services; but see Hirsch (39). If a significant negative relationship is observed between per capita expenditures for a service and population, it is usually argued that there might be economies of scale in the financing of that service. This line of reasoning ignores the fact that differentials in expenditures may reflect differentials in quality as well as in cost. Secondly, when this analogy to the economies of scale concept is carried to its logical extreme, it seems to be based on the assumption that population of a governmental unit is a measure of output. Consequently a negative relationship between per capita expenditures and population size gives very little information about the existence or non-existence of economies of scale, *i.e.,* about the nature of the underlying production function. Moreover, the statistical analyses have been made on cross-sections of data, therefore, any conclusions reached must be based on the finding that at a point in time larger government units in the sample spend significantly less per capita than smaller government units. It does not necessarily follow that an increase in the population of any given governmental unit will be accompanied by a decline in per capita costs.

One further conceptual difficulty with using an economy of scale analogy in the public sector concerns the confusion between movements along the long-run average cost curve and shifts to lower long-run average cost curves. Cross-section studies may suggest shifts, since the arguments for governmental consolidation, particularly within standard metropolitan statistical areas, are based on the theory that a lower-cost combination of inputs will result from consolidation if the same size population will be served. However, the concept of economies of scale as developed in the theory of the firm assumes a least cost combination of inputs for any given level of output and relates to movements along this particular long-run average cost curve.

THE DETERMINANTS STUDIES*

This section is a brief survey of the determinants literature, organized around the unit of government considered, and including most of the major contributions. The objective here is to describe, synthesize (if possible), and evaluate what has been done.

STATE AND LOCAL STUDIES

Although Colm (17) and Berolzheimer (12) statistically investigated the determinants of state and local government expenditures in earlier works, Fabricant's analysis (21) of 1941 data was the first comprehensive attempt (in a geographic sense) to explain the pattern of such government expenditures. Consequently, Fabricant is usually given the credit, or blame, for starting the rash of determinants studies. His unit of analysis is per capita state and local government expenditures, and therefore the problem of interstate differences in the division of state-local financial responsibility is avoided. But aggregating expenditures in this manner does not result in analysis that explains the factors affecting the decisions of individual governmental units. In explaining approximately 72 percent of the variation in per capita operating expenditures, and 28 to 85 percent for other functions, he concludes that interstate differences in income are primarily responsible for state-to-state spending differentials. Fabri-

---

* Robin Barlow has compiled an extensive tabular summary of the statistical results of determinants studies: "Multivariate Studies of the Determinants of State and Local Government Expenditures," paper prepared for the Ford Foundation Workshop in State Local Finance, Ann Arbor, Michigan, June 1966.

cant's three "basic variables" are income, population density, and urbanization, of which he finds urbanization to be the least important explanatory factor.

Fisher (22, 23) extended Fabricant's analysis on 1957 data to consider a number of additional economic, demographic, and socio-political variables and found that interstate spending disparities are closely associated with the distribution of income within states. However, Fisher recognizes that the strong negative correlation between the percentage of families with income less than $3,000 and per capita expenditures may be attributable to either (1) greater political resistance among low income groups to increased government expenditures and to higher taxes, or (2) the high correlation between income level and income distribution.

Sacks and Harris (55) test the hypothesis that the level of government expenditures is not independent of the source of the revenues, and find differentials in per capita federal and state aid to be closely associated with expenditure disparities. In contrasting the results of their 1957 and 1960 regressions with Fabricant's 1942 analysis, they conclude that the substantial decline in the explanatory power of the three basic variables is a result of the increasing importance of intergovernmental flows of funds. However, Bahl and Saunders more recent paper (9) shows that the marginal contribution of federal aid between 1942 and 1962 was approximately the same; hence the explanation—the declining importance of the three basic variables—is not supported by the data. It is hypothesized that the reduction in the explanatory power of Fabricant's basic factors is due to the increasing complexities of public expenditure decisions, i.e., the level of public spending has become increasingly responsive to particular needs.

Spangler (63) has found a significant and positive correlation coefficient between linear rate of population growth between 1950 and 1960 and per capita expenditures for education, health and hospitals, police, interest expense, general control, and capital outlays. He contends that the most efficient rate of output may well be the present one—the one to which the workers are accustomed—and that the disruptive effects of expansion result in rising per capita expenditures. However, his suggestion that there exists a rising long-run average cost curve for state and local government is not supported by empirical analyses for other levels of government; e.g., Brazer (15) found a negative relationship between per capita city expenditures and rate of population growth. Therefore it may be hypothesized that Spangler's interpretation was distorted by collinearities in the data,* or by inadequacies in the technique, or alternatively, that the reasons for the observed diseconomies are to be found at the state rather than the local level.

One final contribution deserves mention: it is Kurnow's argument (43) that the additive, or linear, regression model is not appropriate and should be replaced by a model that accounts for joint effects. Whereas a model of the form

$$y_i = a + (\Sigma \, b_i x_i) + u$$

may result in explaining the effect of x_i on y given that n-1 remaining variables are held constant, a multiplicative form such as

$$y = a x_1^{b1} \, x_2^{b2} \ldots x_n^{bn} \, u$$

enables a measurement of the effect on x_i on y given the *level* of n-1 other

---

* For example, interstate differences in per capita income in 1962 and rate of population growth between 1950 and 1960 are significantly correlated (r=.54); see Bahl and Saunders (9).

independent variables. Kurnow's point is conceded if one grants the assumption, for example, that the effect of income on expenditures is not independent of the *level* of population density. He has tested this thesis with apparently satisfactory results, increasing the determination coefficient from .72 to .88 on 1942 data and from .53 to .78 on 1957 data.

In summary, it may be concluded that interstate disparities in the level and distribution of income and in the level of per capita intergovernmental revenues account for most of the interstate variability in per capita state and local government expenditures. Again, the appropriateness of using a source of funds such as federal aid as an explanatory factor must be questioned on both conceptual and methodological grounds. More will be said about this later.

CITY EXPENDITURES

To date, Brazer's analysis (15) of the pattern of municipal expenditures in 1951 has been the definitive empirical work on city government spending. In analyzing spending by 462 cities of over 25,000 population he was able to explain approximately 60 percent of the among-city variability in per capita operating expenditures and 6 to 27 percent for various functional categories. He found that the association between population size and per capita expenditures was significant only with respect to police protection, while population density was significantly associated with most expenditure categories. He observed "economies of density" (a significant negative regression coefficient) only for the functions of police protection and street maintenance and found rate of population growth to be a minor factor in determining the level of municipal expenditures. Median family income was significant for all expenditure classes except per capita operating expenses, while per capita intergovernmental revenue was significant in every case. Brazer concludes that the determinants of the level of city expenditures are neither few in number nor readily identifiable, and he points to factors peculiar to state of location as major determinants.

Hawley (32) had earlier regressed a number of socioeconomic and demographic variables on the 1940 per capita expenditures of 76 central cities with metropolitan area populations of 100,000 or more. He found, as did Brazer, no statistical evidence of economies or diseconomies of scale, and he concluded that expenditures by the central city are more closely related to urban fringe population than to central city population. While the possible implications of Hawley's finding must be tempered by recognition of the existing multicollinearity and incomparabilities in the data, the finding demonstrates clearly that an appropriate fiscal and physical planning unit for the central city must include the entire metropolitan area.

A number of additional similarities in the results regarding per capita current expenditures in the above two studies are worth noting. The magnitudes of explained variations are extremely close—57 percent for Brazer and 59 percent for Hawley. Both found evidence of economies of population density and an inverse relation with population growth rate, and both reached the conclusion that the level of central city expenditures is more closely associated with metropolitan area population than with central city population.

Bahl (6) has updated the Brazer-Hawley type of analysis by statistically investigating the pattern of public expenditures among 198 central cities of metropolitan areas. Data were analyzed cross sectionally for 1950 and 1960, and for the changes in per capita expenditures between 1950 and 1960. The conclusions were, in general, quite similar to those reached in the earlier studies: the level of per capita central city expenditures is closely related to the size of the central city population, *relative* to that of the entire Standard Metropolitan

Statistical Area; spending for some functions (notably for police and fire protection, and highways) shows a close association with population density and much of the intercity variation can be attributed to variations in intergovernmental revenues. However, the analysis of expenditure changes and the comparison of 1960 and 1950 results indicates a possible change in the structure of expenditure determinants; i.e., the same factors account for considerably more of the intercity variation for a given function in the later year. For example, per person police expenditures can be explained to a much greater extent in the later year by factors that could be hypothesized to reflect needs for police, and to a much lesser extent by the level of per capita total expenditures. This finding may suggest that expenditure requirements for certain functions are being viewed much less in terms of a given fraction of the public budget, and much more in terms of changes in the level of needs.

Examinations of within-state municipal per capita spending differentials have been carried out in Washington, New Jersey, California, Ohio, and Massachusetts. Brazer (15) investigated the spending patterns of thirty five cities in California, thirty in Massachusetts, and thirty two in Ohio and found that in every case the expenditure variation that could be explained within the states was greater than when cities of various states were considered together. This strongly supports his contention that intermunicipal spending comparisons are distorted substantially when state lines are crossed. Further evidence of the distortion created by interstate comparison is his finding that, while variability in spending among Ohio cities was closely associated with the level of intergovernmental aids, no such significant correlation was observed for cities in Massachusetts, a state in which municipalities are responsible for both the education and the public welfare functions.

Each of four separate analyses of California cities showed that differences in internal fiscal ability and in the level of intergovernmental revenue were the major factors accounting for intercity spending differentials. Brazer (15) found per capita intergovernmental revenues to be highly significant for California cities, while Scott and Feder (59), Shelton, and Davies (64), and Elsner and Sosnick (20), found per capita assessed valuation to be a highly significant explanatory factor. Since, in addition to per capita assessed value, each of the latter three studies used as an independent variable some indicator of the yield of sales or use taxes, the models are subject to the circularity error, i.e., their findings may show only that expenditures are higher because revenues are higher.

The statistical results of these intrastate studies would seem to indicate that the relationship between per person municipal spending and demographic factors is dependent on state of location and perhaps on the year considered. While Brazer found among-city expenditure variations in Ohio and in Massachusetts to be significantly and positively associated with population size, neither Brazer nor Scott and Feder observed significant economies or diseconomies of size for California cities. Conversely, both Shelton-Davies and Elsner-Sosnick found significant diseconomies among California cities in a later period.

In the analyses carried out on California cities by Brazer, Scott-Feder, and Elsner-Sosnick, rate of population growth was found to be a significant determinant of expenditure level and in each study the relation was found to be inverse. Since no similar significant partial relationship is observed for cities in Ohio, Massachusetts, or (48) Washington, it might tentatively be concluded that rate of population growth exerts a significant influence on the level of public spending *only in the more rapidly growing cities*. Arithmetically, the inverse expenditure-growth rate relationship may be explained by a spreading effect, i.e., the fact that in rapidly growing municipalities the denominator of the per capita expenditure figure has increased much faster than has the numerator, which may well mean a decline in the quality and/or scope of services.

INTER AND INTRA METROPOLITAN STUDIES

The value of an analysis of spending differentials among metropolitan areas is that it abstracts from the problem of *intra*-local differences in the distribution of functional responsibilities. Brazer (15) combined 1953 expenditures of overlapping governments within the forty largest central cities, thereby effecting an analysis of the determinants of expenditures *in the city area* by all local governments as opposed to expenditures *by the city government*. While he found neither population size nor rate of growth to be statistically significant, he did find the ratio of city population to metropolitan area population to be a significant explainer of expenditure variations. This reinforces Hawley's contention (32) that central city spending is strongly influenced by the characteristics of the population of the urban fringe. In addition, Brazer found per capita intergovernmental revenues to be a major force in determining expenditure levels, but he also found that differences in the level of income exerted a much smaller influence on the level of aggregate expenditures in large cities than on expenditures of 462 cities with population in excess of 25,000.

Kee (42) analyzed 1957 per person expenditures of thirty six central cities and overlapping units of governments in what is essentially a replication of the Brazer analysis for a later year. The results of his study parallel Brazer's in that differences in income, intergovernmental revenues, and the distribution of population within the Standard Metropolitan Statistical Area are significantly associated with intermetropolitan differences in per capita expenditures. Further, a comparison of his net regression and multiple correlation coefficients for 1957 data with Brazer's for 1951 suggests a fairly high degree of stability between the two years in the relative importance of the explanatory factors.

Prescott (52) found variations in income level and variations in the level of per capita federal and state aids explained most of the variations in per capita expenditures among Standard Metropolitan Statistical Areas in a twelve-state midwestern region. He found population density, growth rate, and property valuation to be generally nonsignificant.

Several intensive studies of the public finances of specific metropolitan areas have included multiple regression analyses of per capita expenditures of governmental units within the standard metropolitan statistical area. The advantages of intrametropolitan analysis are primarily (1) that certain environmental factors may be held constant by examining data for only a single SMSA, (2) that disparities in the quality of service might be smaller within a given metropolitan area than among metropolitan areas, and (3) that the division of fiscal responsibility between the state and local governments may be held constant.

Bollens' analysis (14) of 1954-55 data on expenditures by eighty seven governmental units within the St. Louis SMSA revealed that the level of per capita expenditures was significantly affected by the level of assessed value per capita, and by some index of the quality of services. The statistical results did not reveal the existence of any major economies or diseconomies of scale.

Hirsch (36, 37) has approached the problem of economies of size on an intrametropolitan basis by comparing the governmental unit to the firm and thus developing a clever theoretical framework in which to answer the question: "What are the likely expenditure effects of metropolitan growth and consolidation?" He assumes that the partial relationship between per capita expenditures for various functions and some measure of population will approximate the

LRAC curve of the firm; or in terms of his cross-sectional analysis of 149 St. Louis government units, that a movement along the static per capita expenditure-population function could approximate the effects of consolidation of local governments. Hirsch views this consolidation as differing among functions and taking the form of horizontal integration (for education, for fire, police, and refuse collection services), vertical integration (for water and sewer services), or circular integration (for general control). The results of his regression analysis may be summarized as follows: (1) for the horizontally integrated functions, he found that growth and consolidation had little if any significant effects on per capita expenditures; (2) for circularly integrated services he found evidence of a "U" shape long-run average cost curve; (3) for vertically integrated functions he found that per capita expenditures declined with population size. However, since the horizontally integrated functions account for approximately 80-85 percent of all expenditures, efficiency considerations do not appear to warrant across-the-board consolidation of metropolitan area governments. As was pointed out above, this approach is subject to the dual limitations that (1) quality of service cannot be eliminated from the expenditure side of the equation and (2) the high degree of collinearity present makes the partial relationship between population and expenditures an unreliable measure.

Sacks and Hellmuth (56) investigated the variability of per capita expenditures within the Cleveland metropolitan area in 1956 by separating the governmental units into twenty cities and thirty eight villages. Because of vastly different program responsibilities, little of the variability in per person total spending by cities could be attributed to size of population, per person assessed valuation, or wealth; but when individual functions were analyzed, substantial proportions of the expenditure variability could be explained. Conversely, they found that among villages, where the package of services offered is much more homogeneous, substantial proportions of the variation in per person total spending could be explained. Though collinearity obscures much of the true separate effect of the independent variables, differences in per capita assessed valuation clearly account for a substantial proportion of the differences in among-village spending. As with the cities, no evidence of economies of size was uncovered.

Williams (65) has analyzed 1960 per person expenditures for 225 municipalities (90 suburbs, 41 towns, and 94 townships) in the Philadelphia standard metropolitan statistical area. The results indicate that the suburbs differed in expenditures according to land use pattern and economic role. Industrial and commercial centers have a specialized economic function in the metropolitan area and spend for activities that serve the needs generated by their role. Low density residential suburbs have little need for many services but evidence concern for planning, and high density residential suburbs respond to congestion by developing more services. In all cases, wealth and status generated higher demands. With regard to municipalities, significant correlation between population and expenditures is explained as reflecting other characteristics of the towns such as the degree of economic specialization. This seems a plausible argument since the larger towns are commercial and industrial centers and no doubt provide public services to a large nonresident population (i.e., shoppers, commuters). In addition to the importance of the economic nature and land use pattern of the governmental unit considered, the regression showed the level of per capita spending in residential areas to be closely related to social rank and personal wealth, as measured by the value of the home.

In the Schmandt-Stephens (58) study of nineteen Milwaukee County municipalities, it was found that the level of per capita expenditures was unrelated to the level of public services (number of subfunctions) or to population. However, the level of public services was significantly and positively related to population, a finding that the authors suggest implies the existence of economies of scale. That is to say, if a greater population can be provided a greater number of services than can a smaller population, but at the same per unit cost, some economies of scale exist.

OTHER LEVELS OF GOVERNMENT ANALYZED

Vieg, *et. al.* (64), regressed selected independent variables on 1957 per capita expenditures of county governments in California. The authors were able to explain 63 percent of the variation, and found per capita assessed value, percentage of county population residing outside incorporated areas, and per capita taxable sales to be significant. Because of the importance of the property tax as a source of revenue for California county governments, per capita assessed value reflects capacity to finance services and therefore enables one to conclude that the level of per capita county government spending is partially determined by the size of the property tax base. The significant positive association between per capita county government expenditures and percentage of county population living in unincorporated areas may mean that county residents living outside cities provide the greatest drain on county government services.

An intercounty analysis of per capita expenditures made *in* counties by all governments enables a better evaluation of the extent to which socio-economic factors determine service levels. Adams (2, 4) treats per capita expenditures by all local governments in each of 478 county areas as a dependent variable. To avoid problems arising from interstate differences in the division of state-local fiscal responsibility, he excludes from the analysis functions characterized by high levels of intergovernmental assistance (welfare, highways, education). He uses as independent factors variables reflecting intercounty differences in socioeconomic environment, in physical environment, in income and wealth, in individual characteristics (e.g., percent nonwhite), and political or institutional characteristics. The partial correlation coefficients obtained show variables reflecting differences in socioeconomic environment were the primary determinants of the level of per capita police, fire, sanitation, sewage disposal, and recreation expenditures, while the income variable was found to be relatively unimportant. Adams' findings also show per capita expenditures to be significantly lower in counties experiencing large amounts of in-migration, a result that suggests that the public sector undervalues the preferences and tastes for public services of newcomers. Alternative explanations of this result are that local governments allow quality of services to drop by not expanding public programs to meet the needs of larger populations, or that the relationship between population growth, and increments in the level of public expenditures, is a lagged one.

Schmandt and Stephens (57) examined per capita expenditures by local governments in county areas. Their study included 3,096 counties; the relationship between per capita expenditures and selected economic and demographic variables were analyzed with a simple correlation technique. The results showed that variations in state aids explained most of the variability in per capita expenditures for the aided functions (welfare, highways, and public education) and that family income level explained most of the variance in the traditionally locally financed functions (police and fire). However, the Schmandt-Stephens analysis suffers from the serious weakness of data incomparability to the extent that the distribution of state-local fiscal responsibility differs among states in the sample.

A more recent expenditure analysis by Bahl and Saunders (10) focuses on the pattern of public expenditures within an underdeveloped state—West Virginia—and also uses county area expenditures as the dependent variable. However, in addition to county aggregate expenditures from all local sources, expenditures by all local governments within West Virginia county areas are examined. The results indicate that the level of per capita total public expenditures in counties bore little if any relation to the level of wealth and in fact, was negatively correlated with per capita income level. Over 75 percent of the intercounty variation in per person expenditures was attributable to intercounty variations in per capita state and federal aids and in direct expenditures. Expenditures from local sources were found to be positively related to income level, but did not vary significantly with other socioeconomic or demographic factors. One could reconcile this conclusion with Adams' finding (4) that socioeconomic environment factors are important determinants while income is not by arguing that income is a representative proxy of environmental differences among counties in West Virginia.

Adams has also (3) investigated the activities of the public sector in Appalachia by regressing per capita state and federal aids on local fiscal effort (general revenue less intergovernmental transfers) for county areas. The sample was composed of 1,249 low income counties (a prerequisite for inclusion was a population density between 15 and 50 per square mile) including 146 of the 354 counties located in the Appalachian region. Local fiscal effort in Appalachia was found to be low relative to that in the rest of the country, and negatively related to state aid, within most Appalachian states. When county areas are analyzed by state, for about half of the states a positive correlation was found between local effort and aid. This suggests that an increase in per capita state aid leads to a more than proportionate increase in local public expenditures, that is, to an increase in the share of personal income going to the public sector.

EXPLAINING VARIATIONS IN SPECIFIC CLASSES OF EXPENDITURES

Most of the studies described in the preceding section involve analysis of per capita total expenditures of the government considered, but many also include separate analyses of individual functional categories of government expenditures. It is this latter form of the dependent variable that has the most to offer by way of identifying the underlying structure of public expenditures. The following is a brief summary and synthesis of the empirical conclusions as to the determinants of the level of spending for the major public programs.

EDUCATION

Most studies of the structure of public expenditures have included a separate analysis of education spending since this function accounts for such a large proportion of the public budget. These statistical analyses have concentrated primarily on measuring the degree of association between per capita or per pupil education spending and income, state aid, and certain needs factors.

There is general agreement that income level exerts a significant and positive effect on the level of spending for education. Hirsch (33) estimates the income elasticity of demand for education as 1.09 for the period 1950-58; McLoone (45) estimates the national average at 1.34 for the period 1947-57; James

(40) estimates the 1946-58 elasticities for Washington, California, New Jersey, Nebraska, and Wisconsin as ranging from a high of 2.2 for Nebraska to a low of 1.49 for New Jersey. Though the actual comparability of these results is limited because of differences in the statistical techniques, or the specification of the model, or the form of the variable used, the common conclusion that income exerts a strong positive influence on the growth in education spending is clear. Further, the results of cross-section regressions on interstate variations in per capita (or per pupil) education expenditures lends weight to the importance of the income effect. Fabricant (21), Fisher (23), and Brazer (15) have found interstate (or, in Brazer, intermetropolitan) income differences and per capita education expenditure differences to be significantly and positively associated. Hirsch's cross-sectional analysis of per pupil current education expenditures by St. Louis County school districts in 1951-52 and 1954-55 reveals that, "a district's financial ability to afford education measured in terms of per pupil assessed valuation of real property, was by far the most important determinant" (35). He states, however, that assessed value and income are highly intercorrelated.

It is interesting to note that cross-section estimates have generally shown the income elasticity of public education expenditures to be less than unity, e.g., Fabricant, 0.78, Brazer, 0.73, and Hirsch, 0.56 (21, 15, 35). However, these statistics do not justify Hirsch's conclusion (for the St. Louis area) that "as income *increases* by 1 percent, expenditures for public education *increase* by merely 0.56 percent. . . . Thus, the income elasticity for public education is distinctly below 1; it is inelastic" (35, P. 37). (Italics added by Bahl.) Hirsch's data were cross-sectional, not time series; consequently his coefficient provides no information about the temporal variability between education expenditures and income. What his elasticity figure does show is that at a given point in time, interdistrict differences in education expenditures are proportionately smaller than the differences in income among these districts.

In a more extensive work, Sherman Shapiro (61) has applied cross-section regression analysis to education expenditure data in each of four years for forty eight states, and separately for southern and nonsouthern states. He finds that per capita personal income was the major explanatory factor of interstate differences (among 48 states) in three of the years considered, and though it was a significant determinant of interstate differences among nonsouthern states, it was not an important explainer of education spending levels of southern states.

Miner (47) has examined the spending pattern of 1,127 school districts in 21 states with a regression model in which the independent variables (he initially considers 26) are specified as demand or supply factors "to reflect the underlying determinants of the quantity, cost, and quality of the education services provided in individual school systems which, in turn, determine levels of expenditures" (P. 74). However, the high degree of intercorrelation among the explanatory factors prevents him from attributing the statistical importance of a variable to a supply or demand effect. Miner concludes that the explanatory power of his model is not strong and attributes this to the possibility that agencies that determine local school expenditures are not motivated by rational economic objectives, and hence do not respond to similar preference patterns in similar fashion. The statistical analysis does show that education spending differences within states were largely a result of differences in factors that reflect the level of state aids, and Miner notes that the effects of factors that reflect local preferences seem to be virtually obliterated. Finally, his conclusions lend some support to the hypothesis that expenditures are lower in dependent school systems, even when ability-to-pay and cost elements are taken into account.

Another question regarding the structure of spending for public education that has been investigated with the regression technique relates to whether state education aids are *stimulative* or *substitutive* for local resources. This is generally approached by regressing per capita (or per pupil) state aids and other independent variables on per capita (or per pupil) education expenditures (including intergovernmental aids). If the regression coefficient exceeds unity, i.e., if a one dollar increment in per capita state aid is accompanied by an increment in per capita education expenditures greater than one dollar, the effect is stimulative. If the regression coefficient is less than one, the effect is substitutive. Brazer (15), in analyzing per capita education spending in 40 large cities, found a coefficient of .29, which implies substitution. Renshaw (53), in examining per pupil data for the forty eight continental states, found a coefficient of .16, which also implies substitutibility, as did Bishop (13) in investigating the effects of state aids on 1,400 New England towns and cities in 1962.

POLICE, FIRE, SANITATION

The results of the determinants analyses are generally consistent in concluding that the level of police, fire, and sanitation-related services is fairly responsive to the physical and economic characteristics of the community. Three hypotheses have been tested about the determinants of expenditures for these functions. First, that the cost of providing these services is related to the physical area that must be served, i.e., all other things being equal, the smaller the land area that must be served, the smaller are per capita expenditures. Second, that service requirements are greater to the extent that larger proportions of the resident population are in lower income brackets, i.e., low income level results in, among other things, higher crime rates and a greater amount of dilapidated housing and consequently greater police and fire expenditures. A third hypothesis is that the government expenditure decision for these functions is sensitive to the demands of both higher income residents and commercial users of the services.

Analyses of the variation in per capita fire expenditures among governmental units has focused on both cost and demand factors. Bollens (14) found that larger land areas resulted in higher expenditures for fire services, Brazer (15) found a positive relationship with population density, Wood (66) with housing density, and Williams (65) with percentage of single family dwelling units. (Williams' variable is also a measure of needs since a lower proportion of single family dwelling units implies a more congested population and a higher proportion of dilapidated housing.) Conversely, Brazer found a positive association of fire services with income; Bollens, with assessed value, and Wood, with the level of industrialization—all implying that the level of fire services provided is also affected by the level of demand generated in the residential and commercial sectors.

Statistical examinations of sanitation, refuse collection, and sewage disposal expenditures have not yielded consistent results primarily because of much incomparability in the data. The governmental responsibility and financing arrangements for this function vary greatly between states and even between communities; hence results obtained from cross-sectional analyses must be viewed with much suspicion. Hirsch (34) has attempted to get at the determinants of "refuse collection cost per pickup" by regressing selected demographic, quality and financial arrangement variables on 1960 data for twenty five St. Louis municipalities. He concludes that quality variables such as collection frequency and pickup location (curb or rear of house) have significant cost effects. Brazer (15), Williams (65), and Bahl (6) have found that per capita sanitation expenditures were positively related to population density, possibly indicating more intensive collection and disposal services required by heavy pedestrian and automobile traffic. Further, refuse collection was more regular and more complete in densely populated areas.

The pattern of expenditures for police protection is similar to that for fire protection in that factors reflecting greater levels of need for law enforcement and traffic control services, and factors that might reflect a demand for greater scope and quality of police services have been consistently identified as significant determinants. Bollens (14) found that the percentage of nonwhites was significant at a positive level, and Brazer and Williams found that population density was a significant, positive determinant. Further, Brazer's results show a significant positive association between per capita police expenditures and the ratio of city employment to city population, while Wood's results (66) show a similar relationship between such expenditures and his index of industrialization. It may be hypothesized that percentage of nonwhites and population density reflect a higher level of requirements for law enforcement because of the low income status of residents of crowded areas and of Negroes, while the role of the city as a center of employment and trade probably results in increased requirements for traffic control functions.

Interstate analyses of the Fabricant type do not enable close examination of the specific factors reflecting needs because of the degree to which the data are aggregated. However, this approach does indicate the extent to which among-state differences in fiscal capacity affect differences in the level of spending for police, fire, and sanitation services. Fabricant (21) found income positively related to interstate differences in police and fire (but not sanitation) expenditures in 1942, however, neither Fisher (23) nor Sacks-Harris (55) found income to exert a significant influence on any of these three types of expenditure in 1960.

HIGHWAYS

Statistical analyses of highway expenditures have taken the form of (1) cross-section regressions of per capita local government expenditures for roads and streets, usually excluding capital expenditures, and (2) regression analyses of interstate differences in per capita expenditures by all levels of government. Interstate statistical examinations of the former type generally may not yield reliable results because of the varying division of state-local responsibility.

For central cities, both Brazer (15) and Bahl (6) have found a significant negative relationship between highway expenditures and population density, which may mean either (1) that higher densities reflect lower ability to pay, which results in lower per capita expenditures on local roads and streets, and/or (2) that higher densities reduce the physical mileage per person that must be maintained and that therefore per resident expenditures are lower. Statistical analyses of interstate variations in aggregated state and local government spending have yielded consistent results in that population density (negatively) and per capita income (positively) are significantly related to the level of highway expenditures. The latter indicates that residents of higher income states both demand and can afford a higher level of highway services, while the former suggests the existence of certain economies in constructing and maintaining highways for densely populated areas (which in many cases are states having relatively small land areas).

Finally, Sacks-Harris (55) and Osman (50) have suggested that forms of intergovernmental assistance are determinants of the level of state and local government highway spending. Osman, in regressing per capita federal aid for highways on per capita highway expenditures from own sources finds a regression coefficient that exceeds unity (1.37) and hence is interpreted as showing a stimulative effect. However, since the regression technique does not enable an accurate measure of the separate effect of federal aids when collinearities in the data exist, and because of the circulatory issue, the conclusion as to the stimulative effects of intergovernmental aids is at best tentative.

PUBLIC WELFARE

Variations in per capita expenditures for public assistance clearly must be associated with variations in need (income level) and with variations in the level of intergovernmental aids for welfare. Fisher (23, 24) is able to explain a significant amount of the interstate variation in recipient rates for aid to dependent children (i.e., number of recipients per 100,000 under 18 years of age) with the independent variables being urban percent of population (positive), percent of labor force unemployed (positive), and percent of families with incomes under $3,000 (positive). He notes that these results are not surprising since high recipient rates for aid to dependent children are associated with urbanization, poverty, and low levels of employment. The results of Fisher's analysis of *average per capita aid to dependent children payments* show that states that make high nonwelfare expenditures also make generally higher aid to dependent children payments per capita, whereas states with large proportions of low income families make lower payments. Wood (66) found that variations in the degree of "low income prevalence" were positively related to the level of variations in public welfare expenditures among New Jersey municipalities.

As might be expected, a significant positive association between per capita federal welfare aid and per capita state and local welfare expenditures has been observed. Osman (50), in an analysis parallel to that on highways described above, found welfare aids to be stimulative (regression coefficient of 1.34) while Kee (42) found empirical evidence that per capita welfare expenditures in metropolitan areas were significantly higher where responsibility for the welfare program lies with the local rather than the state government.

CONCLUSIONS

Determinants analyses reflect in part an attempt to construct a positive theory of public expenditures, i.e., to explain the allocation of resources between the public and the private sector and the allocation of resources among public functions.* The multiple regression analyses described above are efforts to develop this theory by examining, over a large number of either governmental or spatial units, the covariability between expenditures and a wide range of economic, demographic, and sociopolitical factors. Where some factor explains a significant portion of the public expenditure variance, it has been inferred that this factor "reveals" the community's preference for the public good in question. However, limitations in the data and in the statistical technique used are such that empirical studies do not enable an accurate measurement of the factors that affect the government expenditure decision. Moreover, few of the studies appear to be based on a logical theoretical structure. Miner (47) points out that the positive theory aims at explaining actual levels of public spending and therefore must identify each of the major determinants of public spending and

---

* For a review and critique of the determinants studies as a method for developing a positive theory, see Siegel (62).

estimate the direction and magnitude of its effect. "Also, if implications of cause and effect rather than associative relationships are to be drawn, a further requisite of a positive theory is that the distinction between dependent and independent variables be based on a logical, theoretical structure that explains the distinction" (Miner, p. 74). A general lack of this kind of theoretical structure has left these studies open to the criticism—for example, from Siegel (62), Fisher (23), and Bahl-Saunders (9)—that the search for explanatory variables is almost casual and that the direction of causation between independent and dependent variables is either unsure or meaningless.

The empirical studies considered in the sections above may be grouped into two general classes: (1) those concerned with explaining spatial differences in the level of public sector activity and (2) those concerned with explaining intergovernmental differences in the level of public sector activity. The first class is weak in that it is overaggregated and consequently provides little information about the factors that affect the expenditure decisions of a particular governmental unit. The alternative—the intergovernment variations approach—is weak as a basis for empirical examination because of broad differences in the division of state-local and interlocal functional responsibility and because of externalities, e.g., the difference between expenditures *in the city* and expenditures *by the city government,* or the difference between the resident population of the city and the population to be served by city government facilities. Both approaches are subject to the limitations created by collinearities in the data, and the lack of an adequate method for isolating quality of service variations.

If this approach to the study of public expenditures is to yield meaningful results, certain refinements and adjustments must be made. First, quantitative measures of the value of urban services must be derived in order to evaluate objectively alternative fiscal development plans and in order to explain intergovernmental or spatial variances in the level of public sector activity; see Ackoff (1). Secondly, the nature of the underlying production function for public goods must be examined before much serious work can be done on the critical question of measuring the cost and efficiency of urban services and before informed judgments can be passed concerning the efficiency argument for governmental consolidation. Thirdly, the question of budget structures needs to be given more attention, i.e., the focus of the empirical works described in the sections above has been largely on the question of variations in the per capita levels of government expenditures, and the reasons for the resulting distribution of funds among alternative functions has been largely ignored.

One method of getting at certain of these unanswered questions is to abandon the macro statistical approach in favor of intensive case studies of specific states, or better yet, metropolitan areas; see, for example, Advisory Commission on Intergovernmental Relations (5) and Committee for Economic Development (18). The advantages of this approach—for example, a case study of a metropolitan area—over the macro approach are numerous: (1) Quality variations within a given metropolitan area are smaller and perhaps may even be measured by factors such as achievement tests of students, crime rates, traffic congestion rates, and so on. (2) Externalities associated with the public sector (such as the urban-suburban exploitation hypothesis) may be examined more intensively and their effects more readily evaluated if the unit of analysis is a particular standard metropolitan statistical area. (3) More accurate and more detailed data for longer periods of time may be collected from local sources. (4) The problems in the data created by differing intergovernmental fiscal arrangements may be eliminated by confining the analysis to a particular standard metropolitan statistical area.

Finally, many of the determinants studies purport to offer conclusions that are of some utility in evaluating alternative public policies. Most often mentioned in this connection are the effects of intergovernmental aids on the magnitude of public spending by lower level governments. But while these studies describe what exists—e.g., the degree to which the existing grant distribution equalizes—they may not be used validly to predict the effects of additional federal aids on state and local spending. The response of state and local governments to more federal aid depends on some combination of the nature of the grant (conditional, unconditional, tax credit, matching, etc.), the relative preferences of residents for certain types of public goods, the preferences of residents for public as against private goods, and the existing levels of public services, fiscal capacity, and fiscal effort. Until these kinds of factors can be properly included in the statistical model, the implications of the results of these analyses for public policy will be extremely limited.

LIST OF REFERENCES*

1. Ackoff, Russell, "Toward a Quantitative Evaluation of Urban Services," in *Public Expenditure Decisions in the Urban Community*, Howard Schaller, editor (Resources for the Future, 1963), pp. 91-117.

2. Adams, Robert F., "Determinants of Local Government Expenditures" (unpublished doctoral dissertation, University of Michigan, 1963).

3. —————————, "Local Fiscal Effort and Intergovernmental Transfers in the Less Developed Areas of the United States," *Review of Economics and Statistics*, Vol. 48 (August 1966) pp. 308-13.

4. —————————, "On the Variation in the Consumption of Public Services," *Review of Economics and Statistics*, Vol. 47 (November 1965), pp. 400-05.

5. Advisory Commission on Intergovernmental Relations, *Fiscal Balance in the American Federal System: Vol. 2, Metropolitan Fiscal Disparities* (Government Printing Office, October 1967).

6. Bahl, Roy W., *Metropolitan City Expenditures: A Comparative Analysis* (University of Kentucky Press, 1968).

7. Bahl, Roy W. and Saunders, Robert J., "Determinants of Changes in State and Local Government Expenditures," *National Tax Journal*, Vol. 18 (March 1965), pp. 50-57.

8. —————————, "Fabricant's Determinants After Twenty Years: A Critical Reappraisal," *American Economist*, Vol. 10 (Spring 1966), pp. 27-42.

9. —————————, "Factors Associated with Variations in State and Local Government Spending," *Journal of Finance*, Vol. 21 (September 1966), pp. 523-34.

10. —————————, *Intercounty Differences in West Virginia Government Spending* (Office of Research and Development, West Virginia University, 1967).

11. Beck, Morris, "Determinants of the Property Tax Level: A Case Study of Northeastern New Jersey," *National Tax Journal*, Vol. 18 (March 1965), pp. 74-77. (N)

12. Beroltzheimer, Josef, "Influences Shaping Expenditure for Operation of State and Local Governments," *Bulletin of the National Tax Association*, Vol. 32 (March, April, May 1947), pp. 170-71, 213-19, 237-44.

---

* The letter N following a citation indicates "No explicit comment," but that the study was part of the background of our review.

13. Bishop, George A., "Stimulative Versus Substitutive Effects of State School Aid in New England," *National Tax Journal,* Vol. 17 (June 1964), pp. 133-43.

14. Bollens, J., *et al., Exploring the Metropolitan Community* (University of California Press, 1961).

15. Brazer, Harvey E., *City Expenditures in the United States* (National Bureau of Economic Research, 1959), p. 25.

16. Carroll, John J. and Sacks, Seymour, "Government Expenditures: The Influence of Industry," *Regional Science Association Papers,* Vol. 9 (1962), pp. 173-91. (N)

17. Colm, Gerhard, *et., al.,* "Public Expenditures and Economic Structure in United States," *Social Research,* Vol. 3 (March 1935), pp. 75-85.

18. Committee for Economic Development, *Fiscal Issues in the Future of Federalism* (Supplementary Paper, No. 23, May 1968).

19. Davis, Otto A., "Empirical Evidence of Political Influences upon the Expenditure Policies of Public Schools," in Julius Margolis (ed.), *The Public Economy of Urban Communities* (Resources for the Future, 1965), pp. 92-111. (N)

20. Elsner, Gary H. and Sosnick, Stephen H., *Municipal Expenditures in California: Statistical Correlates* (Occasional Paper Series, No. 2, Institute of Governmental Affairs, Davis Campus, University of California, 1964).

21. Fabricant, Solomon, *The Trend of Government Activity in the United States Since 1900* (National Bureau of Economic Research, 1952), Chapter 6.

22. Fisher, Glenn W., "Determinants of State and Local Government Expenditures: A Preliminary Analysis," *National Tax Journal,* Vol. 14 (December 1961) pp. 349-55.

23. —————————————, "Interstate Variation in State and Local Government Expenditures," *National Tax Journal,* Vol. 17 (March 1964), pp. 55-74.

24. —————————————, "Public Assistance Expenditures," in *Report of the Commission on Revenue of the State of Illinois* (Springfield, 1963), p. 120.

25. Fredland, J. Eric, Hymans, Saul and Morss, Elliott R., "Fluctuations in State Expenditures: An Econometric Analysis," *Southern Economic Journal,* Vol. 33 (April 1967), pp. 496-517.

26. Frisch, R. and Budgett, B.D., "Statistical Correlation and the Theory of Cluster Types," *Journal of the American Statistical Association,* Vol. 26 (June 1931), p. 275.

27. Gensemer, Bruce L., "Determinants of the Fiscal Policy Decisions of Local Governments in Urban Areas: Public Safety and Public Education" (unpublished doctoral dissertation, University of Michigan, 1966). (N)

28. Gregory, Karl D., "Variations in State and Local Appropriations for Publicly Supported Institutions of Higher Education, by State in 1955-66" (unpublished doctoral dissertation, University of Michigan, 1961). (N)

29. Hansen, Nels, "Economy of Scale as a Cost Factor in Financing Public Schools," *National Tax Journal,* Vol. 17 (March 1964), pp. 92-96. (N)

30. Hansen, Niles, "Municipal Investment Requirements in a Growing Agglomeration," *Land Economics,* Vol. 41 (February 1965), pp. 49-56. (N)

31. —————————————, "The Structure and Determinants of Local Public Investment Expenditures," *Review of Economics and Statistics,* Vol. 47 (May 1965), pp. 150-62. (N)

32. Hawley, Amos H., "Metropolitan Population and Municipal Government Expenditures in Central Cities," reprinted in *Cities and Society,* Paul K. Hatt and Albert J. Reiss, Jr. editors (Free Press, revised 1957), pp. 773-82.

33. Hirsch, Werner, *Analysis of the Rising Costs of Public Education*, U.S. Congress, Joint Economic Committee, Study Paper, No. 4 (Government Printing Office, November 1959).

34. ———————————, "Cost Functions of an Urban Government Service," *Review of Economics and Statistics*, Vol. 47 (February 1965), pp. 87-92.

35. ———————————, "Determinants of Public Education Expenditures," *National Tax Journal*, Vol. 13 (March 1960), pp. 29-40.

36. ———————————, "Expenditure Implications of Metropolitan Growth and Consolidation," *Review of Economics and Statistics*, Vol. 41 (August 1959), pp. 232-41.

37. ———————————, "Expenditure Implications of Metropolitan Consolidation Revisited," *Review of Economics and Statistics*, Vol. 44 (August 1962), pp. 344-46.

38. ———————————, "Quality of Government Services," in *Public Expenditures in the Urban Community*, Howard J. Schaller, editor (Resources for the Future, 1963), pp. 163-79.

39. ———————————, "The Supply of Urban Public Services," in *Issues in Urban Economics*, Harvey S. Perloff and Lowdon Wingo Jr., editors (Johns Hopkins Press for Resources for the Future, 1968).

40. James H. Thomas, *School Revenue Systems in Five States* (School of Education, Stanford University, 1961).

41. James, H. Thomas, Thomas, J. Alan and Dyck, Harold J., *Wealth, Expenditures and Decision-Making for Education* (School of Education, Stanford University, 1963), Chapter 4. (N)

42. Kee, Woo Sik, "Central City Expenditures and Metropolitan Areas," *National Tax Journal*, Vol. 18 (December 1965), pp. 337-53.

43. Kurnow, Ernest, "Determinants of State and Local Expenditures Reexamined," *National Tax Journal*, Vol. 16 (September 1963), pp. 252-55.

44. Lohnes, Paul R., *New England Finances Public Education* (Cambridge, New England School Development Council, 1958).

45. McCloone, Eugene P., "Effects of Tax Elasticity on the Financial Support of Education" (unpublished doctoral dissertation, University of Illinois, 1961).

46. McMahon, Walter W., "The Determinants of Public Expenditure: An Econometric Analysis of the Demand for Public Education" (unpublished paper, Department of Economics, University of Illinois, 1961). (N)

47. Miner, Jerry, *Social and Economic Factors in Spending for Public Education* (Syracuse University Press, 1963).

48. Montgomery, Albert A., *Washington Expenditures, 1941-1957—An Economic Analysis* (Washington State University Press, 1963).

49. Morss, Elliott R., "Some Thoughts on the Determinants of State and Local Expenditures," *National Tax Journal*, Vol. 19 (March 1966), pp. 95-104. (N)

50. Osman, Jack W., "The Dual Impact of Federal Aid on State and Local Government Expenditures," *National Tax Journal*, Vol. 19 (December 1966), pp. 362-72.

51. Pidot, George, Jr., "The Public Finances of Local Government in the Metropolitan U.S." (unpublished doctoral dissertation, Harvard University, 1965). (N)

52. Prescott, James R., "SMSA Expenditures in the North Central Region: Some Preliminary Results" (paper delivered at the Midwest Economics Association Meetings, April 1966, Columbus, Ohio).

53. Renshaw, Edward F., "A Note on the Expenditure Effect of State Aid to Education," *Journal of Political Economy*, Vol. 68 (April 1960), pp. 170-74.

54. Sacks, Seymour, "Spatial and Locational Aspects of Local Government Expenditures," in *Public Expenditures Decisions in the Urban Community,,* Howard Schaller, editor (Resources for the Future, 1963) pp. 180-98. (N)

55. Sacks, Seymour and Harris, Robert, "The Determinants of State and Local Government Expenditures and Intergovernmental Flows of Funds," *National Tax Journal,* Vol. 17 (March 1964), pp. 75-85.

56. Sacks, Seymour and Hellmuth, William F., Jr. *Financing Government in a Metropolitan Area* (Free Press of Glencoe, 1961), pp. 87-132.

57. Schmandt, Henry J. and Stephens, G. Ross, "Local Government Expenditure Patterns in the United States," *Land Economics,* Vol. 39 (November 1963), pp. 397-407.

58. ————————————, "Measuring Municipal Output," *National Tax Journal,* Vol. 13 (December 1960), pp. 369-75.

59. Scott, Stanley and Fender, Edward L., *Factors Associated with Variations in Municipal Expenditures Levels* (Bureau of Public Administration, University of California, 1957).

60. Shapiro, Harvey, "Measuring Local Government Output: A Comment," *National Tax Journal,* Vol. 14 (December 1961), pp. 394-97. (N)

61. Shapiro, Sherman, "Some Socioeconomic Determinants of Expenditures for Education: Southern and Other States Compared," *Comparative Education Review,* Vol. 6 (October 1962), pp. 160-66.

62. Siegel, Barry N., "On the Positive Theory of State and Local Expenditures," in *Public Finance and Welfare,* Paul Kleinsorge, editor (University of Oregon Books, 1966).

63. Spangler, Richard, "The Effect of Population Growth upon State and Local Government Expenditures," *National Tax Journal,* Vol. 16 (June 1963), pp. 193-96.

64. Vieg, John A., *et. al., California Local Finance* (Stanford University Press, 1960).

65. Williams, Oliver P., *Suburban Differences and Metropolitan Policies* (University of Pennsylvania Press, 1965).

66. Wood, Robert C., *1400 Governments* (Harvard University Press, 1961).